Sources of
Western Society

**VOLUME I: FROM ANTIQUITY
TO THE ENLIGHTENMENT**

Sources of
Western Society

**VOLUME I: FROM ANTIQUITY
TO THE ENLIGHTENMENT**

BEDFORD/ST. MARTIN'S   BOSTON ◆ NEW YORK

For Bedford/St. Martin's

Publisher for History: Mary Dougherty
Executive Editor for History: Traci Mueller
Director of Development for History: Jane Knetzger
Associate Editor for History: Lynn Sternberger
Assistant Production Manager: Joe Ford
Executive Marketing Manager: Jenna Bookin Barry
Project Management: DeMasi Design and Publishing Service
Text Design: DeMasi Design and Publishing Service
Cover Design: Sara Gates
Cover Art: Portrait of a Man by Antonello da Messina, ca. 1475. National Gallery,
   London/Bridgeman Art Library. *Market Scene* (detail with vendors and women),
   Anonymous, fifteenth century. Late fifteenth-century fresco, Castello d'Issogne,
   Italy. Scala/Art Resource.
Composition: Jeff Miller Book Design
Printing and Binding: RR Donnelley & Sons Company

President: Joan E. Feinberg
Editorial Director: Denise B. Wydra
Director of Marketing: Karen R. Soeltz
Director of Editing, Design, and Production: Marcia Cohen
Assistant Director of Editing, Design, and Production: Elise S. Kaiser
Manager, Publishing Services: Emily Berleth

Manufactured in the United States of America.

4 3 2 1 0 9
f e d c b a

For information, write: Bedford/St. Martin's, 75 Arlington Street, Boston, MA 02116
(617-399-4000)

ISBN-10: 0-312-59250-7
ISBN-13: 978-0-312-59250-9

Acknowledgments

PREFACE

Sources of Western Society is a compilation of primary sources recorded by those who shaped and experienced the development of the Western world — among them rulers and subjects alike, men and women, philosophers, revolutionaries, economists, and laborers, from ancient times to the present. With a parallel chapter structure and documents hand-picked to complement the text, this reader is designed to complement either *A History of Western Society*, ninth edition, or *Western Society: A Brief History*. *Sources of Western Society* aspires to animate the past for students, providing resonant accounts of the people and events that changed the face of Western history, from myths of creation to tallies of the spoils and fatalities of war.

While a good textbook offers a clear framework of major historical figures and movements, *Sources* evokes the experiences of historical times at the moments they were lived and creates a dynamic connection for students, bridging the events of the past with their own understandings of power and its abuses, of the ripple effects of human agency, and of the material conditions of life. For example, John Locke's *Second Treatise of Civil Government* is cited in the textbook for its crucial role in the development of citizens' rights. In *Sources*, Locke himself makes a convincing case for the need for individual empowerment, as well as the study of history: "For he that thinks *absolute Power purifies Mens Bloods*, and corrects the baseness of Humane Nature, need read but the History of this, or any other Age to be convinced of the contrary."

With input from the textbook authors, as well as from current instructors of the Western civilization survey course, we have compiled these documents with one goal foremost in mind: to make history's most classic and compelling voices accessible to students, from the most well-known thinkers of their times to the galvanized or introspective commoner. In Chapter 24, for example, Darwin presents his defense of natural selection and Spencer applies that same "survival of the fittest" theory to human populations with disquieting insight, while home etiquette writer Isabella

Beeton and socialist feminist Clara Zetkin argue for two dramatically different visions of a woman's working life.

We have stepped back from drawing conclusions and instead provide just enough background to enable students' own analyses of the sources at hand. Chapter-opening paragraphs briefly review the major events of the time and place the documents that follow within the framework of the corresponding textbook chapter. A concise headnote for each document provides context about the author and the circumstances surrounding the document's creation, while glossary notes supply information to aid comprehension of unfamiliar terms and references. Each document is followed by Reading and Discussion Questions that spur deep student analysis of the material, while chapter-concluding Comparative Questions encourage students to contemplate the harmony and discord among the sources within and, when called for, between the chapters. The excerpts range widely in length to allow for a range of class assignments.

ACKNOWLEDGMENTS

Instrumental to the creation of this primary source reader were Jay Boggis's contributions to the first volume. For their availability and insight, many thanks to the *History of Western Society* authors John P. McKay, John Buckler, Clare Crowston, and Merry Wiesner-Hanks. Lynn Sternberger at Bedford/St. Martins has been a paragon of editorial ability, efficiency, and tact. Working with her has been an unalloyed pleasure. Kathryn Abbott's editorial guidance and insight was immensely helpful. Emily Berleth of Bedford/St. Martin's and Linda DeMasi of DeMasi Design made production of this reader possible with remarkable finesse.

CONTENTS

Sources of
Western Society

VOLUME I: FROM ANTIQUITY
TO THE ENLIGHTENMENT

CHAPTER 1

Origins

ca. 400,000–1100 B.C.E.

B y 3000 B.C.E., two contrasting agricultural societies had developed in Mesopotamia and Egypt. Mesopotamia was located between the great Tigris and Euphrates Rivers, which were a challenge to navigate and needed to be channeled into complicated irrigation systems. The area possessed few natural defenses against invasion. Egypt, on the other hand, was largely protected by desert, and the flooding of the Nile was fairly regular and could be managed with relative ease. The pharaohs were able to create a unified kingdom at an early point in Egypt's history, in part because the current of the Nile made travel up and down the river feasible. In Mesopotamia, various city-states warred against one another for domination, although larger states eventually dominated the region. The writings these cultures left are among the earliest records of Western society. The following documents are concerned with two basic questions: how did the gods create and govern the world, and what sort of life should mortals lead to fulfill their duties to the gods and one another?

DOCUMENT 1-1

A Mesopotamian Creation Myth

ca. 2000–1000 B.C.E.

Creation myths offer religious or myth-based explanations for the origins of the earth, heavens, and life. In societies where the workings of the natural world were mysterious, creation myths could provide people with a sense of understanding, even comfort. This Mesopotamian creation myth portrays the struggle of the Sun-God Marduk with Tiamat the Sea-Goddess, mother

James B. Pritchard, ed., *Ancient Near Eastern Texts Relating to the Old Testament*, 3d ed. (Princeton, N.J.: Princeton University Press, 1969), 60–68.

of all gods. Marduk defeats Tiamat to become the chief of all the gods, but in earlier times he had simply been the patron god of Babylon. As Babylon came to dominate the other cities of the Euphrates Valley, however, Marduk became the chief god of the pantheon.

Nothing there was but primordial Fresh-Water (Apsu), their begetter,
And Mother-Sea (Mummu-Tiamat), she who bore them all,
Their waters commingling as a single body;
No reed hut had been matted, no marsh land had appeared,
When no gods whatever had been brought into being,
Uncalled by name, their destinies undetermined —
Then it was that the gods were formed within them. . . .
Then struggled the Sea-Goddess (Tiamat) and the Sun-God (Marduk),
    wisest of gods.
They strove in single combat, locked in battle. . . .
He released the arrow, it tore her belly,
It cut through her insides, splitting the heart.
Having thus subdued her, he extinguished her life.
He cast down her carcass to stand upon it. . . .
He split her like a shellfish into two parts:
Half of her he set up as the sky,
Pulled down the bar and posted guards.
He bade them to allow not her waters to escape.
He crossed the heavens and surveyed the regions. . . .
Opening his mouth, he addresses his father (Ea)
To impart the plan he had conceived in his heart:
"Blood I will mass and cause bones to be.
I will establish a savage, man shall be his name.
Truly, savage-man I will create.
He shall be charged with the service of the gods
That they might be at ease!"

READING AND DISCUSSION QUESTIONS

1. According to this account, how is the world created?

2. Central to this creation story is a struggle to the death between two gods. What might the focus on battle reveal about Mesopotamian beliefs?

3. What might we learn about daily life in Mesopotamia based on the details in this story?

4. Why have human beings been created, and what is their duty?

DOCUMENT 1-2

The Code of Hammurabi

ca. 1780 B.C.E.

As king of Babylon, Hammurabi (r. ca. 1792–1750 B.C.E.) created an empire that extended throughout Mesopotamia, although his successors were not able to hold it together. During his reign, Babylon was one of the first great cities in the world. Hammurabi compiled one of the best-known law codes of ancient times and ordered it to be carved on stone tablets and set up in a public space. The inscriptions were in Akkadian, the daily language of the people. Although it is not known how many Babylonians were literate at this time, ordinary people might have had a general sense of what was written there, and they would know that a scribe or other literate person could read the laws in detail.

3. If any one bring an accusation of any crime before the elders, and does not prove what he has charged, he shall, if it be a capital offense charged, be put to death. . . .

5. If a judge try a case, reach a decision, and present his judgment in writing; if later error shall appear in his decision, and it be through his own fault, then he shall pay twelve times the fine set by him in the case, and he shall be publicly removed from the judge's bench, and never again shall he sit there to render judgment. . . .

15. If anyone take a male or female slave of the court, or a male or female slave of a freed man, outside the city gates, he shall be put to death.

James B. Pritchard, ed., *Ancient Near Eastern Texts Relating to the Old Testament,* 3d ed. (Princeton, N.J.: Princeton University Press, 1969), 176–178.

16. If anyone receive into his house a runaway male or female slave of the court, or of a freedman, and does not bring it out at the public proclamation of the major domus, the master of the house shall be put to death.

17. If anyone find runaway male or female slaves in the open country and bring them to their masters, the master of the slaves shall pay him two shekels of silver. . . .

25. If fire break out in a house, and some one who comes to put it out cast his eye upon the property of the owner of the house, and take the property of the master of the house, he shall be thrown into that self-same fire. . . .

30. If a chieftain or a man leave his house, garden, and field and hires it out, and some one else takes possession of his house, garden, and field and uses it for three years: if the first owner return and claims his house, garden, and field, it shall not be given to him, but he who has taken possession of it and used it shall continue to use it. . . .

108. If a tavern-keeper (feminine) does not accept corn according to gross weight in payment of drink, but takes money, and the price of the drink is less than that of the corn, she shall be convicted and thrown into the water.

109. If conspirators meet in the house of a tavern-keeper, and these conspirators are not captured and delivered to the court, the tavern-keeper shall be put to death.

110. If a "sister of a god" open a tavern, or enter a tavern to drink, then shall this woman be burned to death. . . .

128. If a man take a woman to wife, but have no intercourse with her, this woman is no wife to him.

129. If a man's wife be surprised with another man, both shall be tied and thrown into the water, but the husband may pardon his wife and the king his slaves.

130. If a man violate the wife (betrothed or child-wife) of another man, who has never known a man, and still lives in her father's house, and sleep with her and be surprised, this man shall be put to death, but the wife is blameless.

131. If a man bring a charge against one's wife, but she is not surprised with another man, she must take an oath and then may return to her house.
132. If the "finger is pointed" at a man's wife about another man, but she is not caught sleeping with the other man, she shall jump into the river for her husband. . . .

137. If a man wish to separate from a woman who has borne him children, or from his wife who has borne him children: then he shall give that wife her dowry, and a part of the usufruct of field, garden, and property, so that she can rear her children. When she has brought up her children, a portion of all that is given to the children, equal as that of one son, shall be given to her. She may then marry the man of her heart.
138. If a man wishes to separate from his wife who has borne him no children, he shall give her the amount of her purchase money and the dowry which she brought from her father's house, and let her go.
139. If there was no purchase price he shall give her one mina of gold as a gift of release. . . .

141. If a man's wife, who lives in his house, wishes to leave it, plunges into debt, tries to ruin her house, neglects her husband, and is judicially convicted: if her husband offer her release, she may go on her way, and he gives her nothing as a gift of release. If her husband does not wish to release her, and if he take another wife, she shall remain as servant in her husband's house. . . .

144. If a man take a wife and this woman give her husband a maid-servant, and she bear him children, but this man wishes to take another wife, this shall not be permitted to him; he shall not take a second wife.
145. If a man take a wife, and she bear him no children, and he intend to take another wife: if he take this second wife, and bring her into the house, this second wife shall not be allowed equality with his wife. . . .

195. If a son strike his father, his hands shall be hewn off.
196. If a man put out the eye of another man, his eye shall be put out.
197. If he break another man's bone, his bone shall be broken.

198. If he put out the eye of a freed man, or break the bone of a freed man, he shall pay one gold mina.

199. If he put out the eye of a man's slave, or break the bone of a man's slave, he shall pay one-half of its value.

200. If a man knock out the teeth of his equal, his teeth shall be knocked out.

201. If he knock out the teeth of a freed man, he shall pay one-third of a gold mina.

202. If anyone strike the body of a man higher in rank than he, he shall receive sixty blows with an ox-whip in public.

203. If a free-born man strike the body of another free-born man of equal rank, he shall pay one gold mina.

204. If a freed man strike the body of another freed man, he shall pay ten shekels in money.

205. If the slave of a freed man strike the body of a freed man, his ear shall be cut off. . . .

209. If a man strike a free-born woman so that she lose her unborn child, he shall pay ten shekels for her loss.

210. If the woman die, his daughter shall be put to death.

211. If a woman of the free class lose her child by a blow, he shall pay five shekels in money.

212. If this woman die, he shall pay half a mina.

213. If he strike the maid-servant of a man, and she lose her child, he shall pay two shekels in money.

214. If this maid-servant die, he shall pay one-third of a mina. . . .

READING AND DISCUSSION QUESTIONS

1. Why might people hesitate before going to court?

2. When is it especially important who the victim is? The accused?

3. What do these laws reveal about contemporary family life? What do they reveal about the status of women?

4. What can we surmise about a man's responsibilities to his community as a whole?

DOCUMENT 1-3

A Hymn to the Nile

ca. 1350–1100 B.C.E.

Around 3000 B.C.E., the two separate kingdoms of Egypt — Lower Egypt, the delta land where the Nile emptied into the Mediterranean, and Upper Egypt, the bank land surrounding the Nile as it ran north through the desert — were united under one pharaoh. By the time of this document, all of Egypt had long shared a common ruler and an economy entirely dependent upon the success of crops and trade along the river. As this hymn extols the river's virtues, it becomes a catalogue of daily life in Egypt. The rise and fall of the Nile shaped every aspect of life in ancient Egypt, from the health of crops and animals to the religious and moral state of its people.

Hail to thee, O Nile, that issues from the earth and comes to keep Egypt alive! Hidden in his form of appearance, a darkness by day, to whom minstrels have sung. He that waters the meadows which Re[1] created, in order to keep every kid alive. He that makes to drink the desert and the place distant from water: that is his dew coming down (from) heaven. . . .

The lord of fishes, he who makes the marsh-birds to go upstream. There are no birds which come down because of the hot winds. He who makes barley and brings emmer [wheat] into being, that he may make the temples festive. If he is sluggish, . . . the nostrils are stopped up, and everybody is poor. If there be (thus) a cutting down in the food-offerings of the gods, then a million men perish among mortals, covetousness is practiced, the entire land is in a fury, and great and small are on the execution-block. (But) people are different when he approaches. Khnum[2] constructed him. When he rises, then the land is in jubilation, then every belly is in joy, every backbone takes on laughter, and every tooth is exposed.

James B. Pritchard, ed., *Ancient Near Eastern Texts Relating to the Old Testament*, 3d ed. with supplement (Princeton, N.J.: Princeton University Press, 1969), 372–373.

[1] **Re**: Egyptian sun god also known as Ra.

[2] **Khnum**: God of the source of the River Nile; also a potter who shapes the human form from clay.

The bringer of food, rich in provisions, creator of all good, lord of majesty, sweet of fragrance. What is in him is satisfaction. He who brings grass into being for the cattle and (thus) gives . . . sacrifice to every god, whether he be in the underworld, heaven, or earth, him who is under his authority. He who takes in possession the Two Lands, fills the magazines, makes the granaries wide, and gives things (to) the poor.

He who makes every beloved tree to grow, without lack of them. He who brings a ship into being by his strength, without hewing in stone. The enduring image with the White Crown. He cannot be seen; (he has) no taxes; he has no levies; no one can read of the mystery; no one knows the place where he is; he cannot be found by the power of writing. (He has) no shrines; he has no portion. He has no service of (his) desire. (But) generations of thy children jubilate for thee, and men give thee greeting as a king, stable of laws, coming forth (at) his season and filling Upper and Lower Egypt. . . . (Whenever) water is drunk, every eye is in him, who gives an excess of his good.

He who was sorrowful is come forth gay. . . . and the Ennead,[3] in which thou art, is exalted. Vomiting forth and making the field to drink. Anointing the whole land. Making one man rich and laying another, (but) there is no coming to trial with him, who makes satisfaction without being thwarted, for whom no boundaries are made.

A maker of light when issuing from darkness, a fat for his cattle. His limits are all that is created. There is no district which can live without him. Men are clothed . . . with flax from his meadows, . . . (He) made anointing with his unguents, being the associate of Ptah[4] in his nature, bringing into being all service in him, all writings and divine words, his responsibility in Lower Egypt.

Entering into the underworld and coming forth above, loving to come forth as a mystery. If thou art (too) heavy (to rise), the people are few, and one begs for the water of the year. (Then) the rich man looks like him who is worried, and every man is seen (to be) carrying his weapons. This is no companion backing up a companion. There are no garments for clothing; there are no ornaments for the children of nobles. There is no listening at night, that one may answer with coolness. There is no anointing for anybody.

He who establishes truth in the heart of men, for it is said: "Deceit

---

[3] **Ennead**: A group of deities often thought to include Re.
[4] **Ptah**: The deification of the primordial earth, included in the Ennead.

comes after poverty." If one compares thee with the great green sea, which does not . . . control the Grain-God, whom all the gods praise, there are no birds coming down from his desert. His hand does not beat with gold, with making ingots of silver. No one can eat genuine lapis lazuli. (But) barley is foremost and lasting.

Men began to sing to thee with the harp, and men sing to thee with the hand. The generations of thy children jubilate for thee. Men equip messengers for thee, who come (back) bearing treasures (to) ornament this land. He who makes a ship to prosper before mankind; he who sustains hearts in pregnant women; he who loves a multitude of all (kinds of) his cattle.

When thou risest in the city of the ruler, then men are satisfied with the goodly produce of the meadows. . . . Oh for the little lotus-blossoms, everything that pours forth upon earth, all (kinds of) herbs in the hands of children! They have (even) forgotten how to eat. Good things are strewn about the houses. The land comes down frolicking.

When the Nile floods, offering is made to thee, oxen are sacrificed to thee, great oblations are made to thee, birds are fattened for thee, lions are hunted for thee in the desert, fire is provided for thee. And offering is made to every (other) god, as is done for the Nile, with prime incense, oxen, cattle, birds, and flame. The Nile has made his cavern in Thebes, and his name is no (longer) known in the underworld. Not a god will come forth in his form, if the plan is ignored.

O all men who uphold the Ennead, . . . fear ye the majesty which his son, the All-Lord, has made, (by) making verdant the two banks. So it is "Verdant art thou!" So it is "Verdant art thou!" So it is "O Nile, verdant art thou, who makest man and cattle to live!"

READING AND DISCUSSION QUESTIONS

1. What are three surprising things for which the Nile is praised? Explain why the Nile should be revered for each.

2. What happens when mortals cut down on their food-offerings to the gods?

3. What happens when the Nile fails to rise, and what does that imply about the role of the river in Egyptian life?

4. Consider the phrase, "His limits are all that is created." Who or what is "he" in the hymn?

DOCUMENT 1-4

The Egyptian Book of the Dead:
The Declaration of Innocence

ca. 2100–1800 B.C.E.

The Egyptian Book of the Dead comprises texts that were placed in tombs describing how a dead person should overcome various obstacles in the afterlife. Although there was no standard Book of the Dead (this was not a name used by the Egyptians), many of the same texts appear in tombs dating from shortly after 2000 B.C.E. until the adoption of Christianity. This "Declaration of Innocence," one such text, is remarkable for the detail with which it describes the possible sins of the deceased Egyptian. In listing the undesirable acts, it creates an outline of what Egyptians considered acceptable social behavior.

To be said on reaching the Hall of the Two Truths[5] so as to purge [name]
    of any sins committed and to see the face of every god:
Hail to you, great God, Lord of the Two Truths!
I have come to you, my Lord,
I was brought to see your beauty.
I know you, I know the names of the forty-two gods
Who are with you in the Hall of the Two Truths,
Who live by warding off evildoers,
Who drink of their blood,
On that day of judging characters before Wennofer [Osiris].
Lo, your name is "He-of-Two-Daughters,"
(And) "He-of-Maat's[6]-Two-Eyes."

Miriam Lichtheim, trans. and ed., *Ancient Egyptian Literature* (Berkeley: University of California Press, 1973).

[5] **Hall of the Two Truths**: A place of judgment after death. Upon reaching the Hall of Two Truths, ancient Egyptians would stand before a jury of gods, hear a recounting of their life's deeds, and have their hearts literally weighed by the god Osiris on the scales of justice. A heart heavy with guilt meant the owner would be devoured by the demon Ammit.

[6] **Maat**: Egyptian goddess who personified truth, cosmic order, and justice. Her followers were considered upholders of the universal order.

Lo, I come before you,
Bringing Maat to you,
Having repelled evil for you.
I have not done crimes against people,
I have not mistreated cattle,
I have not sinned in the Place of Truth,
I have not known what should not be known,
I have not done any harm.
I did not begin a day by exacting more than my due,
My name did not reach the bark of the mighty ruler.
I have not blasphemed a god,
I have not robbed the poor.
I have not done what the god abhors,
I have not maligned a servant to his master.
I have not caused pain,
I have not caused tears.
I have not killed,
I have not ordered to kill,
I have not made anyone suffer.
I have not damaged the offerings in the temples,
I have not depleted the loaves of the gods,
I have not stolen the cakes of the dead.
I have not copulated nor defiled myself.
I have not increased nor reduced the measure,
I have not diminished the arura [land].
I have not cheated in the fields.
I have not added to the weight of the balance,
I have not falsified the plummet of the scales.
I have not taken milk from the mouth of children,
I have not deprived cattle of their pasture.
I have not snared birds in the reeds of the gods,
I have not caught fish in their ponds.
I have not held back water in its season,
I have not dammed a flowing stream,
I have not quenched a needed fire.
I have not neglected the days of meat offerings,
I have not detained cattle belonging to the god,
I have not stopped a god in his procession.
I am pure, I am pure, I am pure, I am pure!

READING AND DISCUSSION QUESTIONS

1. Name three specific offenses that the deceased has not committed. What does each of these reveal about Egyptian social life?

2. Why might the declaration repeatedly state that the Egyptian knows the names of the gods?

3. List two offenses against gods and two offenses against mortals. Then list at least two more offenses for which it is unclear whether they offend gods or mortals. In two or three sentences discuss what these various offenses reveal about Egyptian moral thinking.

COMPARATIVE QUESTIONS

1. In what ways is the relationship between gods and humans in the Mesopotamian creation myth different from the relationship in the Declaration of Innocence?

2. In the Declaration of Innocence, the writer lists a multitude of crimes against the gods and humanity. In what ways are notions of morality in the Book of the Dead and Hammurabi's Code similar to or different from other, nonancient "morality lists"? How many such lists can you think of?

3. Based on the documents, what would you list as the top priorities of a model Egyptian or Mesopotamian citizen? List at least three priorities each for Egyptians and Mesopotamians.

4. Given the depictions of a river-fed earth, what can we assume about ancient conceptions of an afterlife for someone who has violated the society's social and religious customs? Are there helpful descriptions in any of the documents?

CHAPTER 2

Small Kingdoms and Mighty Empires in the Near East

ca. 1100–513 B.C.E.

T he Hebrew people lived in two small kingdoms, Israel and Judah, on the borders of two great empires, Egypt and Assyria. The following documents describe how the Hebrew people came into being and how they struggled for existence. A passage from Genesis in the Old Testament describes the beginning of all creation, before recorded time. Another, also taken from the Hebrew Bible, describes how, sometime between 1700 and 1300 B.C.E., God handed down the Law to the Hebrews, who were unified under one religion but who had not yet found the "promised land" on which to build their nation. By the time of the third document, an Assyrian source from 700 B.C.E., the kingdom of Israel had been established, but had been conquered by Assyria. Later, around 586 B.C.E., the Jews were exiled to Babylon, where they were forced to reside until Babylon was recaptured and its new Persian ruler, Cyrus the Great, issued orders for the treatment of its conquered people.

DOCUMENT 2-1

Book of Genesis: The Hebrews Explain Creation

ca. 950–450 B.C.E.

The following passage is the beginning of Genesis, the first book of the Hebrew Bible, or Torah. The range of dates in the headnote reveals something about the hotly debated issue of how the Hebrew Bible was created. Modern historians believe that by about 450 B.C.E., the book of Genesis

---

Genesis 1:1–31; 2:1–7.

*existed in something close to the form we now possess. At the same time, it is
known that some passages of Genesis are much older.*

In the beginning God created the heaven and the earth. And the earth was
without form, and void; and darkness was upon the face of the deep. And
the Spirit of God moved upon the face of the waters. And God said, Let
there be light: and there was light. And God saw the light, that it was good:
and God divided the light from the darkness. And God called the light
Day, and the darkness he called Night. And the evening and the morning
were the first day.

And God said, Let there be a firmament in the midst of the waters, and
let it divide the waters from the waters. And God made the firmament, and
divided the waters which were under the firmament from the waters which
were above the firmament: and it was so.

And God called the firmament Heaven. And the evening and the
morning were the second day.

And God said, Let the waters under the heaven be gathered together
unto one place, and let the dry land appear: and it was so. And God called
the dry land Earth; and the gathering together of the waters called he Seas:
and God saw that it was good. And God said, Let the earth bring forth
grass, the herb yielding seed, and the fruit tree yielding fruit after his kind,
whose seed is in itself, upon the earth: and it was so. And the earth brought
forth grass, and herb yielding seed after his kind, and the tree yielding fruit,
whose seed was in itself, after his kind: and God saw that it was good. And
the evening and the morning were the third day.

And God said, Let there be lights in the firmament of the heaven to
divide the day from the night; and let them be for signs, and for seasons, and for days, and years: And let them be for lights in the firmament
of the heaven to give light upon the earth: and it was so. And God made
two great lights; the greater light to rule the day, and the lesser light to
rule the night: he made the stars also. And God set them in the firmament
of the heaven to give light upon the earth. And to rule over the day and
over the night, and to divide the light from the darkness: and God saw that
it was good. And the evening and the morning were the fourth day. And
God said, Let the waters bring forth abundantly the moving creature that
hath life, and fowl that may fly above the earth in the open firmament of
heaven. And God created great whales, and every living creature that
moveth, which the waters brought forth abundantly, after their kind, and

every winged fowl after his kind: and God saw that it was good. And God blessed them, saying, Be fruitful, and multiply, and fill the waters in the seas, and let fowl multiply in the earth. And the evening and the morning were the fifth day.

And God said, Let the earth bring forth the living creature after his kind, cattle, and creeping thing, and beast of the earth after his kind: and it was so. And God made the beast of the earth after his kind, and cattle after their kind, and every thing that creepeth upon the earth after his kind: and God saw that it was good.

And God said, Let us make man in our image, after our likeness: and let them have dominion over the fish of the sea, and over the fowl of the air, and over the cattle, and over all the earth, and over every creeping thing that creepeth upon the earth. So God created man in his own image, in the image of God created he him; male and female created he them. And God blessed them, and God said unto them, Be fruitful, and multiply, and replenish the earth, and subdue it: and have dominion over the fish of the sea, and over the fowl of the air, and over every living thing that moveth upon the earth.

And God said, Behold, I have given you every herb bearing seed, which is upon the face of all the earth, and every tree, in the which is the fruit of a tree yielding seed; to you it shall be for meat. And to every beast of the earth, and to every fowl of the air, and to every thing that creepeth upon the earth, wherein there is life, I have given every green herb for meat: and it was so. And God saw every thing that he had made, and, behold, it was very good. And the evening and the morning were the sixth day.

Thus the heavens and the earth were finished, and all the host of them. And on the seventh day God ended his work which he had made; and he rested on the seventh day from all his work which he had made. And God blessed the seventh day, and sanctified it: because that in it he had rested from all his work which God created and made.

These are the generations of the heavens and of the earth when they were created, in the day that the Lord God made the earth and the heavens, And every plant of the field before it was in the earth, and every herb of the field before it grew: for the Lord God had not caused it to rain upon the earth, and there was not a man to till the ground. But there went up a mist from the earth, and watered the whole face of the ground. And the Lord God formed man of the dust of the ground, and breathed into his nostrils the breath of life; and man became a living soul.

READING AND DISCUSSION QUESTIONS

1. Consider the stages of creation. What does their order reveal about the Hebrew faith?

2. God creates man on the sixth day, but a few verses later the text states that "there was not a man to till the ground," then a mist watered the earth and God formed man from the dust of the ground. Why does God seem to create man twice, and what could this indicate about the way the text was created?

3. Explain the following passage: "Be fruitful, and multiply, and replenish the earth, and subdue it."

4. Why does the text state that at the end of various stages of creation, God "saw that it was good"?

DOCUMENT 2-2

Book of Exodus: Moses Descends Mount Sinai with the Ten Commandments

ca. 950–450 B.C.E.

Moses was the greatest of the Hebrew prophets, and is revered by Jews, Christians, and Muslims alike. After Moses led his people out of bondage in Egypt, God revealed a series of commandments to Moses on Mount Sinai. This was not the first occasion when God handed down moral commandments to his people, but it was here that He forbade his people to worship other gods. The passage establishes monotheism, the worship of only one God, as a tenet of the Hebrew religion.

And it came to pass on the third day in the morning, that there were thunders and lightnings, and a thick cloud upon the mount, and the voice of the trumpet exceeding loud; so that all the people that was in the camp trembled. And Moses brought forth the people out of the camp to meet with God; and they stood at the nether part of the mount. And mount

Exodus 19:16–25; 20:1–21.

Sinai was altogether on a smoke, because the Lord descended upon it in fire: and the smoke thereof ascended as the smoke of a furnace, and the whole mount quaked greatly. And when the voice of the trumpet sounded long, and waxed louder and louder, Moses spake, and God answered him by a voice. And the Lord came down upon mount Sinai, on the top of the mount: and the Lord called Moses up to the top of the mount; and Moses went up. And the Lord said unto Moses, Go down, charge the people, lest they break through unto the Lord to gaze, and many of them perish. And let the priests also, which come near to the Lord, sanctify themselves, lest the Lord break forth upon them. And Moses said unto the Lord, The people cannot come up to mount Sinai: for thou chargedst us, saying, Set bounds about the mount, and sanctify it. And the Lord said unto him, Away, get thee down, and thou shalt come up, thou, and Aaron with thee: but let not the priests and the people break through to come up unto the Lord, lest he break forth upon them. So Moses, went down unto the people, and spake unto them.

And God spake all these words, saying, I am the Lord thy God, which have brought thee out of the land of Egypt, out of the house of bondage. Thou shalt have no other gods before me. Thou shalt not make unto thee any graven image, or any likeness of any thing that is in heaven above, or that is in the earth beneath, or that is in the water under the earth: Thou shalt not bow down thyself to them, nor serve them: for I the Lord thy God am a jealous God, visiting the iniquity of the fathers upon the children unto the third and fourth generation of them that hate me; And shewing mercy unto thousands of them that love me, and keep my commandments. Thou shalt not take the name of the Lord thy God in vain; for the Lord will not hold him guiltless that taketh his name in vain. Remember the sabbath day, to keep it holy. Six days shalt thou labor, and do all thy work: But the seventh day is the sabbath of the Lord thy God: in it thou shalt not do any work, thou, nor thy son, nor thy daughter, thy manservant, nor thy maidservant, nor thy cattle, nor thy stranger that is within thy gates: For in six days the Lord made heaven and earth, the sea, and all that in them is, and rested the seventh day: wherefore the Lord blessed the sabbath day, and hallowed it.

Honor thy father and thy mother: that thy days may be long upon the land which the Lord thy God giveth thee. Thou shalt not kill. Thou shalt not commit adultery. Thou shalt not steal. Thou shalt not bear false witness against thy neighbor. Thou shalt not covet thy neighbor's house, thou shalt not covet thy neighbor's wife, nor his manservant, nor his maidservant, nor his ox, nor his ass, nor any thing that is thy neighbor's.

And all the people saw the thunderings, and the lightnings, and the noise of the trumpet, and the mountain smoking: and when the people saw it, they removed, and stood afar off. And they said unto Moses, Speak thou with us, and we will hear: but let not God speak with us, lest we die. And Moses said unto the people, Fear not: for God is come to prove you, and that his fear may be before your faces, that ye sin not. And the people stood afar off, and Moses drew near unto the thick darkness where God was.

READING AND DISCUSSION QUESTIONS

1. Consider the description of God's descent upon Mount Sinai and the following passage: "And the Lord said unto Moses, Go down, charge the people, lest they break through unto the Lord to gaze, and many of them perish." What do they reveal about the Hebrews' conception of God's power?

2. Why are priests required to sanctify themselves?

3. How does the command "Honor thy father and thy mother" and those that follow differ from the earlier commandments?

4. Why does God forbid the creation and worship of graven images?

DOCUMENT 2-3

SENNACHERIB, KING OF ASSYRIA

Jerusalem Besieged

701 B.C.E.

Around 930 B.C.E., the kingdom of Israel, which had been ruled by David and Solomon, split into a northern kingdom (which retained the name Israel) and the southern kingdom of Judah. Approximately two hundred years later, Israel was conquered by the Assyrians and many of its people

James B. Pritchard, ed., *Ancient Near Eastern Texts Relating to the New Testament*, 3d ed. (Princeton, N.J.: Princeton University Press, 1969), 287–288.

dispersed. Hezekiah (r. 716/5–687 B.C.E.) ruled the independent kingdom of Judah, and kept the peace by paying tribute to the kings of Assyria. In 705 B.C.E., after the death of Sargon II of Assyria, Hezekiah ceased paying tribute and formed an alliance with Egypt instead. The following passage, translated from a clay prism unearthed from the ruins of the Assyrian capital city of Ninevah, describes how the Assyrian king Sennacherib, Sargon II's son, reconquered the area.

In my third campaign I marched against Hatti. Luli, king of Sidon, whom the terror-inspiring glamor of my lordship had overwhelmed, fled far overseas and perished. The awe-inspiring splendor of the "Weapon" of Ashur, my lord, overwhelmed his strong cities (such as) Great Sidon, Little Sidon, Bit-Zitti, Zaribtu, Mahalliba, Ushu, Akzib (and) Akko, (all) his fortress cities, walled (and well) provided with feed and water for his garrisons, and they bowed in submission to my feet. I installed Ethbaal upon the throne to be their king and imposed upon him tribute (due) to me (as his) overlord (to be paid) annually without interruption.

As to all the kings of Amurru-Menahem from Samsimuruna, Tubalu from Sidon, Abdiliti from Arvad, Urumilki from Byblos, Mitinti from Ashdod, Buduili from Beth-Ammon, Kammusun-adbi from Moab (and) Aiarammu from Edom, they brought sumptuous gifts and-fourfold-their heavy tamartu-presents to me and kissed my feet. Sidqia, however, king of Ashkelon, who did not bow to my yoke, I deported and sent to Assyria, his family-gods, himself, his wife, his children, his brothers, all the male descendants of his family. I set Sharruludari, son of Rukibtu, their former king, over the inhabitants of Ashkelon and imposed upon him the payment of tribute (and of) katru-presents (due) to me (as) overlord-and he (now) pulls the straps (of my yoke)![1]

In the continuation of my campaign I besieged Beth-Dagon, Joppa, Banai-Barqa, Azuru, cities belonging to Sidqia who did not bow to my feet quickly (enough); I conquered (them) and carried their spoils away. The officials, the patricians and the (common) people of Ekron-who had thrown Padi, their king, into fetters (because he was) loyal to (his) solemn oath (sworn) by the god Ashur, and had handed him over to Hezekiah, the Jew (and) he (Hezekiah) held him in prison, unlawfully, as if he (Padi) be an enemy-had become afraid and had called (for help) upon the kings of Egypt (and) the bowmen, the chariot(-corps) and the cavalry of the king of

---

[1] **pulls the straps (of my yoke)**: As in servitude, like a draft animal harnessed to a plow.

Ethiopia, an army beyond counting-and they (actually) had come to their assistance. In the plain of Eltekeh, their battle lines were drawn up against me and they sharpened their weapons. Upon a trust(-inspiring) oracle (given) by Ashur, my lord, I fought with them and inflicted a defeat upon them. In the melee of the battle, I personally captured alive the Egyptian charioteers with the(ir) princes and (also) the charioteers of the king of Ethiopia. I besieged Eltekeh (and) Timnah, conquered (them) and carried their spoils away. I assaulted Ekron and killed the officials and patricians who had committed the crime and hung their bodies on poles surrounding the city. The (common) citizens who were guilty of minor crimes, I considered prisoners of war. The rest of them, those who were not accused of crimes and misbehavior, I released. I made Padi, their king, come from Jerusalem and set him as their lord on the throne, imposing upon him the tribute (due) to me (as) overlord.

As to Hezekiah, the Jew, he did not submit to my yoke, I laid siege to 46 of his strong cities, walled forts and to the countless small villages in their vicinity, and conquered (them) by means of well-stamped (earth-) ramps, and battering-rams brought (thus) near (to the walls) (combined with) the attack by foot soldiers, (using) mines, breeches as well as sapper work. I drove out (of them) 200,150 people, young and old, male and female, horses, mules, donkeys, camels, big and small cattle beyond counting, and considered (them) booty. Himself I made a prisoner in Jerusalem, his royal residence, like a bird in a cage. I surrounded him with earthwork in order to molest those who were leaving his city's gate. His towns which I had plundered, I took away from his country and gave them (over) to Mitinti, king of Ashdod, Padi, king of Ekron, and Sillibel, king of Gaza. Thus I reduced his country, but I still increased the tribute and the katru-presents (due) to me (as his) overlord which I imposed (later) upon him beyond the former tribute, to be delivered annually. Hezekiah himself, whom the terror-inspiring splendor of my lordship had overwhelmed and whose irregular and elite troops which he had brought into Jerusalem, his royal residence, in order to strengthen (it), had deserted him, did send me, later, to Nineveh, my lordly city, together with 30 talents of gold, 800 talents of silver, precious stones, antimony, large cuts of red stone, couches (inlaid) with ivory, nimedu-chairs (inlaid) with ivory, elephant-hides, ebony-wood, boxwood (and) all kinds of valuable treasures, his (own) daughters, concubines, male and female musicians. In order to deliver the tribute and to do obeisance as a slave he sent his (personal) messenger.

READING AND DISCUSSION QUESTIONS

1. Why was Padi the king deposed by the people of Ekron, and why was he restored by the Assyrians? What does this reveal about Assyrian methods of rule?

2. The capture of Jerusalem was one incident in a larger war. What were some of Sennacherib's most successful military strategies?

3. If you were a ruler or citizen of one of the lands that the Assyrians captured, what were your possible fates?

4. Why might the passage end with a list of gifts that Hezekiah sent to Sennacherib?

DOCUMENT 2-4

Inscription Honoring Cyrus, King of Persia

ca. 550 B.C.E.

Cyrus the Great (died 530/529 B.C.E.) was a king of Persia who expanded his rule to create one of the largest empires in the world up to that time. He conquered the Medes (to whom the Persians had been subject), the Lydians (in what is now western Turkey), and the Neo-Babylonians in the heart of Mesopotamia. He also established his rule over vast areas of central Asia. Cyrus followed a policy of fair treatment for conquered peoples, freeing the Jews from their "Babylonian captivity" and allowing them to return to their homeland. Cyrus had his legacy inscribed in a clay cylinder, dubbed by some "the first charter of human rights."

I am Cyrus, king of the world, great king, legitimate king, king of Babylon, king of Sumer and Akkad, king of the four rims [of the earth], son of Cambyses, great king, king of Anshan, grandson of Cyrus, great king, king of Anshan, descendant of Teispes, great king, king of Anshan, of a family

James B. Pritchard, ed., *Ancient Near Eastern Texts Relating to the Old Testament*, 3d ed. (Princeton, N.J.: Princeton University Press, 1969), 315–316.

[which] always [exercised] kingship; whose rule Bel and Nabu love, whom they want as king to please their hearts.

When I entered Babylon as a friend and [when] I established the seat of government in the palace of the ruler under jubilation and rejoicing. Marduk, the great lord (induced) the magnanimous inhabitants of Babylon (to love me), and I was daily endeavoring to worship him. My numerous troops walked around in Babylon in peace, I did not allow anybody to terrorize [any place] of the [country of Sumer] and Akkad. I strove for peace in Babylon, [I abolished] the [labor tribute] which was against their [social] standing. I brought relief to their dilapidated housings, putting an end to their complaints. Marduk, the great Lord, was well pleased with my deeds and sent friendly blessings to myself, Cyrus, the king who worships him, to Cambyses, my son, the offspring of my loins, as well as to all my troops, and we all [praised] his great [godhead] joyously, standing before him in peace.

All the kings of the entire world from the Upper to the Lower Sea, those who are seated in throne rooms, [those who] live in other [types of buildings as well as] all the kings of the West land living in tents, brought their heavy tributes and kissed my feet in Babylon. [As to the region] from . . . as far as Ashur and Susa, Agade, Eshnuna, the towns of Zamban, Me-Turnu, Der, as well as the region of the Gutium, I returned to [these] sacred cities on the other sides of the Tigris, the sanctuaries of which have been ruins for a long time, the images which [used] to live therein and established for them permanent sanctuaries. I [also] gathered all their [former] inhabitants and returned [to them] their habitations. Furthermore, I resettled upon the command of Marduk, the great lord, all the gods of Sumer and Akkad who Nabonidus[2] has brought into Babylon to the anger of the lord of the gods, unharmed, in the [former] chapels, the places which make them happy.

May all the gods whom I have resettled in their sacred cities ask daily Bel and Nebo for a long life for me and may they recommend me [to him]; to Marduk, my lord, they may say this: "Cyrus, the king who worships you, and Cambyses, his son. . . ." . . . all of them I settled in a peaceful place . . . ducks and doves . . . I endeavored to repair their dwelling places. . . .

---

[2] **Nabonidus**: The last king of the Neo-Babylonian empire, whom Cyrus overthrew.

READING AND DISCUSSION QUESTIONS

1. Why does Cyrus claim that he entered Babylon as a friend, and what orders did he give his troops about treating the Babylonians?

2. What reforms and improvements did Cyrus bring to Babylon? Why would Cyrus solve problems that he had not created in the first place?

3. How did Cyrus treat people who had been displaced from their homes?

4. How did Cyrus seem to regard the many religious foundations of his new subjects?

COMPARATIVE QUESTIONS

1. What are some differences or similarities between the Mesopotamian creation myth (Document 1-1) and the Hebrew creation myth in this chapter? What are their tones like?

2. What, if any, differences can you find between man as created by God in Genesis and man as commanded by God in Exodus? What kind of God is the God in each document?

3. Independent sources exist that describe the conquests that Sennacherib recounts in the third document, whereas the authorship of the biblical accounts in the first two documents is hotly debated. What are some reasons scholars may be unable to reach consensus?

4. Compare and contrast the proclamations of Sennacherib and Cyrus. Why did the two rulers present themselves in such different ways? How do these documents reflect the contrasting ways in which the Assyrians and Persians treated conquered peoples?

CHAPTER 3

Classical Greece

ca. 1650–338 B.C.E.

H omer (ca. 800 B.C.E.) was credited with composing the *Iliad* and the *Odyssey*, two of the most famous epic poems of all time. The thoughts of the earliest Greek philosophers, the Pre-Socratics, generally remain only in fragments, often in the form of remarks that later writers made about them. Plato (427–347 B.C.E.), his mentor Socrates (ca. 470–399 B.C.E.), and their contemporaries lived later than Homer, in Classical Greece, a period of burgeoning public interest in art and philosophy. The philosophers and writers of Classical Greece were greatly concerned with ethics and man's place in the world, and they questioned conventional values and assumptions. Plato advanced arguments in the form of "dialogues" to spread his philosophical debates beyond his own circle. The playwright Aristophanes' work reveals that in his own time, a philosopher like Socrates could be a figure of great controversy. Homer, Socrates, and Plato are the ancestors of modern Western literature and philosophy, and many of the questions they explored are questions that people are still attempting to answer today.

DOCUMENT 3-1

HOMER

From Odyssey: Odysseus Is Rescued

ca. 800 B.C.E.

Homer's Odyssey, *a masterwork of Western literature and an important cultural, religious, and social record of Greek civilization, is one of our few historical documents from the early period of Greek history. Composed in*

The Odyssey of Homer, translated with Introduction and Notes by S. H. Butcher and A. Lang (New York: Collier, 1909). The Harvard Classics, v. 22.

dactylic hexameter, a form of verse that is usually sung, the Odyssey *was probably passed down orally. It tells the story of hero Odysseus's 10-year journey home to Ithaca after his victory in the Trojan War (possibly 1200 or 1100 B.C.E.). The* Odyssey *begins in the middle of this journey, and Homer uses flashback to supply background information as his protagonist's struggles unfold. In the following passage, Odysseus has just been cast ashore on a strange island and needs food, shelter, and clothing.*

The goodly Odysseus came forth from beneath the bushes, and with his stout hand he broke from the thick wood a leafy branch, that he might hold it about him and hide therewith his nakedness. Forth he came like a mountain-nurtured lion trusting in his might, who goes forth, beaten with rain and wind, but his two eyes are ablaze: into the midst of the kine [cows] he goes, or of the sheep, or on the track of the wild deer, and his belly bids him go even into the close-built fold, to make an attack upon the flocks. Even so Odysseus was about to enter the company of the fair-tressed maidens, naked though he was, for need had come upon him. But terrible did he seem to them, all befouled with brine, and they shrank in fear, one here, one there, along the jutting sand-spits. Alone the daughter of Alcinous kept her place, for in her heart Athene[1] put courage, and took fear from her limbs. She fled not, but stood and faced him; and Odysseus pondered whether he should clasp the knees of the fair-faced maid, and make his prayer, or whether, standing apart as he was, he should beseech her with gentle words, in hope that she might show him the city and give him raiment. And, as he pondered, it seemed to him better to stand apart and beseech her with gentle words, lest the maiden's heart should be wroth with him if he clasped her knees; so straight-way he spoke a gentle word and crafty:

"I beseech thee, O queen, — a goddess art thou, or art thou mortal? If thou art a goddess, one of those who hold broad heaven, to Artemis, the daughter of great Zeus,[2] do I liken thee most nearly in comeliness and in stature and in form. But if thou art one of mortals who dwell upon the earth, thrice-blessed then are thy father and thy honored mother, and thrice-blessed thy brethren. Full well, I ween, are their hearts ever warmed with joy because of thee, as they see thee entering the dance, a plant so fair. But he again is blessed in heart above all others, who shall prevail with

---

[1] **Athene**: An armed warrior goddess and patroness of heroic endeavor.
[2] **Zeus**: King of the gods.

his gifts of wooing and lead thee to his home. For never yet have mine eyes looked upon a mortal such as thou, whether man or woman; amazement holds me as I look on thee. On a truth in Delos once I saw such a thing, a young shoot of a palm springing up beside the altar of Apollo[3] — for thither, too, I went, and much people followed with me, on that journey on which evil woes were to be my portion; — even so, when I saw that, I marvelled long at heart, for never yet did such a tree spring up from the earth. And in like manner, lady, do I marvel at thee, and am amazed, and fear greatly to touch thy knees; but sore grief has come upon me. Yesterday, on the twentieth day, I escaped from the wine-dark sea, but ever until then the wave and the swift winds bore me from the island of Ogygia; and now fate has cast me ashore here, that here too, haply, I may suffer some ill. For not yet, methinks, will my troubles cease, but the gods ere that will bring many to pass. Nay, O queen, have pity; for it is to thee first that I am come after many grievous toils, and of the others who possess this city and land I know not one. Shew me the city, and give me some rag to throw about me, if thou hadst any wrapping for the clothes when thou camest hither. And for thyself, may the gods grant thee all that thy heart desires; a husband and a home may they grant thee, and oneness of heart — a goodly gift. For nothing is greater or better than this, when man and wife dwell in a home in one accord, a great grief to their foes and a joy to their friends; but they know it best themselves."

Then white-armed Nausicaä answered him; "Stranger, since thou seemest to be neither an evil man nor a witless, and it is Zeus himself, the Olympian, that gives happy fortune to men, both to the good and the evil, to each man as he will; so to thee, I ween, he has given this lot, and thou must in any case endure it. But now, since thou hast come to our city and land, thou shalt not lack clothing or aught else of those things which befit a sore-tried suppliant when he cometh in the way. The city will I shew thee, and will tell thee the name of the people. The Phaeacians possess this city and land, and I am the daughter of great-hearted Alcinous, upon whom depend the might and power of the Phaeacians."

She spoke, and called to her fair-tressed handmaids: "Stand, my maidens. Whither do ye flee at the sight of a man? Ye do not think, surely, that he is an enemy? That mortal man lives not, nor exists nor shall ever be born who shall come to the land of the Phaeacians as a foe-man, for we are

---

[3] **Apollo**: Son of Zeus and Artemis's twin brother. In Homer's *Illiad*, Apollo defended the Apollo-worshipping Trojans in the Trojan War.

very dear to the immortals. Far off we dwell in the surging sea, the furthermost of men, and no other mortals have dealings with us. Nay, this is some hapless wanderer that has come hither. Him must we now tend; for from Zeus are all strangers and beggars; and a gift, though small, is welcome. Come, then, my maidens, give to the stranger food and drink, and bathe him in the river in a spot where there is shelter from the wind."

So she spoke, and they halted and called to each other. Then they set Odysseus in a sheltered place, as Nausicaä, the daughter of great-hearted Alcinous, bade, and beside him they put a cloak and a tunic for raiment, and gave him soft olive oil in the flask of gold, and bade him bathe in the streams of the river. Then among the maidens spoke goodly Odysseus: "Maidens, stand yonder apart, that by myself I may wash the brine from my shoulders, and anoint myself with olive oil; for of a truth it is long since oil came near my skin. But in your presence will I not bathe, for I am ashamed to make me naked in the midst of fair-tressed maidens."

READING AND DISCUSSION QUESTIONS

1. Why does Odysseus flatter Nausicaä? What do his descriptions of her beauty tell us about the Greek ideal of beauty?

2. When Odysseus asks whether Nausicaä is a goddess or a mortal woman, he is not simply flattering her. Throughout both the *Iliad* and *Odyssey*, gods and goddesses frequently appear to mortals, often in the form of a mortal. What does this reveal about Greek notions about the relationships between humans and the gods?

3. Of all the Greek heroes, Odysseus is described as the most resourceful. In what ways does this passage support this assessment?

4. Why might Homer have composed this story? Is it meant to be a history lesson, or is it instructional, for entertainment, or some other purpose?

DOCUMENT 3-2

ARISTOPHANES

From The Clouds

ca. 410 B.C.E.

Aristophanes (ca. 446–386 B.C.E.) was one of the greatest Greek playwrights, authoring upwards of forty plays between 427 and 386 B.C.E. Unlike his older contemporaries who specialized in tragedies, Aristophanes wrote comedies, usually about current, often political, events. In this excerpt from Clouds, *which originally won Aristophanes last place at a religious festival, Strepsiades is a fictional citizen of Athens who converses with a farcical Socrates. Although many fellow philosophers and citizens of Athens admired Socrates (at least until he criticized powerful Athenians), Attic comedy often mocked powerful and respected citizens.*

STREPSIADES: Then, woe to you! And who is this man suspended up in a basket?

DISCIPLE: 'Tis *he himself.*

STREPSIADES: Who himself?

DISCIPLE: Socrates.

STREPSIADES: Socrates! Oh! I pray you, call him right loudly for me.

DISCIPLE: Call him yourself; I have no time to waste.

STREPSIADES: Socrates! my little Socrates!

SOCRATES: Mortal, what do you want with me?

STREPSIADES: First, what are you doing up there? Tell me, I beseech you.

SOCRATES: I traverse the air and contemplate the sun.

STREPSIADES: Thus 'tis not on the solid ground, but from the height of this basket, that you slight the gods, if indeed . . .

SOCRATES: I have to suspend my brain and mingle the subtle essence of my mind with this air, which is of the like nature, in order to clearly penetrate the things of heaven. I should have discovered nothing, had I remained on the ground to consider from below the things that are above; for the earth by its force attracts the sap of the mind to itself. 'Tis just the same with the water-cress.

Aristophanes, *The Clouds*, in *Eleven Comedies*, trans. anon. (New York: Liveright, 1943), 310–314.

STREPSIADES: What? Does the mind attract the sap of the water-cress? Ah! my dear little Socrates, come down to me! I have come to ask you for lessons.

SOCRATES: And for what lessons? . . .

SOCRATES: Do you really wish to know the truth of celestial matters?

STREPSIADES: Why, truly, if 'tis possible.

SOCRATES: . . . and to converse with the clouds, who are our genii?

STREPSIADES: Without a doubt.

SOCRATES: Then be seated on this sacred couch.

STREPSIADES: I am seated.

SOCRATES: Now take this chaplet [wreath].

STREPSIADES: Why a chaplet? Alas! Socrates, would you sacrifice me, like Athamas?[4]

SOCRATES: No, these are the rites of initiation.

STREPSIADES: And what is it I am to gain?

SOCRATES: You will become a thorough rattle-pate [whimsical person], a hardened old stager [actor], the fine flour of the talkers. . . . But come, keep quiet.

STREPSIADES: By Zeus! You lie not! Soon I shall be nothing but wheat-flour, if you powder me in this fashion.

SOCRATES: Silence, old man, give heed to the prayers. . . . Oh! most mighty king, the boundless air, that keepest the earth suspended in space, thou bright Aether[5] and ye venerable goddesses, the Clouds, who carry in your loins the thunder and the lightning, arise, ye sovereign powers and manifest yourselves in the celestial spheres to the eyes of the sage.

STREPSIADES: Not yet! Wait a bit, till I fold my mantle double, so as not to get wet. And to think that I did not even bring my travelling cap! What a misfortune!

SOCRATES: Come, oh! Clouds, whom I adore, come and show yourselves to this man, whether you be resting on the sacred summits of Olympus, crowned with hoar-frost, or tarrying in the gardens of Ocean, your father, forming sacred choruses with the Nymphs; whether you be gathering the waves of the Nile in golden vases or dwelling in the Maeotic marsh or on the snowy rocks of Mimas, hearken to my prayer and accept my offering. May these sacrifices be pleasing to you.

---

[4] **Athamas**: A mythological Greek king who was told he must be sacrificed to the gods, and was led to the altar wearing a wreath upon his head.

[5] **Aether**: The personification of heaven, or sky.

CHORUS: Eternal Clouds, let us appear, let us arise from the roaring depth of Ocean, our father; let us fly towards the lofty mountains, spread our damp wings over their forest-laden summits, whence we will dominate the distant valleys, the harvest fed by the sacred earth, the murmur of the divine streams and the resounding waves of the sea, which the unwearying orb lights up with its glittering beams. But let us shake off the rainy fogs, which hide our immortal beauty and sweep the earth from afar with our gaze.

SOCRATES: Oh, venerated goddesses, yes, you are answering my call! (*To Strepsiades.*) Did you hear their voices mingling with the awful growling of the thunder?

STREPSIADES: Oh! adorable Clouds, I revere you and I too am going to let off *my* thunder, so greatly has your own affrighted me. Faith! whether permitted or not, I must, I must crap!

SOCRATES: No scoffing; do not copy those accursed comic poets. Come, silence! a numerous host of goddesses approaches with songs. . . .

READING AND DISCUSSION QUESTIONS

1. Why does Socrates need to "mingle the subtle essence of my mind with this air"? What is the point of Aristophanes' joke?

2. Why is Socrates studying the clouds?

3. What is the function of the Chorus in this scene? Who are they?

4. How can Aristophanes get away with telling dirty jokes at a religious festival? What does this tell you about Greek religion?

DOCUMENT 3-3

THALES, ANAXIMANDER, EMPEDOCLES,

AND DEMOCRITUS

The Pre-Socratic Philosophers Seek Answers

ca. 500 B.C.E.–250 C.E.

The teachings of many early Greek philosophers survive only in fragments. Often we know about them primarily through casual mentions of their theories in the writings of Classical philosophers like Aristotle (384–322 B.C.E.), a student of Plato's, and Diogenes Laertius (ca. 200–250 C.E.). Apart from the thin historical record, one difficulty is that the Greeks sometimes attribute different meanings to words we commonly use. For instance, it may seem reasonable to think that the notions of love and strife have remained the same for centuries, but Empedocles (ca. 490–430 B.C.E.) writes about them as though they are principles of nature, such as the laws of gravity or chemistry.

THALES

Some say that the earth rests on water. We have ascertained that the oldest statement of this character is the one accredited to Thales the Milesian, to the effect that it rests on water, floating like a piece of wood or something else of that sort. (Aristotle, *On the Heavens*)

And Thales, according to what is related of him, seems to have regarded the soul as something endowed with the power of motion, if indeed he said that the loadstone[6] has a soul because it moves iron. (Aristotle, *On the Soul*)

ANAXIMANDER

The beginning of that which is, is the boundless but whence that which is arises, thither must it return again of necessity; for the things give

Fairbanks, Arthur, ed. and trans., *The First Philosopher of Greece* (London: K. Paul, Trench, Trubner, 1898), 157–234.

T. V. Smith, *From Thales to Plato* (Chicago: University of Chicago Press, 1934), 6–7, 28–31, 45.

[6]**loadstone**: A magnetic stone used in early compasses.

satisfaction and reparation to one another for their injustice, as is appointed according to the ordering of time.

For some who hold that the real, the underlying substance, is a unity, either one of the three (elements) or something else that is denser than fire and more rarefied than air, teach that other things are generated by condensation and rarefaction. . . . And others believe that existing opposites are separated from the unity, as Anaximander says. . . .

There is no beginning of the infinite, for in that case it would have an end. But it is without beginning and indestructible, as being a sort of first principle; for it is necessary that whatever comes into existence should have an end, and there is a conclusion of all destruction. Wherefore as we say, there is no first principle of this (i.e., the infinite), but it itself seems to be the first principle of all other things and to surround all and to direct all, as they say who think that there are no other causes besides the infinite (such as mind, or friendship), but that it itself is divine; for it is immortal and indestructible, as Anaximander and most of the physicists say. (Aristotle, *Physics*)

EMPEDOCLES

33. Hear first the four roots of all things: bright Zeus [fire], life-giving Hera (air), and Aidoneus (earth), and Nestis (water) who moistens the springs of men with her tears.

36. And a second thing I will tell thee: There is no origination of anything that is mortal, nor yet any end in baneful death; but only mixture and separation of what is mixed, but men call this "origination."

40. But when light is mingled with air in human form, or in form like the race of wild beasts or of plants or of birds, then men say that these things have come into being; and when they are separated, they call them evil fate; this is the established practice, and I myself also call it so in accordance with the custom.

45. Fools! for they have no far-reaching studious thoughts who think that what was not before comes into being or that anything dies and perishes utterly.

48. For from what does not exist at all it is impossible that anything come into being, and it is neither possible nor perceivable that

being should perish completely; for things will always stand wherever one in each case shall put them. . . .

60. Twofold is the truth I shall speak; for at one time there grew to be one alone out of many, and at another time, however, it separated so that there were many out of the one. Twofold is the coming into being, twofold the passing away, of perishable things; for the latter (i.e., passing away) the combining of all things both begets and destroys, and the former (i.e., coming into being), which was nurtured again out of parts that were being separated, is itself scattered. . . .

66. And these (elements) never cease changing place continually, now being all united by Love into one, now each borne apart by the hatred engendered of Strife, until they are brought together in the unity of the all, and become subject to it. Thus inasmuch as one has been wont to arise out of many and again with the separation of the one the many arise, so things are continually coming into being and there is no fixed age for them; and farther inasmuch as they [the elements] never cease changing place continually, so they always exist within an immovable circle. . . .

96. But come, gaze on the things that bear farther witness to my former words, if in what was said before there be anything defective in form. Behold the sun, warm and bright on all sides, and whatever is immortal and is bathed in its bright ray, and behold the raincloud, dark and cold on all sides; from the earth there proceed the foundations of things and solid bodies. In Strife all things are, endured with form and separate from each other, but they come together in Love and are desired by each other.

104. For from these (elements) come all things that are or have been or shall be; from these there grew up trees and men and women, wild beasts and birds and water-nourished fishes, and the very gods, long-lived, highest in honor.

139. But when mighty Strife was nurtured in its members and leaped up to honor at the completion of the time, which has been driven on by them both in turn under a mighty oath. . . .

210. And if your faith be at all lacking in regard to these (elements), how from water and earth and air and sun (fire) when they are mixed, arose such colours and forms of mortals things, as many as now have arisen under the uniting power of Aphrodite.[7] . . .

236. Hair and leaves and thick feathers of birds are the same thing in origin, and reptiles' scales, too, on strong limbs. . . .

247. This is indeed remarkable in the mass of human members; at one time all the limbs which form the body, uniting into one by Love, grow vigorously in the prime of life; but yet at another time, separated by evil Strife, they wander each in different directions along the breakers of the sea of life. Just so it is with plants and with fishes dwelling in watery halls, and beasts whose lair is in the mountains, and birds borne on wings. . . . (Empedocles, *Fragments*)

DEMOCRITUS

The first principles of the universe are atoms and empty space; everything else is merely thought to exist. The worlds are unlimited; they come into being and perish. Nothing can come into being from that which is not nor pass away into that which is not. Further, the atoms are unlimited in size and number, and they are borne along in the whole universe in a vortex, and thereby generate all composite things — fire, water, air, earth; for even these are conglomerations of given atoms. And it is because of their solidity that these atoms are impassive and unalterable. The sun and the moon have been composed of such smooth and spherical masses, i.e., atoms, and so also the soul, which is identical with reason. We see by virtue of the impact of images upon our eyes.

All things happen by virtue of necessity, the vortex being the cause of the creation of all things, and this he calls necessity. The end of action is tranquility, which is not identical with pleasure, as some by a false interpretation have understood, but a state in which the soul continues calm and strong, undisturbed by any fear of superstition or any other emotion. This he (Democritus) calls wellbeing and many other names; the qualities of things exist merely by convention; in nature there is nothing but atoms and void space. These, then, are his opinions. (Diogenes Laertius, *Lives of Eminent Philosophers*)

---

[7] **Aphrodite:** Greek goddess of love and beauty.

READING AND DISCUSSION QUESTIONS

1. Describe the Pre-Socratic philosophers' different explanations for the origin of all things.

2. Explain what Empedocles means when he claims that "it is neither possible nor perceivable that being should perish completely."

3. Sometimes these philosophers speak of gods or goddesses as though they were elements or principles of nature. Give two examples and explain the role of these divine beings, according to each philosopher.

4. Choose a passage in which science seems to intermingle with philosophy. Why might these thinkers seem to reject drawing boundaries between these areas of thought?

5. What common threads seem to run between the different passages? What, if any, similar terminology do they use?

DOCUMENT 3-4

PLATO

From The Republic: *On the Equality of Women*

ca. 380 B.C.E.

Plato wrote The Republic *approximately twenty years after the death of his mentor Socrates in 399 B.C.E. Socrates had described himself as a midwife, someone who helped others give birth to their own ideas, and Plato likewise adopts a dialogue form in which characters argue, debate, and exchange ideas to arrive at reasoned conclusions. Although it is not clear to what extent Plato was representing Socrates' own ideas, it may be significant that Glaucon, the other participant in the dialogue, was Plato's older brother. In the exchange, Socrates and Glaucon are trying to define what justice truly is, and to do so Socrates suggests that they first try to define an ideal city and ideal rulers.*

Plato, *Republic* 5, trans. Benjamin Jowett, *Dialogues of Plato* (Oxford: Clarendon Press, 1892), 147–150.

SOCRATES: Next, we shall ask our opponent how, in reference to any of the pursuits or arts of civic life, the nature of a woman differs from that of a man?

GLAUCON: That will be quite fair.

SOCRATES: And perhaps he, like yourself, will reply that to give a sufficient answer on the instant is not easy; but after a little reflection there is no difficulty.

GLAUCON: Yes, perhaps.

SOCRATES: Suppose then that we invite him to accompany us in the argument, and then we may hope to show him that there is nothing peculiar in the constitution of women which would affect them in the administration of the State.

GLAUCON: By all means. . . .

SOCRATES: And can you mention any pursuit of mankind in which the male sex has not all these gifts and qualities in a higher degree than the female? Need I waste time in speaking of the art of weaving, and the management of pancakes and preserves, in which womankind does really appear to be great, and in which for her to be beaten by a man is of all things the most absurd?

GLAUCON: You are quite right, he replied, in maintaining the general inferiority of the female sex: although many women are in many things superior to many men, yet on the whole what you say is true.

SOCRATES: And if so, my friend, I said, there is no special faculty of administration in a state which a woman has because she is a woman, or which a man has by virtue of his sex, but the gifts of nature are alike diffused in both; all the pursuits of men are the pursuits of women also, but in all of them a woman is inferior to a man.

GLAUCON: Very true.

SOCRATES: Then are we to impose all our enactments on men and none of them on women?

GLAUCON: That will never do.

SOCRATES: One woman has a gift of healing, another not; one is a musician, and another has no music in her nature?

GLAUCON: Very true.

SOCRATES: And one woman has a turn for gymnastic and military exercises, and another is unwarlike and hates gymnastics?

GLAUCON: Certainly.

SOCRATES: And one woman is a philosopher, and another is an enemy of philosophy; one has spirit, and another is without spirit?

GLAUCON: That is also true.

SOCRATES: Then one woman will have the temper of a guardian,[8] and another not. Was not the selection of the male guardians determined by differences of this sort?

GLAUCON: Yes.

SOCRATES: Men and women alike possess the qualities which make a guardian; they differ only in their comparative strength or weakness.

GLAUCON: Obviously.

SOCRATES: And those women who have such qualities are to be selected as the companions and colleagues of men who have similar qualities and whom they resemble in capacity and in character?

GLAUCON: Very true.

SOCRATES: And ought not the same natures to have the same pursuits?

GLAUCON: They ought.

SOCRATES: Then, as we were saying before, there is nothing unnatural in assigning music and gymnastic to the wives of the guardians — to that point we come round again.

GLAUCON: Certainly not. . . .

SOCRATES: Well, and may we not further say that our guardians are the best of our citizens?

GLAUCON: By far the best.

SOCRATES: And will not their wives be the best women?

GLAUCON: Yes, by far the best.

SOCRATES: And can there be anything better for the interests of the State than that the men and women of a State should be as good as possible?

GLAUCON: There can be nothing better.

SOCRATES: And this is what the arts of music and gymnastic, when present in such manner as we have described, will accomplish?

GLAUCON: Certainly.

SOCRATES: Then we have made an enactment not only possible but in the highest degree beneficial to the State?

GLAUCON: True.

SOCRATES: Then let the wives of our guardians strip, for their virtue will be their robe, and let them share in the toils of war and the defense of their country; only in the distribution of labors the lighter are to be assigned to the women, who are the weaker natures, but in other respects their duties are to be the same. And as for the man who laughs

---

[8] **guardian:** Socrates believed a perfect society would have three classes of citizens. Guardians, comprising the top class, represent reason and rationality, and are the only citizens qualified to govern.

at naked women exercising their bodies from the best of motives, in his laughter he is plucking a fruit of unripe wisdom, and he himself is ignorant of what he is laughing at, or what he is about; — for that is, and ever will be, the best of sayings, *That the useful is the noble and the hurtful is the base.*

READING AND DISCUSSION QUESTIONS

1. Does Socrates appear to think that women are generally equal to men in their abilities? What does he mean by "comparative strength or weakness"? Explain your reasoning.

2. What point is Socrates trying to make when he compares women to one another?

3. In what, if any, instances does Socrates stop asking questions and instead reach a conclusion? Is there a significance?

4. Explain whether Socrates believes that some women are fit to be guardians. Why or why not?

COMPARATIVE QUESTIONS

1. Compare and contrast the thinking of *one* figure from this chapter to *one* figure who appears in Chapters 1 or 2.

2. Discuss the differing portrayals of Socrates by Aristophanes and Plato.

3. Compare and contrast the depiction of women in Homer and Plato.

4. Discuss the following claim: "In *The Clouds*, Aristophanes was making fun of philosophers in general, not only Socrates." Cite at least one of the Pre-Socratic philosophers in support of your argument.

The Hellenistic World

336–146 B.C.E.

I n 338 B.C.E., Philip II, king of Macedonia, defeated the armies of Athens and Thebes at the battle of Chaeronea and established a Common Peace, a new political system that maintained each Greek city-state's right to its own laws and customs. Following Philip II's assassination in 336 B.C.E., his young son Alexander set about to finish his father's plans and conquer Persia. By the time of his premature death in 323 B.C.E., Alexander had conquered the entire Persian Empire and taken his army through Afghanistan into what is now northwestern India. The newly connected reaches of the expanded Greek Empire became a melting pot of culture in what is commonly referred to as the Hellenistic Period (336–146 B.C.E.). Although Alexander's empire quickly broke up into smaller states, Greek rulers dominated most of the eastern Mediterranean and spread Greek culture, or Hellenism, far into the East. The city of Alexandria, on the Nile delta, became the center of Greek science and learning and the Greek language spread among educated people throughout the Mediterranean world.

DOCUMENT 4-1

On the Burial of Alexander and Hephaestion: Ephippus of Olynthus Remembers Alexander the Great

ca. 323 B.C.E.

Even before his death in 323 B.C.E., Alexander the Great had become a legend. A former student of Aristotle's, Alexander was known not for his philosophical

G. W. Botsford and E. G. Sihler, eds., *Hellenic Civilization* (New York: Columbia University Press, 1915), 682–683.

inquiry but for his prolific military conquests for Greece, including vast stretches of the Persian-ruled Middle East, Central Asia, and India. Alexander was deified, although some historians tried to describe him as the flawed mortal he was. Alexander is known to have appointed a certain Ephippus as a superintendent in Egypt, but it is uncertain whether this man was the Ephippus of Olynthus mentioned in the following passage.

Concerning the luxury of Alexander the Great, Ephippus of Olynthus, in his treatise *On the Burial of Alexander and Hephaestion*, relates that he had in his park a golden throne and couches with silver feet, on which he used to sit while transacting business with his companions. Nicobule[1] says, moreover, that while he was at supper all the dancers and athletes sought to amuse the king. At his very last banquet, Alexander, remembering an episode in the *Andromeda*[2] of Euripides, recited it in a declamatory manner, and then drank a cup of unmixed wine with great zest, and compelled all the rest to do the same. Ephippus tells us, too, that Alexander used to wear at his entertainments even the sacred vestments. Sometimes he would put on the purple robe, cloven sandals, and horns of Ammon,[3] as if he had been the god. Sometimes he would imitate Artemis,[4] whose dress he often wore while driving in his chariot; at the same time he had on a Persian robe, which displayed above his shoulders the bow and javelin of the goddess. At times also he would appear in the guise of Hermes;[5] at other times, and in fact nearly every day, he would wear a purple cloak, a chiton shot with white, and a cap with a royal diadem attached. When too he was in private with his friends he wore the sandals of Hermes, with the petasus on his head and the caduceus in hand. Often however he wore a lion's skin and carried a club like Heracles.[6] . . .

Alexander used also to have the floor sprinkled with exquisite perfumes and with fragrant wine; and myrrh and other kinds of incense were burned before him, while all the bystanders kept silence or spoke words

---

[1] **Nicobule**: A female historian to whom a biography of Alexander is ascribed.
[2] **Andromeda**: Euripides' play of approximately 412 B.C.E., in which the hero Perseus saves Andromeda from being sacrificed to a sea monster.
[3] **horns of Ammon**: Ammon's horns symbolized the Greco-Egyptian "composite god" Zeus-Ammon, a king of all other gods.
[4] **Artemis**: Daughter of Zeus and goddess of fertility and the hunt.
[5] **Hermes**: Messenger of the gods.
[6] **Heracles**: A half-god and the son of Zeus, Heracles was worshipped for his uncomparable strength, courage, and cleverness.

only of good omen because of fear. For he was an extremely violent man with no regard for human life, and gave the impression of a man of choleric temperament. . . .

READING AND DISCUSSION QUESTIONS

1. According to this source, in what ways did Alexander seek to glorify himself? What do his choices reveal about Greek attitudes toward the gods?
2. Why would Alexander recite from the *Andromeda* during the banquet described? What does his selection suggest about Alexander's attitudes toward himself and his subjects?
3. How would you describe the author's (or authors') view of Alexander? Point to specific passages to support your argument.

DOCUMENT 4-2

DIOGENES LAERTIUS

On Hipparchia, A Woman of Intellectual Merit

ca. 300–200 B.C.E.

Hipparchia, born ca. 350 B.C.E., moved with her family to Athens as a young child. As a resident of the capital at the onset of Hellenism, her brother Metrocles enrolled in the Lyceum, the school founded by Aristotle. He eventually left and became a dedicated follower of the philosopher Crates the Cynic, with whom sister Hipparchia fell in love. The Cynics claimed that they had learned much of their style of philosophy from Socrates. Principally concerned with ethics, they were more interested in putting their ideas into practice than in constructing a systematic philosophy. As the philosophical radicals of their times, they were famous for their unconventional ways of life.

G. W. Botsford and E. G. Sihler, eds., *Hellenic Civilization* (New York: Columbia University Press, 1915), 665.

Hipparchia, the sister of Metrocles, was charmed along with others by the doctrines of this school. She and Metrocles were natives of Maroneia.[7] She fell in love with the doctrines and the manners of Crates, and could not be diverted from her regard for him either by the wealth or the high birth or the personal beauty of any of her suitors; but Crates was everything to her. She threatened her parents to make away with herself, if she were not given in marriage to him. When entreated by her parents to dissuade her from this resolution, Crates did all he could; and at last, as he could not persuade her, he arose and placing all his furniture before her, he said: "This is the bridegroom whom you are choosing, and this is the whole of his property. Consider these facts; for it will not be possible for you to become his partner, if you do not apply yourself to the same studies and conform to the same habits as he does." The girl chose him; and assuming the same dress as he wore, went with him as her husband, and appeared with him in public everywhere, and went to all entertainments in his company.

Once when she went to sup at the house of Lysimachus, she attacked Theodorus, who was surnamed the Atheist. To him she proposed the following sophism:[8] "What Theodorus could not be called wrong for doing, that same thing Hipparchia could not be called wrong for doing. But Theodorus does no wrong when he beats himself; therefore Hipparchia does no wrong when she beats Theodorus." He made no reply to what she said, but only pulled her gown. Hipparchia was neither offended nor ashamed, as many a woman would have been; but when he said to her: —

Who is the woman who has left the shuttle
So near the warp?[9]

She replied: "I, Theodorus, am the person; but do I seem to you to have come to a wrong decision, if I devote that time to philosophy which otherwise I should have spent at the loom?" These and many other sayings are reported of this female philosopher.

---

[7] **Maroneia**: A Greek municipality.
[8] **sophism**: A plausible but false argument.
[9] **shuttle so near the warp**: A mistake of the unpracticed weaver.

READING AND DISCUSSION QUESTIONS

1. How much freedom did wealthy Hellenistic women like Hipparchia have to choose their own husbands, judging from this source?

2. Why is it significant that Hipparchia "appeared with [Crates] in public everywhere, and went to all entertainments in his company"? Based on her exchange with Theodorus, was this behavior typical of women Cynics?

3. Why did Crates first try to dissuade Hipparchia from marriage?

DOCUMENT 4-3

EPICURUS

The Principal Doctrines of Epicureanism

ca. 306 B.C.E.

Epicurus, founder of the Epicurean school of philosophy, lived from 341 to 270 B.C.E., primarily in Athens. The central principle of his teachings was to live a life that was free of pain and fear (the bad), and filled with pleasure and friendship (the good). He presented arguments that helped establish numerous principles of scientific and religious study, including the idea that you should believe only that which can be observed. His sometimes unpopular theories challenged Greek notions of the gods' power in their lives. Few of his works survive — the quotes below were recorded by Diogenes Laertius, the great Greek biographer and a likely Epicurean.

1. The blessed and immortal nature knows no trouble itself nor causes trouble to any other, so that it is never constrained by anger or favor. For all such things exist only in the weak.

2. Death is nothing to us: for that which is dissolved is without sensation; and that which lacks sensation is nothing to us. . . .

Whitney H. Oates, ed., *The Stoic and Epicurean Philosophers* (New York: Modern Library, 1940), 35–39.

4. Pain does not last continuously in the flesh, but the acutest pain is there for a very short time, and even that which just exceeds the pleasure in the flesh does not continue for many days at once. But chronic illnesses permit a predominance of pleasure over pain in the flesh.

5. It is not possible to live pleasantly without living prudently and honorably and justly, nor again to live a life of prudence, honor, and justice without living pleasantly. And the man who does not possess the pleasant life, is not living prudently and honorably and justly, and the man who does not possess the virtuous life, cannot possibly live pleasantly. . . .

7. Some men wished to become famous and conspicuous, thinking that they would thus win for themselves safety from other men. Wherefore if the life of such men is safe, they have obtained the good which nature craves; but if it is not safe, they do not possess that for which they strove at first by the instinct of nature.

8. No pleasure is a bad thing in itself: but the means which produce some pleasures bring with them disturbances many times greater than the pleasures. . . .

10. If the things that produce the pleasures of profligates[10] could dispel the fears of the mind about the phenomena of the sky and death and its pains, and also teach the limits of desires and of pains, we should never have cause to blame them: for they would be filling themselves full with pleasures from every source and never have pain of body or mind, which is the evil of life. . . .

12. A man cannot dispel his fear about the most important matters if he does not know what is the nature of the universe but suspects the truth of some mythical story. So that without natural science it is not possible to attain our pleasures unalloyed.[11] . . .

15. The wealth demanded by nature is both limited and easily procured; that demanded by idle imaginings stretches on to infinity. . . .

17. The just man is most free from trouble, the unjust most full of trouble. . . .

21. He who has learned the limits of life knows that that which removes the pain due to want and makes the whole of life complete is easy to obtain; so that there is no need of actions which involve competition. . . .

---

[10] profligates: Wasteful and extravagant people.
[11] unalloyed: Purely and completely.

27. Of all the things which wisdom acquires to produce the blessedness of the complete life, far the greatest is the possession of friendship. . . .

31. The justice which arises from nature is a pledge of mutual advantage to restrain men from harming one another and save them from being harmed. . . .

33. Justice never is anything in itself, but in the dealings of men with one another in any place whatever and at any time it is a kind of compact not to harm or be harmed. . . .

READING AND DISCUSSION QUESTIONS

1. According to Epicurus, what is the relationship between pain and pleasure? What is true pleasure?

2. How does natural science contribute to true pleasure?

3. How does Epicurus define justice?

4. According to Epicurus, what principles should a human being follow to lead a fulfilled life? Which of his principles might have upset his contemporaries, and why?

DOCUMENT 4-4

CLEOMEDES

Concerning the Circular Motion of the Heavenly Bodies: Eratosthenes Computes the Earth's Circumference

ca. 230 B.C.E.

Cleomedes, Greek philosopher and astronomer, wrote a popular astronomy textbook in which this story of the great mathematician and astronomer Eratosthenes originally appears. Eratosthenes was born in Cyrene, in modern

Cleomedes, "Concerning the Circular Motion of the Heavenly Bodies," in G. W. Botsford and E. G. Sihler, eds., *Hellenic Civilization* (New York: Columbia University Press, 1915), 636–637.

Libya, and eventually became head of the library of Alexandria, the greatest institution of learning in the Hellenistic world. In addition to calculating the circumference of the earth with a great deal of accuracy, Eratosthenes determined the tilt of the earth's axis. It is also possible that he made a good estimate of the distance from the earth to the sun, but the texts that support such a claim are questionable.

Under the same meridian,[12] he [Eratosthenes] says, lie Syene[13] and Alexandria.[14] Since then the greatest (lines) in the universe are the meridians, the spherical lines lying under them on the earth must necessarily be the greatest. Consequently whatever extent the theory (of Eratosthenes) will demonstrate for the spherical line running through Syene and Alexandria, so extensive also will be the greatest spherical line of the earth. He then says: And it is so, that Syene lies under the summer solstice. Whenever therefore the sun, having passed into Cancer and, effecting the summer solstice, is precisely at the zenith point of the sky, the gnomon[15] of the sundial necessarily becomes shadowless, in accordance with the exact perpendicular of the sun standing overhead; and it is reasonable that this should happen to the extent of three hundred stadia[16] in diameter. At Alexandria at the same hour the gnomons of the sun-dials cast a shadow, since this city lies more to the north than Syene. Inasmuch as these cities lie under the same meridian and the greatest spherical line, if we draw the arc from the apex of the shadow of the sun-dial to the base itself of the sun-dial which is in Alexandria, this arc will prove a segment of the greatest spherical line in the concave sun-dial, since the concave surface of the sun-dial lies under the largest spherical line. If consequently we were to conceive straight lines extended through the earth from each of the sun-dials, they will meet at the center of the earth. Since then the sun-dial at Syene lies perpendicularly under the sun, if we conceive in addition a straight line drawn from the sun to the apex of the style of the sun-dial, then the line drawn from the sun to the center of the earth will prove one straight line. If then we conceive another straight line from the apex of the shadow of the gnomon drawn up to the sun from the concave dial in

---

[12] **meridian**: A circle around the earth, passing through both poles.

[13] **Syene**: An ancient city in the South of modern-day Egypt.

[14] **Alexandria**: The capital of ancient Egypt, located on the Nile Delta.

[15] **gnomon**: The triangular blade of the sundial that casts a shadow.

[16] **stadia**: An ancient unit length. One stade was approximately 600 feet. However, the length of one foot, and therefore one stade, varied by culture and location.

Alexandria, this one and the aforesaid straight line will prove to be parallel, passing from different parts of the sun to different parts of the earth. Into these (lines), which are parallel, the line drawn from the center of the earth to the dial at Alexandria falls as a straight line, so as to render the alternate angles equal. Of these (angles) the one is at the center of the earth through the meeting of the straight lines which were drawn from the apex of its shadow. The other angle results through the meeting of (the lines drawn) from the apex of the dial at Alexandria and the line drawn upward from the apex of its shadow to the sun through the contact with it. Upon this is constructed the circular line which has been circumscribed from the apex of the shadow of the gnomon to its base; and upon that at the center of the earth the (line) which passes from Syene to Alexandria. Similar then are the arcs to each other, namely, those based on equal angles. The relation therefore which the line in the concave has to its own circle is the same as the relation of the line drawn from Syene to Alexandria. The line in the concave is to be 1/50 of its own circle; therefore necessarily also the distance from Syene to Alexandria must be 1/50 of the largest circle of earth; and this is (a distance) of 5,000 stadia. The whole circle herefore amounts to 250,000 stadia. Such is the computation of Eratosthenes.

READING AND DISCUSSION QUESTIONS

1. Before Eratosthenes formulated his proof, what assumptions had he made about the physical properties of the earth?

2. Based on Cleomedes' description, what can we deduce the Greeks knew of geometry by the time that Eratosthenes developed his proof?

3. Although Christopher Columbus had avidly studied other ancient geographers, it seems he was unfamiliar with Eratosthenes and ended up thinking that the earth is considerably smaller than it is. How could such a simple proof have been forgotten? Why do you suppose it was not re-created independently?

COMPARATIVE QUESTIONS

1. Consider points of similarity and difference among the teachings of Epicurus and either the Declaration of Innocence in the Egyptian

Book of the Dead (Document 1-4) or the Ten Commandments (Document 2-2). Why do you suppose prohibitions and commandments played little role in Epicurus' teachings?

2. Consider the description of Alexander in relation to the work of Eratosthenes. Why, in an age of increasing scientific inquiry and discovery, might a ruler be able to claim divinity and still be worshipped as a demigod?

3. In Document 3-4, Socrates discusses the role of female guardians in his ideal state. Do you think Socrates would have considered Hipparchia to be a good candidate for guardian? Why or why not?

CHAPTER 5

The Rise of Rome

ca. 750–44 B.C.E.

ounded around 750 B.C.E. Rome was first ruled by kings. In 509 B.C.E. the last king was expelled and Rome became a republic. Over the next two hundred years, Rome gained rule of the whole Italian peninsula, partly by conquest and partly in alliance with other states. In the course of three wars (264 to 146 B.C.E.) with Carthage, the greatest power in the western Mediterranean, the Romans destroyed their great rival. Even while fighting Carthage, the Romans undertook conquests in Greece, Asia Minor, the eastern Mediterranean, and North Africa. Julius Caesar himself conquered Gaul and invaded Britain. By the time of Caesar's assassination in 44 B.C.E., Rome ruled the whole of the Mediterranean basin and much of Western Europe. Unlike the empire of Alexander, however, the Roman Empire would endure for another five hundred years in the West and fifteen hundred years in the East.

DOCUMENT 5-1

LIVY

The Rape of Lucretia

ca. 27–25 B.C.E.

The story of Lucretia, excerpted from Livy's (59 B.C.E.–17 C.E.) comprehensive history of Rome, is a foundational myth that describes how the Roman republic came into being. The story illustrates complicated Roman attitudes toward both suicide and female virtue. For example, Roman generals who were defeated in battle sometimes killed themselves, essentially taking responsibility

Livy, *Ab Urbe condita* (*History*) 1:58–59, trans. George Baker (Philadelphia: T. Wardle, 1840).

for their military failures. The Romans believed this was a noble gesture.
Lucretia's story has long been an important theme in Western art. Titian,
Rembrandt, Dürer, Raphael, Botticelli, Shakespeare, Handel, and many
others subsequently created works in her honor.

A few days after, Sextus Tarquinius,[1] without the knowledge of Collatinus,
went to Collatia, with only a single attendant: he was kindly received by
the family, who suspected not his design, and, after supper, conducted
to the chamber where guests were lodged. Then, burning with desire, as
soon as he thought that every thing was safe, and the family all at rest, he
came with his sword drawn to Lucretia, where she lay asleep, and, holding
her down, with his left hand pressed on her breast, said, "Lucretia, be
silent: I am Sextus Tarquinius; my sword is in my hand, if you utter a word,
you die."

Terrified at being thus disturbed from sleep, she saw no assistance
near, and immediate death threatening her. Tarquinius then acknowledged his passion, entreated, mixed threats with entreaties, and used every
argument likely to have effect on a woman's mind: but finding her inflex-
ible, and not to be moved, even by the fear of death, he added to that fear,
the dread of dishonor, telling her that, after killing her he would murder
a slave, and lay him naked by her side, that she might be said to have been
slain in base adultery. The shocking apprehension, conveyed by this men-
ace, overpowering her resolution in defending her chastity, his lust became
victorious; and Tarquinius departed, applauding himself for this triumph
over a lady's honor.

But Lucretia plunged by such a disaster into the deepest distress,
despatched a messenger to Rome to her father, with orders to proceed to
Ardea to her husband, and to desire them to come to her, each with one
faithful friend; to tell them, that there was a necessity for their doing so,
and speedily, for that a dreadful affair had happened. Spurius Lucretius
came with Publius Valerius, the son of Volesus; Collatinus with Lucius
Junius Brutus, in company with whom he chanced to be returning to
Rome, when he was met by his wife's messenger.

They found Lucretia sitting in her chamber, melancholy and
dejected: on the arrival of her friends, she burst into tears, and on her husband's asking, "Is all well?" "Far from it," said she, "for how can it be well

---

[1] **Sextus Tarquinius**: Prince of Rome, son of king L. Tarquinius Superbus (r. 535–510
B.C.E.).

with a woman who has lost her chastity? Collatinus, the impression of another man is in your bed; yet my person only has been violated, my mind is guiltless as my death will testify. But give me your right hands, and pledge your honor that the adulterer shall not escape unpunished. He is Sextus Tarquinius, who, under the appearance of a guest, disguising an enemy, obtained here last night, by armed violence, a triumph deadly to me, and to himself also, if ye be men."

They all pledged their honor, one after another, and endeavored to comfort her distracted mind, acquitting her of blame, as under the compulsion of force, and charging it on the violent perpetrator of the crime, told her, that "the mind alone was capable of sinning, not the body, and that where there was no such intention, there could be no guilt."

"[It is] your concern," said she, "to consider what is due to him; as to me, though I acquit myself of the guilt, I cannot dispense with the penalty, nor shall any woman ever plead the example of Lucretia, for surviving her chastity." Thus saying, she plunged into her heart a knife which she had concealed under her garment, and falling forward on the wound, dropped lifeless. The husband and father shrieked aloud.

But Brutus, while they were overpowered by grief, drawing the knife, from the wound of Lucretia, and holding it out, reeking with blood, before him, said, "By this blood, most chaste until injured by royal insolence, swear, and call you, O ye gods, to witness, that I will prosecute to destruction, by sword, fire, and every forcible means in my power, both Lucius Tarquinius the proud, and his impious wife, together with their entire race, and never will suffer one of them, nor any other person whatsoever, to be king in Rome." He then delivered the knife to Collatinus, afterwards to Lucretius, and Valerius, who were filled with amazement, as at a prodigy, and at a loss to account for this unusual elevation of sentiment in the mind of Brutus.

However, they took the oath as directed, and converting their grief into rage, followed Brutus, who put himself at their head, and called on them to proceed instantly to abolish kingly power.

They brought out the body of Lucretia from the house, conveyed it to the forum, and assembled the people, who came together quickly, in astonishment, as may be supposed at a deed so atrocious and unheard of. Every one exclaimed with vehemence against the villany and violence of the prince: they were deeply affected by the grief of her father, and also by the discourse of Brutus, who rebuked their tears and ineffectual complaints, and advised them, as became men, as became Romans, to take up arms against those who had dared to treat them as enemies. The most spirited among the youth offered themselves with their arms, and the rest followed their example. On which, leaving half their number at the gates to defend Collatia, and fixing guards to prevent any intelligence of the commotion being carried to the princes, the rest, with Brutus at their head, marched to Rome.

When they arrived there, the sight of such an armed multitude spread terror and confusion wherever they came: but, in a little time, when people observed the principal men of the state marching at their head, they concluded, that whatever the matter was, there must be good reason for it. Nor did the heinousness of the affair raise less violent emotions in the minds of the people at Rome, than it had at Collatia: so that, from all parts of the city, they hurried into the forum; where, as soon as the party arrived, a crier summoned the people to attend the tribune of the celeres, which office happened at that time to be held by Brutus.

He there made a speech, no way consonant to that low degree of sensibility and capacity, which until that day, he had counterfeited; recounting the violence and lust of Sextus Tarquinius, the shocking violation of Lucretia's chastity, and her lamentable death; the misfortune of Tricipitinus, in being left childless, who must feel the cause of his daughter's death as a greater injury and cruelty, than her death itself: to these representations he added the pride of the king himself, the miseries and toils of the commons, buried under ground to cleanse sinks and sewers, saying, that ". . . citizens of Rome, the conquerors of all the neighboring nations, were, from warriors, reduced to laborers and stone cutters"; mentioned the barbarous murder of king Servius Tullius, his abominable daughter driving in her carriage over the body of her father, and invoked the gods to avenge the cause of parents.

By descanting on these and other, I suppose, more forcible topics, which the heinousness or present injuries suggested at the time, but which it is difficult for writers to repeat, he inflamed the rage of the multitude to such a degree, that they were easily persuaded to deprive the king of his government, and to pass an order for the banishment of Lucius Tarquinius, his wife, and children. Brutus himself, having collected and armed such of the young men as voluntarily gave in their names, set out for the camp at Ardea, in order to excite the troops there to take part against the king. The command in the city he left to Lucretius, who had some time before been appointed by the king to the office of prefect of the city. During this tumult Tullia fled from her house; both men and women, wherever she passed, imprecating curses on her head, and invoking the furies, the avengers of parents . . .

READING AND DISCUSSION QUESTIONS

1. How did Tarquinius frighten Lucretia into having sex with him?
2. How did the men in Lucretia's family react to what had happened to her?
3. What reason did Lucretia give for killing herself? What other motive may also have driven her?
4. Describe the speech that Brutus gave to the multitude. Was it in any way surprising, and why or why not?

DOCUMENT 5-2

Manumissions of Hellenistic Slaves: The Process of Freedom

ca. 167–101 B.C.E.

In the ancient world, slavery was not always a permanent condition. The father of the Roman poet Horace had been born a slave but was eventually freed and became a rich man. The documents that follow illustrate that the often blurry boundaries between servitude and freedom in Roman society. In the first case, one of unconditional manumission (emancipation), the slave Sosus is released immediately and forever. In the second instance, one of conditional manumission, the slaves Maiphatas and Ammia are required to stay with their owner Critodamus until he dies, at which point they will become free persons.

Unconditional Manumission

In the archonship of Tharres, in the month of Panagyrius, as reckoned by the people of Amphissa, and in the archonship of Damostratus at Delphi, in the month of Poitropius (144 B.C.E.), Telon and Cleto, with the approval of their son Straton, sold to Pythian Apollo a male slave whose name is

M. M. Austin, ed., *The Hellenistic World from Alexander to the Roman Conquest: A Selection of Ancient Sources in Translation* (Cambridge, UK: Cambridge University Press, 1981), 221–222.

Sosus, of Cappadocian origin, for the price of 3 minas of silver. Accordingly Sosus entrusted the sale to the god, on condition of his being free and not to be claimed as a slave by anyone for all time. Guarantor in accordance with the law and the contract: Philoxenus son of Dorotheus of Amphissa. The previous sale of Sosus to Apollo which took place in the archonship of Thrasycles at Delphi, and the provisions of the sale, namely that Sosus should remain with Telon and Cleto for as long as they live, shall be null and void. Witnesses: the priests of Apollo, Praxias and Andronicus, and the archon Pyrrhias son of Archelaus, and the Amphissians Charixenus son of Ecephylus, Polycritus, Aristodamus son of Callicles, Euthydamus son of Polycritus, Dorotheus son of Timesius, Demetrius son of Monimus. The contract is kept by the priest Praxias and Andronicus, and the Amphissians Polycritus and (Charixenus) son of Ecephylus.

CONDITIONAL MANUMISSION

When Panaetolus and Phytaeus were generals of the Aetolians, in the month of Homoloius, and in the archonship of Xeneas at Delphi and the month Bysius (167 B.C.E.), Critodamus son of Damocles, of Physce, sold to Pythian Apollo a male slave whose name is Maiphatas, of Galatian origin, and a female (slave) whose name is Ammia, of Illyrian origin, for the price of seven minas of silver. Maiphatas and Ammia shall remain with Critodamus for as long as Critodamus lives, doing for Critodamus what they are told to; if they do not remain and do what they are told to, the sale shall be null and void. When Critodamus dies, Maiphatas and Ammia shall be free and the sale shall remain with the god on condition that they are free and not to be claimed as slaves by anyone for their whole life, doing whatever they wish and going wherever they wish. Guarantors in accordance with the law and the contract: Philon son of Aristeas, Astoxenus son of Dionysius. Witnesses: the priests Amyntas and Tarantinus; private citizens: Dexicrates, Sotimus, Callimachus, Euangelus, . . . chaeus, of Delphi, Lyciscus and Menedamus, of Physce.

READING AND DISCUSSION QUESTIONS

1. Why do you think it is mentioned that Telon and Cleto's son Straton also approved of Solus' manumission?
2. Why might there be so many witnesses to these transactions?
3. Based on this document, what seems to be the main difference between conditional and unconditional manumission?

DOCUMENT 5-3

SENECA

The Sounds of a Roman Bath

ca. 50 C.E.

Personal cleanliness was imperative to both Greeks and Romans. The Greeks in particular frequently complained that barbarians were dirty. Public baths were central gathering places for Romans of many classes. The well-off frequently had baths in their own houses, but even so they might visit the public baths to meet friends or partake in other activities. The baths often had a questionable reputation. Even so, men and women generally bathed together as ordained by the Principate, although emperors such as Trajan and Marcus Aurelius sometimes forbade it. Seneca (ca. 4 B.C.E.–65 C.E.), who recorded this sketch of a bath's commotion, was a philosopher, orator, and eventually the chief adviser to the emperor.

I live over a bath. Imagine the variety of voices, enough noise to make you sick. When the stronger fellows are working out with heavy weights, when they are working hard or pretending to work hard, I hear their grunts; and whenever they exhale, I hear their hissing and panting. Or when some lazy type is getting a cheap rubdown, I hear the slap of the hand pounding his shoulders. . . . If a serious ballplayer comes along and starts keeping score out loud, that's the end for me. . . . And there's the guy who always likes to hear his own voice when washing, or those people who jump into the swimming pool with a tremendous splash. . . . The hair plucker keeps up a constant chatter to attract customers, except when he is plucking armpits and making his customer scream instead of screaming himself. It would be disgusting to list all the cries from the sausage seller, and the fellow hawking cakes, and all the food vendors yelling out what they have to sell, each with own special intonation.

Naphtali Lewis and Meyer Reinhold, eds., *Roman Civilization: Selected Readings* (New York: Columbia University Press, 1951), 2:228.

READING AND DISCUSSION QUESTIONS

1. What other activities took place at the public baths besides bathing?

2. In what ways do all these activities go together?

3. How would you describe Roman notions of privacy and personal space?

4. What does it reveal about Roman urban life that someone like Seneca would live so close to the public baths?

DOCUMENT 5-4

PLUTARCH

On Julius Caesar, A Man of Unlimited Ambition

ca. 44 B.C.E.

The historian Plutarch wrote long after Caesar's death, but he seems to have drawn on contemporary accounts. By 44 B.C.E., Rome had suffered genera-tions of civil war, and Caesar had become dictator for life. Throughout his political career, Caesar and his family had been partisans of the popular party, and he was generally well-liked among the Roman populace. How-ever, by the time of his death, Caesar's individual powers overshadowed the Roman polity, and not all citizens tolerated having their governments usurped. One of the most telling points is that some of Caesar's closest asso-ciates became his assassins.

But that which brought upon him the most apparent and mortal hatred was his desire of being king; which gave the common people the first occa-sion to quarrel with him, and proved the most specious pretence to those who had been his secret enemies all along. Those who would have pro-cured him that title gave it out that it was foretold in the Sibyls' books[2] that the Romans should conquer the Parthians when they fought against them under the conduct of a king, but not before. And one day, as Caesar was

---

A. H. Clough, trans., *Plutarch's Lives, Vol. 4* (Boston: Little, Brown and Company, 1859), 316–320.

[2] **Sibyls' books**: Prophetic writings, widely read in ancient Rome.

coming down from Alba to Rome, some were so bold as to salute him by the name of king; but he, finding the people disrelish it, seemed to resent it himself, and said his name was Caesar, not king. Upon this there was a general silence, and he passed on looking not very well pleased or contented. Another time, when the senate had conferred on him some extravagant honors, he chanced to receive the message as he was sitting on the rostra, where, though the consuls and praetors themselves waited on him, attended by the whole body of the senate, he did not rise, but behaved himself to them as if they had been private men, and told them his honors wanted rather to be retrenched then increased. This treatment offended not only the senate, but the commonalty too, as if they thought the affront upon the senate equally reflected upon the whole republic; so that all who could decently leave him went off, looking much discomposed. Caesar, perceiving the false step he had made, immediately retired home; and laying his throat bare, told his friends that he was ready to offer this to any one would give the stroke. But afterwards he made the malady from which he suffered (epilepsy) the excuse for his sitting, saying that those who are attacked by it lose their presence of mind if they talk much standing; that they presently grow giddy, fall into convulsions, and quite lose their reason. But this was not the reality, for he would willingly have stood up to the senate, had not Cornelius Balbus, one of his friends, or rather flatterers, hindered him. "Will you not remember," said he, "you are Caesar, and claim the honor which is due to your merit?"

He gave a fresh occasion of resentment by his affront to the tribunes. The Lupercalia were then celebrated, a feast at the first institution belonging, as some writers say, to the shepherds, and having some connection with the Arcadian Lycae. Many young noblemen and magistrates run up and down the city with their upper garments off, striking all they meet with thongs of hide, by way of sport; and many women, even of the highest rank, place themselves in the way, and hold out their hands to the lash, as boys in a school do to the master, out of a belief that it procures an easy labor to those who are with child, and makes those conceive who are barren. Caesar, dressed in a triumphal robe, seated himself in a golden chair at the rostra to view this ceremony. Antony, as consul, was one of those who ran this course, and when he came into the forum, and the people made way for him, he went up and reached to Caesar a diadem wreathed with laurel. Upon this there was a shout, but only a slight one, made by the few who were planted there for that purpose; but when Caesar refused it, there was universal applause. Upon the second offer, very few, and upon the second refusal, all again applauded. Caesar finding it would not take,

rose up, and ordered the crown to be carried into the capitol. Caesar's statues were afterwards found with royal diadems on their heads. Flavius and
Marullus, two tribunes of the people, went presently and pulled them off,
and having apprehended those who first saluted Caesar as king committed
them to prison. The people followed them with acclamations, and called
them by the name of Brutus,[3] because Brutus was the first who ended the
succession of kings, and transferred the power which before was lodged in
one man into the hands of the senate and people. Caesar so far resented
this, that he displaced Marullus and Flavius; and in urging his charges
against them, at the same time ridiculed the people, by himself giving the
men more than once the names of Bruti and Cumaei.

This made the multitude turn their thoughts to Marcus Brutus, who,
by his father's side, was thought to be descended from that first Brutus, and
by his mother's side from the Servilii, another noble family, being besides
nephew and son-in-law to Cato. But the honors and favors he had received
from Caesar took off the edge from the desires he might himself have felt
for overthrowing the new monarchy. For he had not only been pardoned
himself after Pompey's defeat at Pharsalia, and had procured the same
grace for many of his friends, but was one in whom Caesar had a particular confidence. He had at that time the most honorable praetorship for
the year, and was named for the consulship four years after, being preferred before Cassius, his competitor. Upon the question as to the choice,
Caesar, it is related, said that Cassius had the fairer pretensions, but that he
could not pass by Brutus. Nor would he afterwards listen to some who
spoke against Brutus, when the conspiracy against him was already afoot,
but laying his hand on his body, said to the informers, "Brutus will wait for
this skin of mine," intimating that he was worthy to bear rule on account
of his virtue, but would not be base and ungrateful to gain it. Those who
desired a change, and looked on him as the only, or at least the most
proper, person to effect it, did not venture to speak with him; but in the
night-time laid papers about his chair of state, where he used to sit and
determine causes, with such sentences in them as, "You are asleep, Brutus," "You are no longer Brutus." Cassius, when he perceived his ambition
a little raised upon this, was more instant than before to work him yet further, having himself a private grudge against Caesar for some reasons that
we have mentioned in the Life of Brutus. Nor was Caesar without suspi-

---

[3] **Brutus:** A reference to Marcus Brutus's ancestor, who had been instrumental in the
Roman rebellion against Etruscan domination in the fifth century B.C.E.

cions of him, and said once to his friends, "What do you think Cassius is aiming at? I don't like him, he looks so pale." And when it was told him that Antony and Dolabella were in a plot against him, he said he did not fear such fat, luxurious men, but rather the pale, lean fellows, meaning Cassius and Brutus.

READING AND DISCUSSION QUESTIONS

1. Which segments of the Roman population wanted Caesar to become king, and why?

2. How did Caesar treat those who had taken the side of his enemy Pompey earlier in the civil wars?

3. Why is it significant that Caesar did not conceal his epilepsy?

4. What were the motives of the conspirators against Caesar?

DOCUMENT 5-5

CICERO

From Philippius: *Faint Praise for Antony*

44 B.C.E.

Cicero (106–43 B.C.E.) was a Roman statesman, lawyer, and philosopher whose letters, speeches, and treatises have been models of Latin prose style for 2,000 years. Cicero aspired to defend the traditional Roman constitution, which often put him in opposition to Caesar, although at times Caesar sought his support. Following Caesar's death, Cicero became one of Rome's leading politicians and tried to turn Octavian, Caesar's great-nephew, against Marc Antony, who Cicero feared was becoming too powerful. In the end, however, Octavian and Marc Antony became allies, and Cicero was condemned and killed.

Cicero, *Philippius*, trans. Walter A. C. Ker, Loeb Classical Library (Cambridge, Mass.: Harvard University Press, 1926), 21–25.

The speech Marcus Antonius made that day was a noble one; his good will too was conspicuous; in a word, it was through him and his sons that peace was established with our most illustrious citizens.

And with these beginnings the sequel agreed. To the deliberations he held at his house on public affairs he invited the chief men of the State; to this our body he made the most favorable reports; nothing then but what was known to all men was being found in Caius Caesar's note-books; with the greatest decision he replied to the questions put to him. Were any exiles recalled? One, he said; beyond the one, nobody. Were any exemptions from taxation given? None, he replied. He even wished us to assent to the motion of Servius Sulpicius, a man of great distinction, that from the Ides of March no notice of any decree or grant of Caesar's should be posted. Much, and that excellent, I pass over, for there is one particular act of Marcus Antonius which I must mention at once. The dictatorship, which had already usurped the might of regal authority, he abolished utterly out of the State; about that we did not even debate. He brought in draft the decree he wished passed, and when this was read we followed his recommendation with the greatest enthusiasm, and passed him a vote of thanks in the most complimentary terms.

It seemed almost as if light had been shed upon us, now there had been removed, not merely despotism — that we had endured — but also the dread of despotism; and a great assurance had been given by him to the State of his wish that it should be free, in that he had utterly abolished the title of dictator — an office often established by law — on account of men's recollection of the perpetual dictatorship. A few days after, the Senate was relieved from the peril of proscription; the fugitive slave who had usurped the name of Marius was executed. And all these things were done jointly with his colleague; other things afterwards were Dolabella's[4] own acts, yet I believe that, had not Dolabella's colleague been absent, they would have been the joint acts of the two. For when an illimitable evil was creeping into the State, and spreading day by day more widely, and when the same men were building an altar in the Forum who had carried out that burial that was no burial, and when daily more and more scoundrels, together with slaves like themselves, were threatening the dwellings and temples of the city, so signal was the punishment Dolabella inflicted not only on audacious and rascally slaves, but also on debauched and wicked freemen, and so prompt was his upsetting of that accursed

---

[4] **Dollabella**: A member of the Senate.

column, that it seems to me marvellous how greatly the time that followed differed from that one day.

For look you: on the Kalends of June,[5] on which they had summoned us to sit, all was changed: nothing was done through the Senate, much — and that important — was done through the people, and in the absence of the people and against its will. The consuls elect said they dared not come into the Senate; the liberators of their country were exiles from the city from whose neck they had struck off the yoke of slavery, while none the less the consuls themselves, both in public meetings and in common talk, were passing eulogies upon them. Those that claimed the name of veterans, for whom this our body had been most carefully solicitous, were being incited, not to preserve what they already possessed, but to hope for new plunder. As I preferred to hear of these things rather than to see them, and held an honorary commission as legate, I departed with the intention of being at home on the Kalends of January, which seemed the first likely date for a meeting of the Senate.

READING AND DISCUSSION QUESTIONS

1. For what reasons does Cicero praise Marc Antony?
2. Who were the people that Cicero calls "the liberators of their country"?
3. Why is Cicero so worried about what "those that claimed the name of veterans" might do?
4. Why is it important that the Senate seems to be losing power and respect?

COMPARATIVE QUESTIONS

1. What attitudes about appropriate social behaviors are illustrated in the first three documents?
2. The Brutus who took part in the assassination of Caesar was a descendant of the Brutus who gave the speech in the first document. How

---

[5] **Kalends of June:** The first day of the month of June.

does this illuminate the ways in which the conspirators may have thought of themselves?

3. What does Cicero's record suggest about why Caesar's actions, as outlined by Plutarch, provided reason enough for his assassins to kill him?

4. Compare and contrast Caesar's behavior in the Senate as illustrated in Document 5-4 to the behavior of Alexander the Great as described in Document 4-1.

CHAPTER 6

The Pax Romana

31 B.C.E.–450 C.E.

T he social, political, and cultural changes that accompanied the Pax
Romana had a long-lasting impact on Western civilization. The principate, in which the leader of the Roman Empire was designated as the
First Citizen rather than the emperor or king, survived for 500 years in the
West and 1,500 years in the East. In the first century C.E., a new religion
from the Judaic tradition emerged on the periphery of the Roman Empire.
Christianity had taken root. Historically, the Romans were generally tolerant of various religions, although at first they persecuted Christians, and
sometimes Jews, because they would not participate in the imperial cult.
In the late fourth century C.E., this tolerant view shifted as Christianity
became the state religion of Rome, and Christians, who believed that the
entire world should convert, began to persecute non-Christians.

DOCUMENT 6-1

AUGUSTUS CAESAR

From Res Gestae: *Propaganda in the*
First Century C.E.

ca. 13 C.E.

The Res Gestae Divi Augusti (Deeds of the Divine Augustus) *is the funeral*
inscription for Augustus Caesar, the first Roman emperor. The inscription
declares that it was written shortly before the emperor's death, although it is
likely that the document was written earlier and revised over the years. In fact,
large portions of it were likely written by Augustus himself. The Res Gestae

Translations and Reprints from the Original Sources of European History, vol. 5
(Philadelphia: University of Pennsylvania Press, 1898).

provides a first-person account of Augustus's achievements and is especially important because it illustrates what Augustus himself thought was most important about his reign.

Below is a copy of the deeds of the divine Augustus, by which he subjected the whole world to the dominion of the Roman people, and of the amounts which he expended upon the commonwealth and the Roman people, as engraved upon two brazen columns which are set up at Rome.

In my twentieth year, acting upon my own judgment and at my own expense, I raised an army by means of which I restored to liberty the commonwealth which had been oppressed by the tyranny of a faction. On account of this the senate by laudatory decrees admitted me to its order, in the consulship of Gaius Pansa and Aulus Hirtius, and at the same time gave me consular rank in the expression of opinion, and gave me the imperium. It also voted that I as propraetor, together with the consuls, should see to it that the commonwealth suffered no harm.

Those who killed my father I drove into exile by lawful judgments, avenging their crime, and afterwards, when they waged war against the commonwealth, I twice defeated them in battle.

I undertook civil and foreign wars by land and sea throughout the whole world, and as victor I showed mercy to all surviving citizens. Foreign peoples, who could be pardoned with safety, I preferred to preserve rather than to destroy. About five hundred thousand Roman citizens took the military oath of allegiance to me. Of these I have settled in colonies or sent back to their municipia, upon the expiration of their terms of service, somewhat over three hundred thousand, and to all these I have given lands purchased by me, or money for farms, out of my own means.

The dictatorship which was offered to me by the people and the senate, both when I was absent and when I was present, in the consulship of Marcus Marcellus and Lucius Arruntius, I did not accept. At a time of the greatest dearth of grain I did not refuse the charge of the food supply, which I so administered that in a few days, at my own expense, I freed the whole people from the anxiety and danger in which they then were. The annual and perpetual consulship offered to me at that time I did not accept. . . .

. . . In my sixth consulship, with Marcus Agrippa as colleague, I made a census of the people. I performed the lustration [census] after forty-one years. In this lustration the number of Roman citizens was four million and sixty-three thousand. . . . By new legislation I have restored many customs of our ancestors which had now begun to fall into disuse, and I have myself also committed to posterity many examples worthy of imitation. . . .

Close to the temples of Honor and Virtue, near the Capena gate, the senate consecrated in honor of my return an altar to Fortune the Restorer, and upon this altar it ordered that the pontifices [priests] and the Vestal virgins should offer sacrifice yearly on the anniversary of the day on which I returned into the city from Syria, in the consulship of Quintus Lucretius and Marcus Vinucius, and it called the day the Augustalia, from our cognomen. . . .

To each man of the Roman *plebs* I paid three hundred sesterces in accordance with the last will of my father; and in my own name, when consul for the fifth time, I gave four hundred sesterces from the spoils of the wars; again, moreover, in my tenth consulship I gave from my own estate four hundred sesterces to each man by way of *congiarium*; and in my eleventh consulship I twelve times made distributions of food, buying grain at my own expense; and in the twelfth year of my tribunitial power I three times gave four hundred sesterces to each man. These my donation have never been made to less than two hundred and fifty thousand men. In my twelfth consulship and the eighteenth year of my tribunitial power I gave to three hundred and twenty thousand of the city plebs sixty denarii apiece. In the colonies of my soldiers, when consul for the fifth time, I gave to each man a thousand sesterces from the spoils; about a hundred and twenty thousand men in the colonies received that triumphal donation. When consul for the thirteenth time I gave sixty denarii to the *plebs* who were at that time receiving public grain; these men were a little more than two hundred thousand in number.

For the lands which in my fourth consulship, and afterwards in the consulship of Marcus Crassus and Cnaeus Lentulus, the augur, I assigned to soldiers, I paid money to the municipia. . . . Of all those who have established colonies of soldiers in Italy or in the provinces I am the first and only one within the memory of my age, to do this. . . .

Four times I have aided the public treasury from my own means, to such extent that I have furnished to those in charge of the treasury one hundred and fifty million sesterces. And in the consulship of Marcus Lepidus and Lucius Arruntius I paid into the military treasury which was established by my advice that from it gratuities might be given to soldiers who have served a term of twenty or more years, one hundred and seventy million sesterces from my own estate.

Beginning with that year in which Cnaeus and Publius Lentulus were consuls, when the imposts failed, I furnished aid sometimes to a hundred thousand men, and sometimes to more, by supplying grain or money for the tribute from my own land and property. . . .

[There follows a list of temples Augustus established in Rome and Palestine.]

The Capitol and the Pompeian theater have been restored by me at enormous expense for each work, without any inscription of my name. Aqueducts which were crumbling in many places by reason of age I have restored, and I have doubled the water which bears the name Marcian by turning a new spring into its course. The Forum Julium and the basilica which was between the temple of Castor and the temple of Saturn, works begun and almost completed by my father, I have finished; and when that same basilica was consumed by fire, I began its reconstruction on an enlarged site, inscribing it with the names of my sons; and if I do not live to complete it, I have given orders that it be completed by my heirs. In accordance with a decree of the senate, while consul for the sixth time, I have restored eighty-two temples of the gods, passing over none which was at that time in need of repair. In my seventh consulship I constructed the Flaminian way from the city to Ariminum, and all the bridges except the Mulvian and Minucian. . . .

[Augustus mentions other temples and other public works that he has restored, built, or endowed.]

Three times in my own name, and five times in that of my sons or grandsons, I have given gladiatorial exhibitions; in these exhibitions about ten thousand men have fought. Twice in my own name, and three times in that of my grandson, I have offered the people the spectacle of athletes gathered from all quarters. I have celebrated games four times in my own name, and twenty-three times in the turns of other magistrates. In behalf of the college of quindecemvirs, I, as master of the college, with my colleague Agrippa, celebrated the Secular Games in the consulship of Gaius Furnius and Gaius Silanus. When consul for the thirteenth time, I first celebrated the Martial games, which since that time the consuls have given in successive years. Twenty-six times in my own name, or in that of my sons and grandsons, I have given hunts of African wild beasts in the circus, the forum, the amphitheaters, and about thirty-five hundred beasts have been killed.

I gave the people the spectacle of a naval battle beyond the Tiber, where now is the grove of the Caesars. For this purpose an excavation was made eighteen hundred feet long and twelve hundred wide. In this contest thirty beaked ships, triremes or biremes, were engaged, besides more of smaller size. About three thousand men fought in these vessels in addition to the rowers. . . .

I have freed the sea from pirates. In that war with the slaves I delivered to their masters for punishment about thirty thousand slaves who had fled from their masters and taken up arms against the state. The whole of Italy voluntarily took the oath of allegiance to me, and demanded me as leader in that war in which I conquered at Actium. The provinces of Gaul, Spain, Africa, Sicily and Sardinia swore the same allegiance to me. There were more than seven hundred senators who at that time fought under my standards, and among these, up to the day on which these words are written, eighty-three have either before or since been made consuls, and about one hundred and seventy have been made priests.

I have extended the boundaries of all the provinces of the Roman people which were bordered by nations not yet subjected to our sway. I have reduced to a state of peace the Gallic and Spanish provinces, and Germany, the lands enclosed by the ocean from Gades to the mouth of the Elbe. The Alps from the region nearest the Adriatic as far as the Tuscan Sea I have brought into a state of peace, without waging an unjust war upon any people. My fleet has navigated the ocean from the mouth of the Rhine as far as the boundaries of the Cimbri, where before that time no Roman had ever penetrated by land or sea; and the Cimbri and Charydes and Semnones and other German peoples of that section, by means of legates, sought my friendship and that of the Roman people. By my command and under my auspices two armies at almost the same time have been led into Ethiopia and into Arabia, which is called "the Happy," and very many of the enemy of both peoples have fallen in battle, and many towns have been captured. Into Ethiopia the advance was as far as Nabata, which is next to Meroe. In Arabia the army penetrated as far as the confines of the Sabaei, to the town Mariba.

I have added Egypt to the empire of the Roman people. Of greater Armenia, when its king Artaxes was killed I could have made a province, but I preferred, after the example of our fathers, to deliver that kingdom to Tigranes, the son of king Artavasdes, and grandson of king Tigranes; and this I did through Tiberius Nero, who was then my son-in-law. And afterwards, when the same people became turbulent and rebellious, they were subdued by Gaius, my son, and I gave the sovereignty over them to king Ariobarzanes, the son of Artabazes, king of the Medes, and after his death to his son Artavasdes. When he was killed I sent into that kingdom Tigranes, who was sprung from the royal house of the Armenians. I recovered all the provinces across the Adriatic Sea, which extend toward the east, and Cyrenaica, at that time for the most part in the possession of kings, together with Sicily and Sardinia, which had been engaged in a servile war.

I have established colonies of soldiers in Africa, Sicily, Macedonia, the two Spains, Achaia, Asia, Syria, Gallia Narbonensis and Pisidia. Italy also has twenty-eight colonies established under my auspices, which within my lifetime have become very famous and populous.

I have recovered from Spain and Gaul, and from the Dalmatians, after conquering the enemy, many military standards which had been lost by other leaders. I have compelled the Parthians to give up to me the spoils and standards of three Roman armies, and as suppliants to seek the friendship of the Roman people. Those standards, moreover, I have deposited in the sanctuary which is in the temple of Mars the Avenger.

The Pannonian peoples, whom before I became princeps, no army of the Roman people had ever attacked, were defeated by Tiberius Nero, at that time my son-in-law and legate; and I brought them under subjection to the empire of the Roman people, and extended the boundaries of Illyricum to the bank of the river Danube. When an army of the Dacians crossed this river, it was defeated and destroyed, and afterwards my army, led across the Danube, compelled the Dacian people to submit to the sway of the Roman people. . . .

[There follows a list of kings and other potentates who have "betaken themselves as suppliants" to Augustus.] . . . Since I have been princeps very many other races have made proof of the good faith of the Roman people, who never before had had any interchange of embassies and friendship with the Roman people.

In my sixth and seventh consulships, when I had put an end to the civil wars, after having obtained complete control of affairs by universal consent, I transferred the commonwealth from my own dominion to the authority of the senate and Roman people. In return for this favor on my part I received by decree of the senate the title Augustus, the door-posts of my house were publicly decked with laurels, a civic crown was fixed above my door, and in the Julian Curia was placed a golden shield, which, by its inscription, bore witness that it was given to me by the senate and Roman people on account of my valor, clemency, justice and piety. After that time I excelled all others in dignity, but of power I held no more than those also held who were my colleagues in any magistracy.

While I was consul for the thirteenth time the senate and the equestrian order and the entire Roman people gave me the title of father of the fatherland, and decreed that it should be inscribed upon the vestibule of my house and in the Curia, and in the Augustan Forum beneath the quadriga which had been, by decree of the senate, set up in my honor. When I wrote these words I was in my seventy-sixth year. . . .

[A supplementary inscription follows, listing other temples that Augustus built or restored.]

READING AND DISCUSSION QUESTIONS

1. Augustus claims that he "restored to liberty the commonwealth which had been oppressed by the tyranny of a faction." Discuss the accuracy of his claim.

2. List the claims that you consider the most important. Explain why you think they are important, and whether you think each claim is justified.

3. Augustus states, "I excelled all others in dignity, but of power I held no more than those also held who were my colleagues in any magistracy." To what extent was this true, and why did he say this?

DOCUMENT 6-2

SUETONIUS

On the Reign of Augustus Caesar

ca. 31 B.C.E.–14 C.E.

The Roman historian Suetonius is best known for The Lives of the Twelve Caesars, *a series of short biographies beginning with Julius Caesar. Suetonius held important posts under the emperors Trajan and Hadrian, and Suetonius's point of view is especially important because he had extensive personal knowledge of Roman government. Suetonius had the advantage of historical perspective. By the time of his death (some time after 130 C.E.), the principate had been in existence for 150 years, and Suetonius had studied and in some cases known the best and the worst of the Roman emperors.*

He was for ten years a member of the triumvirate for restoring the State to order, and though he opposed his colleagues for some time and tried to prevent a proscription, yet when it was begun, he carried it through with greater severity than either of them. . . .

While he was triumvir, Augustus incurred general detestation by many of his acts. For example, when he was addressing the soldiers and a

Suetonius, *Lives of the Caesars*, trans. J. C. Rolfe, Loeb Classical Library (London: Heinemann, 1920), 2:27–35, 37–43.

throng of civilians had been admitted to the assembly, noticing that Pinarius, a Roman knight, was taking notes, he ordered that he be stabbed on the spot, thinking him an eavesdropper and a spy. . . .

He twice thought of restoring the republic; first immediately after the overthrow of Antony, remembering that his rival had often made the charge that it was his fault that it was not restored; and again in the weariness of a lingering illness, when he went so far as to summon the magistrates and the senate to his house, and submit an account of the general condition of the empire. Reflecting, however, that as he himself would not be free from danger if he should retire, so too it would be hazardous to trust the State to the control of the populace, he continued to keep it in his hands; and it is not easy to say whether his intentions or their results were the better. . . .

Since the city was not adorned as the dignity of the empire demanded, and was exposed to flood and fire, he so beautified it that he could justly boast that he had found it built of brick and left it in marble. He made it safe too for the future, so far as human foresight could provide for this.

He built many public works, in particular the following: his forum with the temple of Mars the Avenger, the temple of Apollo on the Palatine, and the fane [temple] of Jupiter the Thunderer on the Capitol. . . .

He divided the area of the city into regions and wards, arranging that the former should be under the charge of magistrates selected each year by lot, and the latter under "masters" elected by the inhabitants of the respective neighbourhoods. To guard against fires he devised a system of stations of night watchmen, and to control the floods, he widened and cleared out the channel of the Tiber, which had for some time been filled with rubbish and narrowed by jutting buildings. . . .

He restored sacred edifices which had gone to ruin through lapse of time or had been destroyed by fire, and adorned both these and the other temples with most lavish gifts. . . .

After he finally had assumed the office of pontifex maximus,[1] . . . he collected whatever prophetic writings of Greek or Latin origin were in circulation anonymously or under the names of authors of little repute, and burned more than two thousand of them. . . . Inasmuch, as the calendar, which had been set in order by the Deified Julius, had later been confused and disordered through negligence, he restored it to its former system; and

---

[1] **pontifex maximus**: High priest. The highest religious authority in the pagan ancient Roman religion.

in making this arrangement he called the month Sextilis by his own surname, rather than his birthmonth September. . . . He increased the number and importance of the priests, and also their allowances and privileges, in particular those of the Vestal virgins. . . .

Next to the immortal Gods he honored the memory of the leaders who had raised the estate of the Roman people from obscurity to greatness. Accordingly he restored the works of such men with their original inscriptions, and in the two colonnades of his forum dedicated statues of all of them in triumphal garb. . . .

Many pernicious practices militating against public security had survived as a result of the lawless habits of the civil wars, or had even arisen in time of peace. Gangs of footpads openly went about with swords by their sides, ostensibly to protect themselves, and travellers in the country, freemen and slaves alike, were seized and kept in confinement in the workhouses of the land owners; numerous leagues, too, were formed for the commission of crimes of every kind, assuming the title of some new guild. Therefore to put a stop to brigandage, he stationed guards of soldiers wherever it seemed advisable, inspected the workhouses, and disbanded all guilds, except such as were of long standing and formed for legitimate purposes. He burned the records of old debts to the treasury, which were by far the most frequent source of blackmail. . . . To prevent any action for damages or on a disputed claim from falling through or being put off, he added to the term of the courts thirty more days, which had before been taken up with honorary games. . . .

He himself administered justice regularly and sometimes up to nightfall, having a litter placed upon the tribunal, if he was indisposed, or even lying down at home. In his administration of justice he was both highly conscientious and very lenient; for to save a man clearly guilty of parricide from being sewn up in the sack, a punishment which was inflicted only on those who pleaded guilty, he is said to have put the question to him in this form: "You surely did not kill your father, did you?" . . .

He revised existing laws and enacted some new ones, for example, on extravagance, on adultery and chastity, on bribery, and on the encouragement of marriage among the various classes of citizens. Having made somewhat more stringent changes in the last of these than in the others, he was unable to carry it out because of an open revolt against its provisions, until he had abolished or mitigated a part of the penalties, besides increasing the rewards and allowing a three years' exemption from the obligation to marry after the death of a husband or wife. . . . And on finding that the spirit of the law was being evaded by betrothal with immature girls and by frequent changes of wives, he shortened the duration of betrothals and set a limit on divorce.

Since the number of the senators was swelled by a low-born and ill-assorted rabble, . . . he restored it to its former limits and distinction by two enrollments. . . . On questions of special importance he called upon the senators to give their opinions, not according to the order established by precedent, but just as he fancied, to induce each man to keep his mind on the alert, as if he were to initiate action rather than give assent to others. . . .

To enable more men to take part in the administration of the State, he devised new offices: the charge of public buildings, of the roads, of the aqueducts, of the channel of the Tiber, of the distribution of grain to the people, as well as the prefecture of the city, a board of three for choosing senators, and another for reviewing the companies of the knights whenever it should be necessary. He appointed censors, an office which had long been discontinued. . . .

He was not less generous in honoring martial prowess, for he had regular triumphs voted to above thirty generals, and the triumphal regalia to somewhat more than that number. . . .

He reviewed the companies of knights at frequent intervals, reviving the custom of the procession after long disuse. But he would not allow an accuser to force anyone to dismount as he rode by, as was often done in the past; and he permitted those who were conspicuous because of old age or any bodily infirmity to send on their horses in the review, and come on foot to answer to their names whenever they were summoned. . . .

Having obtained ten assistants from the senate, he compelled each knight to render an account of his life, punishing some of those whose conduct was scandalous and degrading others; but the greater part he reprimanded with varying degrees of severity. The mildest form of reprimand was to hand them a pair of tablets publicly, which they were to read in silence on the spot. He censured some because they had borrowed money at low interest and invested it at a higher rate. . . .

He revised the lists of the people street by street, and to prevent the commons from being called away from their occupations too often because of the distributions of grain, he determined to give out tickets for four months' supply three times a year. . . .

Considering it also of great importance to keep the people pure and unsullied by any taint of foreign or servile blood, he was most chary of conferring Roman citizenship and set a limit to manumission. . . .

He desired also to revive the ancient fashion of dress, and once when he saw in an assembly a throng of men in dark cloaks, he cried out indignantly, "Behold them, Romans, lords of the world, the nation clad in the toga," and he directed the aediles [local police] never again to allow anyone to appear in the Forum or its neighborhood except in the toga and without a cloak.

He often showed generosity to all classes when occasion offered. For example, by bringing the royal treasures to Rome in his Alexandrian triumph he made ready money so abundant, that the rate of interest fell, and the value of real estate rose greatly; and after that, whenever there was an excess of funds from the property of those who had been condemned, he loaned it without interest for fixed periods to any who could give security for double the amount. He increased the property qualification for senators, requiring one million two hundred thousand sesterces, instead of eight hundred thousand, and making up the amount for those who did not possess it. He often gave largess to the people, but usually of different sums. . . . In times of scarcity too he often distributed grain to each man at a very low figure, sometimes for nothing, and he doubled the money tickets.

But to show that he was a prince who desired the public welfare rather than popularity, when the people complained of the scarcity and high price of wine, he sharply rebuked them. . . . Once indeed in a time of great scarcity when it was difficult to find a remedy, he expelled from the city the slaves that were for sale, as well as the schools of gladiators, all foreigners with the exception of physicians and teachers, and a part of the household slaves; and when grain at last became more plentiful, he writes: "I was strongly inclined to do away forever with distributions of grain, because through dependence on them agriculture was neglected; but I did not carry out my purpose, feeling sure that they would one day be renewed through desire for popular favour." But from that time on he regulated the practice with no less regard for the interests of the farmers and grain-dealers than for those of the populace.

He surpassed all his predecessors in the frequency, variety, and magnificence of his public shows. He says that he gave games four times in his own name and twenty-three times for other magistrates, who were either away from Rome or lacked means. He gave them sometimes in all the wards and on many stages with actors in all languages, and combats of gladiators not only in the Forum or the amphitheatre, but in the Circus and in the Saepta; sometimes however, he gave nothing except a fight with wild beasts. . . . Besides he gave frequent performances of the game of

Troy by older and younger boys, thinking it a time-honored and worthy custom for the flower of the nobility to become known in this way. . . .

He sometimes employed even Roman knights in scenic and gladiatorial performances, but only before it was forbidden by decree of the senate. After that he exhibited no one of respectable parentage. . . . He did however on the day of one of the shows make a display of the first Parthian hostages that had ever been sent to Rome, by leading them through the middle of the arena and placing them in the second row above his own seat. Furthermore, if anything rare and worth seeing was ever brought to the city, it was his habit to make a special exhibit of it in any convenient place on days when no shows were appointed. For example a rhinoceros in the Saepta, a tiger on the stage and a snake of fifty cubits in the Comitium.

READING AND DISCUSSION QUESTIONS

1. Which of Augustus's reforms do you think were most important and why?

2. Why was Augustus "(reluctant to confer) Roman citizenship"? Why did he "set a limit to (emancipation of slaves)"?

3. In what areas do you think Augustus would have agreed with Suetonius' account? Where would he have disagreed?

4. Did Augustus want to restore the Roman Republic? Why or why not?

DOCUMENT 6-3

The Gospel According to Matthew: The Sermon on the Mount

28 C.E.

The Sermon on the Mount is perhaps the best-known summary of Jesus's moral teachings. In Matthew's retelling, while Jesus' disciples were in attendance, most of the audience was Jews. Jesus tells them explicitly that he has

Matthew 5.

not come to destroy the prophets or the traditional interpretation of God's law "Ye have heard. . . ." On the contrary, he is there to fulfill it. As the idea that one should love one's neighbor and hate one's enemies seems to have been a moral commonplace in the ancient world (see Homer in Document 3-1), perhaps the most radical of Jesus's teachings is the injunction to love one's enemies.

Blessed are the poor in spirit: for theirs is the kingdom of heaven. Blessed are they that mourn: for they shall be comforted. Blessed are the meek: for they shall inherit the earth. Blessed are they which do hunger and thirst after righteousness: for they shall be filled. Blessed are the merciful: for they shall obtain mercy. Blessed are the pure in heart: for they shall see God. Blessed are the peacemakers: for they shall be called the children of God. Blessed are they which are persecuted for righteousness' sake: for theirs is the kingdom of heaven. Blessed are ye, when men shall revile you, and persecute you, and shall say all manner of evil against you falsely, for my sake. Rejoice, and be exceeding glad: for great is your reward in heaven: for so persecuted they the prophets which were before you.

Ye are the salt of the earth: but if the salt have lost his savor, wherewith shall it be salted? it is thenceforth good for nothing, but to be cast out, and to be trodden under foot of men. Ye are the light of the world. A city that is set on an hill cannot be hid. Neither do men light a candle, and put it under a bushel, but on a candlestick; and it giveth light unto all that are in the house. Let your light so shine before men, that they may see your good works, and glorify your Father which is in heaven.

Think not that I am come to destroy the law, or the prophets: I am not come to destroy, but to fulfil. For verily I say unto you, Till heaven and earth pass, one jot or one tittle shall in no wise pass from the law, till all be fulfilled. Whosoever therefore shall break one of these least commandments, and shall teach men so, he shall be called the least in the kingdom of heaven: but whosoever shall do and teach them, the same shall be called great in the kingdom of heaven. For I say unto you, That except your righteousness shall exceed the righteousness of the scribes and Pharisees, ye shall in no case enter into the kingdom of heaven.

Ye have heard that it was said by them of old time, Thou shalt not kill; and whosoever shall kill shall be in danger of the judgment: But I say unto you, That whosoever is angry with his brother without a cause shall be in danger of the judgment: and whosoever shall say to his brother, Raca, shall be in danger of the council: but whosoever shall say, Thou fool, shall be in danger of hell fire. Therefore if thou bring thy gift to the altar, and there rememberest that thy brother hath aught against thee; Leave there thy gift before the altar, and go thy way; first be reconciled to thy brother, and then come and offer thy gift. Agree with thine adversary quickly, whiles thou art in the way with him; lest at any time the adversary deliver thee to the judge, and the judge deliver thee to the officer, and thou be cast into prison. Verily I say unto thee, Thou shalt by no means come out thence, till thou hast paid the uttermost farthing.

Ye have heard that it was said by them of old time, Thou shalt not commit adultery: But I say unto you, That whosoever looketh on a woman to lust after her hath committed adultery with her already in his heart. And if thy right eye offend thee, pluck it out, and cast it from thee: for it is profitable for thee that one of thy members should perish, and not that thy whole body should be cast into hell. And if thy right hand offend thee, cut it off, and cast it from thee: for it is profitable for thee that one of thy members should perish, and not that thy whole body should be cast into hell. It hath been said, Whosoever shall put away his wife, let him give her a writing of divorcement: But I say unto you, That whosoever shall put away his wife, saving for the cause of fornication, causeth her to commit adultery: and whosoever shall marry her that is divorced committeth adultery.

Again, ye have heard that it hath been said by them of old time, Thou shalt not forswear thyself, but shalt perform unto the Lord thine oaths: But I say unto you, Swear not at all; neither by heaven; for it is God's throne: Nor by the earth; for it is his footstool: neither by Jerusalem; for it is the city of the great King. Neither shalt thou swear by thy head, because thou canst not make one hair white or black. But let your communication be, Yea, yea; Nay, nay: for whatsoever is more than these cometh of evil.

Ye have heard that it hath been said, An eye for an eye, and a tooth for a tooth: But I say unto you, That ye resist not evil: but whosoever shall smite thee on thy right cheek, turn to him the other also. And if any man will sue thee at the law, and take away thy coat, let him have thy cloak also. And whosoever shall compel thee to go a mile, go with him twain. Give to him that asketh thee, and from him that would borrow of thee turn not thou away.

Ye have heard that it hath been said, Thou shalt love thy neighbor, and hate thine enemy. But I say unto you, Love your enemies, bless them that curse you, do good to them that hate you, and pray for them which despitefully use you, and persecute you; That ye may be the children of your Father which is in heaven: for he maketh his sun to rise on the evil and on the good, and sendeth rain on the just and on the unjust. For if ye love them which love you, what reward have ye? do not even the publicans the same? And if ye salute your brethren only, what do ye more than others? do not even the publicans so? Be ye therefore perfect, even as your Father which is in heaven is perfect.

READING AND DISCUSSION QUESTIONS

1. List at least three places where Jesus's principles are unexpected or difficult to understand. Explain how you would account for them.
2. Why might Jesus's teaching be seen as a threat to Roman law and order?
3. How do you think Jesus expected his teachings to be received by both Jews and Roman authorities?

DOCUMENT 6-4

EUSEBIUS
The Conversion of Constantine
312 C.E.

Eusebius, a contemporary of the emperor Constantine, was one of the most learned of the Christian church fathers, and his Life of Constantine *sometimes approaches veneration for the converted Roman leader. In* The Edict of Milan *(313 C.E.), Constantine ordered toleration for Christianity and the return of confiscated church property. It seems Constantine did not convert due to a moral or spiritual revelation, but came to believe that the Christian god was the most powerful. Christians, both then and later, argued that in times of ignorance, miracles were sometimes the best means to convert unbelievers.*

Being convinced, however, that he needed some more powerful aid than his military forces could afford him, on account of the wicked and magical

---

Eusebius, *Life of Constantine*, in E. C. Richardson, ed., *Library of Nicene and Post-Nicene Fathers*, 2d ser. (New York, 1890), 1:489–491.

enchantments which were so diligently practiced by the tyrant, he sought Divine assistance, deeming the possession of arms and a numerous soldiery of secondary importance, but believing the co-operating power of Deity invincible and not to be shaken. He considered, therefore, on what God he might rely for protection and assistance. While engaged in this enquiry, the thought occurred to him, that, of the many emperors who had preceded him, those who had rested their hopes in a multitude of gods, and served them with sacrifices and offerings, had in the first place been deceived by flattering predictions, and oracles which promised them all prosperity, and at last had met with an unhappy end, while not one of their gods had stood by to warn them of the impending wrath of heaven; while one alone who had pursued an entirely opposite course, who had condemned their error, and honored the one Supreme God during his whole life, had found him to be the Savior and Protector of his empire, and the Giver of every good thing. Reflecting on this, and well weighing the fact that they who had trusted in many gods had also fallen by manifold forms of death, without leaving behind them either family or offspring, stock, name, or memorial among men: while the God of his father had given to him, on the other hand, manifestations of his power and very many tokens: and considering farther that those who had already taken arms against the tyrant, and had marched to the battle-field under the protection of a multitude of gods, had met with a dishonorable end (for one of them had shamefully retreated from the contest without a blow, and the other, being slain in the midst of his own troops, became, as it were, the mere sport of death); reviewing, I say, all these considerations, he judged it to be folly indeed to join in the idle worship of those who were no gods, and, after such convincing evidence, to err from the truth; and therefore felt it incumbent on him to honor his father's God alone.

Accordingly he called on him with earnest prayer and supplications that he would reveal to him who he was, and stretch forth his right hand to help him in his present difficulties. And while he was thus praying with fervent entreaty, a most marvelous sign appeared to him from heaven, the account of which it might have been hard to believe had it been related by any other person. But since the victorious emperor himself long afterwards declared it to the writer of this history, when he was honored with his acquaintance and society, and confirmed his statement by an oath, who could hesitate to accredit the relation, especially since the testimony of after-time has established its truth? He said that about noon, when the day was already beginning to decline, he saw with his own eyes the trophy of a cross of light in the heavens, above the sun, and bearing the inscription,

CONQUER BY THIS. At this sight he himself was struck with amaze-ment, and his whole army also, which followed him on this expedition, and witnessed the miracle.

READING AND DISCUSSION QUESTIONS

1. Eusebius writes that Constantine "considered, therefore, on what God he might rely for protection and assistance." What does this reveal about the religious climate of the time?

2. What persuaded Constantine to put his trust in the Christian god?

3. How would you judge Eusebius' reliability as a witness?

4. Why did miracles and divine portents play such an important part in Constantine's thinking?

COMPARATIVE QUESTIONS

1. Compare and contrast the Sermon on the Mount to the Declaration of Innocence from the Egyptian Book of the Dead (Document 1-4) and the Ten Commandments from the Book of Exodus (Document 2-2). What similarities exist in these documents? What differences are apparent?

2. Compare and contrast the two biographies of Caesar in the *Res Gestae* and Suetonius's *Lives of the Caesars*. Why is it important that Suetonius was able to compare Augustus to the other emperors?

3. What elements in Jesus's teachings might have appealed to Con-stantine?

CHAPTER 7

Late Antiquity

350–600

Beginning in the second half of the second century, the Roman Empire found itself resisting an influx of barbarian tribes, many of them Germanic. In some cases, the Romans fought pitched battles and long campaigns against the outsiders. In other cases, the tribes moved into Roman territory by gradual encroachment. After a series of disasters in the fifth century, the last Roman emperor in the West was deposed in 476. The eastern half of the empire, based in Constantinople, retained considerable strength. The emperor Justinian reconquered considerable portions of Italy and North Africa, although these conquests were generally short-lived. Even before the collapse of the Western empire, the church had become a powerful institution in its own right. As the Western empire disintegrated into a collection of smaller states, the Roman Church increasingly became a center of learning and security.

DOCUMENT 7-1

EMPEROR JUSTINIAN

From Corpus Juris Civilis:
The Problem of Adultery

529–533

The emperor Justinian's (r. 527–565) most enduring accomplishments were in the area of the law. Ruling from the eastern capital of Constantinople, Justinian appointed a committee of jurists to systematize the great mass of Roman laws into the great Code. In the Digest, his legal scholars system-

Mary R. Lefkowitz and Maureen B. Fant, eds., *Women's Life in Greece and Rome* (Baltimore: Johns Hopkins University Press, 1982), 182–184.

atized Roman jurisprudence, or legal thinking. Finally, in the Institutes, *they created a handbook of civil law. Taken together, these three works make up the* corpus juris civilis, *or body of civil law, that is the foundation for the legal codes of most modern European nations.*

The *lex Julia*[1] declares that wives have no right to bring criminal accusations for adultery against their husbands, even though they may desire to complain of the violation of the marriage vow, for while the law grants this privilege to men it does not concede it to women. . . .

The *lex Julia* relating to chastity forbids the two parties guilty of adultery, that is to say, the man and the woman, to be prosecuted at the same time, and in the same case, but they can both be prosecuted in succession. . . .

No one doubts that a husband cannot accuse his wife of adultery if he continues to retain her in marriage. . . . Under the new law, however, he can do so, and if the accusation is proved to be true, he can then repudiate her, and he should file a written accusation against her. If, however, the husband should not be able to establish the accusation of adultery which he brought, he will be liable to the same punishment which his wife would have undergone if the accusation had been proved. . . .

You can resume marital relations with your wife without fear of being liable to the penalty prescribed by the *lex Julia* for the suppression of adultery, as you did nothing more than file the written accusation, for the reason that you assert that you afterwards ascertained that you were impelled by groundless indignation to accuse her; for he alone will be liable to the penalty specifically mentioned by the law who is aware that his wife has been publicly convicted of adultery, or that she is an adulteress, as he cannot simulate ignorance of the fact, and retain her as his wife. . . .

There is no doubt that he who has two wives at once is branded with infamy, for, in a case of this kind, not the operation of the law by which our citizens are forbidden to contract more than one marriage at a time, but the intention, should be considered; and therefore he who pretended to be unmarried, but had another wife in the province, and asked you to marry him, can lawfully be accused of the crime of fornication, for which you are not liable, for the reason that you thought that you were his wife. You can

---

[1] *lex Julia*: This can refer to any Roman law passed by a member of the Julian family, some recorded as early as 18 B.C.E. Justinian cited and modified many of these established laws.

obtain from the governor of the province the return of all your property of which you deplore the loss on account of the fraudulent marriage, and which should be restored to you without delay. But how can you recover what he promised to give you as his betrothed? . . .

The laws punish the detestable wickedness of women who prostitute their chastity to the lusts of others, but do not hold those liable who are compelled to commit fornication through force, and against their will. And, moreover, it has very properly been decided that their reputations are not lost, and that their marriage with others should not be prohibited on this account. . . .

If a woman whom you have carnally known indiscriminately sold herself for money, and prostituted herself everywhere as a harlot, you did not commit the crime of adultery with her. . . . Slaves cannot accuse their wives of adultery for violation of conjugal faith.

If you should be accused of adultery by her with whom you have lived in violation of law, you can defend yourself by an innumerable number of expedients.

READING AND DISCUSSION QUESTIONS

1. How did the laws outlined here treat men and women differently? What do these differences reveal about the status of women?

2. How did the laws about adultery change as they pertained to a man accusing his wife of adultery? Explain whether you think the new provision gives more protection or less protection to women.

3. How are women who are raped treated under the law?

4. Why do you think that slaves are not allowed to accuse their wives of adultery?

SAINT AMBROSE OF MILAN

Emperor Theodosius Brought to Heel

390

Saint Ambrose (ca. 338–397) was the bishop of Milan and one of the most important religious figures of his time. He was an administrator, a theologian, and a significant political voice. In 390, Emperor Theodosius I had 7,000 people massacred in the Greek city of Thessalonica after they staged a rebellion against the imperial garrison. As punishment, Ambrose refused to admit the emperor to the Eucharist until he had done penance for several months. Although Ambrose was not the only church leader to chastise an emperor, he was one of the most successful.

I have written these things, indeed, not to confound you, but that the example of these kings might induce you to put away this sin from your kingdom, which you will accomplish by humiliating your soul to God. You are a man and temptation has come to you; confess it. Sin is not put away except by tears and penitence. Neither an angel can do it nor an archangel; the Lord himself, who alone can say, "I am with you," does not forgive us if we have sinned except we be penitent.

I persuade, I beg, I exhort, I admonish; because it is a grief to me that you who were an example of unusual piety, who were the very personification of clemency, who would not allow guilty individuals to be brought into danger, that you do not grieve at the death of so many innocent persons. Although you have fought battles most successfully, although in other things also you are worthy of praise, yet the crown of all your work was always piety. This the devil envied you, since it was your ever present possession. Conquer him while as yet you have wherewith you may conquer. Do not add another sin to your sin, that you may practice what it has injured many to practice.

I, indeed, though in all other things a debtor to your kindness which I can never be ungrateful for, which kindness surpassed that of many

Translations and Reprints from the Original Sources of European History (Philadelphia: University of Pennsylvania Press, 1898), 4/1:23–24.

emperors and was equalled by the kindness of one only, I, I say, have no cause for a charge of contumacy [resistance to authority] against you, but I have a cause for fear; I dare not offer the sacrifice if you will to be present. Is that which is not allowed after shedding the blood of one innocent person to be allowed after shedding the blood of many? I do not think so.

READING AND DISCUSSION QUESTIONS

1.   How would you describe the tone of Ambrose's letter? How does this tone fit the actual content of the letter?

2.   What does it mean that Ambrose does not dare to offer the sacrifice if the emperor is present?

3.   That Ambrose was able to take the actions described implies what about the power of the church?

DOCUMENT 7-3

SAINT BENEDICT OF NURSIA
The Rule of Saint Benedict
529

By the time of Saint Benedict (ca. 480–547), monasticism was a long-established institution. Some monks (eremites, or hermits) lived on their own; others (cenobites) lived in communities. Benedict's rule for monks living in communities was adopted throughout the Christian world. The rule was widely praised for both its spirituality and its practicality. Benedict was well aware of the need for harmony within monastic communities. According to legend, some of the monks in Benedict's first community tried to murder him, and on one occasion he was saved when a raven made away with a loaf of poisoned bread.

E. F. Henderson, ed., *Select Historical Documents of the Middle Ages* (London: G. Bell, 1892), 597–598.

Concerning the daily manual labor. Idleness is the enemy of the soul. And therefore, at fixed times, the brothers ought to be occupied in manual labor; and again, at fixed times, in sacred reading. Therefore we believe that, according to this disposition, both seasons ought to be arranged; so that, from Easter until the Calends of October, going out early, from the first until the fourth hour they shall do what labor may be necessary. Moreover, from the fourth hour until about the sixth, they shall be free for reading. After the meal of the sixth hour, moreover, rising from table, they shall rest in their beds with all silence; or, perchance, he that wishes to read may so read to himself that he do not disturb another. And the nona [the second meal] shall be gone through with more moderately about the middle of the eighth hour; and again they shall work at what is to be done until Vespers. But, if the exigency or poverty of the place demands that they be occupied by themselves in picking fruits, they shall not be dismayed: for then they are truly monks if they live by the labors of their hands; as did also our fathers and the apostles. Let all things be done with moderation, however, on account of the faint-hearted. . . . [There follows a slightly different schedule for the winter months from October to Easter.] But in the days of Lent, from dawn until the third full hour, they shall be free for their readings; and, until the tenth full hour, they shall do the labor that is enjoined on them. In which days of Lent they shall all receive separate books from the library; which they shall read entirely through in order. These books are to be given out on the first day of Lent. Above all there shall certainly be appointed one or two elders, who shall go round the monastery at the hours in which the brothers are engaged in reading, and see to it that no troublesome brother chance to be found who is open to idleness and trifling, and is not intent on his reading; being not only of no use to himself, but also stirring up others. If such a one — may it not happen — be found, he shall be admonished once and a second time. If he do not amend, he shall be subject under the Rule to such punishment that the others may have fear. . . . On feeble or delicate brothers such a labor or art is to be imposed, that they shall neither be idle, nor shall they be so oppressed by the violence of labor as to be driven to take flight. Their weakness is to be taken into consideration by the abbot.

READING AND DISCUSSION QUESTIONS

1. From this account, describe three practical problems of life in a monastery, and outline how Benedict tries to deal with them.

2.   Why does Benedict think it important that monks should work with their hands?

3.   In what ways does the rule promote learning?

4.   What provisions are made for "feeble or delicate brothers"? Why do they need to be treated carefully?

DOCUMENT 7-4

SAINT AUGUSTINE

From City of God: A Denunciation of Paganism

413–426

Saint Augustine (354–430), bishop of Hippo Regius in what is now Algeria, was one of the most important early church leaders. In 410, Rome was sacked by Alaric the Visigoth. By this time, most of the emperors had been Christian for nearly a hundred years, but pagan religion was still influential, especially in the countryside and among some of the upper classes. Many pagans claimed that Rome had fallen because Christianity had turned people away from the old gods who had once protected the city. The City of God, *among its other purposes, was Augustine's answer to these claims.*

Cicero [ca. 106–43 B.C.E.], a weighty man, and a philosopher in his way, when about to be made edile [a municipal officer], wished the citizens to understand that, among the other duties of his magistracy, he must propitiate Flora[2] by the celebration of games. And these games are reckoned devout in proportion to their lewdness. In another place, and when he was now consul, and the state in great peril, he says that games had been celebrated for ten days together, and that nothing had been omitted which could pacify the gods: as if it had not been more satisfactory to irritate the gods by temperance, than to pacify them by debauchery; and to provoke their hate by honest living, than soothe it by such unseemly grossness. . . .

Augustine, *City of God*, 27–29, in Philip Schaff, ed., *Library of Nicene and Post-Nicene Fathers*, 1st ser. (New York, 1890), 3:41–43.

[2] **Flora**: Goddess of flowers and spring.

They, then, are but abandoned and ungrateful wretches, in deep and fast bondage to that malign spirit, who complain and murmur that men are rescued by the name of Christ from the hellish thraldom of these unclean spirits, and from a participation in their punishment, and are brought out of the night of pestilential ungodliness into the light of most healthful piety. Only such men could murmur that the masses flock to the churches and their chaste acts of worship, where a seemly separation of the sexes is observed; where they learn how they may so spend this earthly life, as to merit a blessed eternity hereafter; where Holy Scripture and instruction in righteousness are proclaimed from a raised platform in presence of all, that both they who do the word may hear to their salvation, and they who do it not may hear to judgment. And though some enter who scoff at such precepts, all their petulance is either quenched by a sudden change, or is restrained through fear or shame. For no filthy and wicked action is there set forth to be gazed at or to be imitated; but either the precepts of the true God are recommended, His miracles narrated, His gifts praised, or His benefits implored.

This, rather, is the religion worthy of your desires, O admirable Roman race, — the progeny of your Scaevolas and Scipios, of Regulus, and of Fabricius.[3] This rather covet, this distinguish from that foul vanity and crafty malice of the devils. If there is in your nature any eminent virtue, only by true piety is it purged and perfected, while by impiety it is wrecked and punished. Choose now what you will pursue, that your praise may be not in yourself, but in the true God, in whom is no error. For of popular glory you have had your share; but by the secret providence of God, the true religion was not offered to your choice. Awake, it is now day; as you have already awaked in the persons of some in whose perfect virtue and sufferings for the true faith we glory: for they, contending on all sides with hostile powers, and conquering them all by bravely dying, have purchased for us this country of ours with their blood; to which country we invite you, and exhort you to add yourselves to the number of the citizens of this city, which also has a sanctuary of its own in the true remission of sins. Do not listen to those degenerate sons of thine who slander Christ and Christians, and impute to them these disastrous times, though they desire times in which they may enjoy rather impunity for their wickedness than a peaceful life. Such has never been Rome's ambition even in regard to her earthly country. Lay hold now on the celestial country, which is easily

---

[3] **Saevolas and Scipios . . . Fabricius**: Noble Roman political men of the day.

won, and in which you will reign truly and for ever. For there shalt thou find no vestal fire, no Capitoline[4] stone, but the one true God.

No date, no goal will here ordain:

But grant an endless, boundless reign.

No longer, then, follow after false and deceitful gods; abjure them rather, and despise them, bursting forth into true liberty. Gods they are not, but malignant spirits, to whom your eternal happiness will be a sore punishment.

READING AND DISCUSSION QUESTIONS

1. How does Augustine describe the morality of the pagan religion?

2. For what reason does Augustine cite Cicero, who had a reputation as a virtuous man?

3. How does Augustine contrast the practice of Christianity with pagan rites?

DOCUMENT 7-5

TACITUS

From Germania: *Rome Encounters the Noble Savages*

ca. 100

Tacitus (ca. 56–117) was the greatest Roman historian and wrote at a time when Rome had reached the zenith of its power. In addition to his works on imperial politics, the Annals *and the* Histories, *Tacitus wrote a study of the Germanic tribes who lived beyond the borders of the empire. In his studies of*

Tacitus, *Germania*, in *Translation and Reprints from the Original Sources of European History* (Philadelphia: University of Pennsylvania Press, 1898), vol. 6/2:5–14.

[4] **Capitoline**: One of two hills surrounding the Roman Forum, and a symbol of Roman fortitude. Ironically, given Augustine's defense of Christianity, the Capitoline was also the sight of the greatest temple constructed in ancient Rome, the Temple of Jupiter.

Roman politics, he described abundant examples of corruption and tyranny, but among the Germanic tribes he found a good deal to admire. Tacitus never lived among Germanic peoples but got his information from writers who had.

In general the country, though varying here and there to appearance, is covered over with wild forests or filthy swamps, being more humid on the side of Gaul but bleaker toward Noricum and Pannonia.[5] It is suitable enough for grain but does not permit the cultivation of fruit trees; and though rich in flocks and herds these are for the most part small, the cattle not even possessing their natural beauty nor spreading horns. The people take pride in possessing a large number of animals, these being their sole and most cherished wealth. Whether it was in mercy or wrath that the gods denied them silver and gold, I know not. . . .

They choose their kings on account of their ancestry, their generals for their valor. The kings do not have free and unlimited power and the generals lead by example rather than command, winning great admiration if they are energetic and fight in plain sight in front of the line. But no one is allowed to put a culprit to death or to imprison him, or even to beat him with stripes except the priests, and then not by way of a punishment or at the command of the general but as though ordered by the god who they believe aids them in their fighting. Certain figures and images taken from their sacred groves they carry into battle, but their greatest incitement to courage is that a division of horse or foot is not made up by chance or by accidental association but is formed of families and clans; and their dear ones are close at hand so that the wailings of the women and the crying of the children can be heard during the battle. These are for each warrior the most sacred witnesses of his bravery, these his dearest applauders. They carry their wounds to their mothers and their wives, nor do the latter fear to count their number and examine them while they bring them food and urge them to deeds of valor.

It is related how on certain occasions their forces already turned to flight and retreating have been rallied by the women who implored them by their prayers and bared their breasts to their weapons, signifying thus the captivity close awaiting them, which is feared far more intensely on account of their women than for themselves; to such an extent indeed that those states are more firmly bound in treaty among whose hostages maidens of

---

[5] **toward Noricum and Pannonia**: Toward what is today Austria, Hungary, and Croatia.

noble family are also required. Further, they believe that the sex has a certain sanctity and prophetic gift, and they neither despise their counsels nor disregard their answers. . . .

Concerning minor matters the chiefs deliberate, but in important affairs all the people are consulted, although the subjects referred to the common people for judgment are discussed beforehand by the chiefs. Unless some sudden and unexpected event calls them together they assemble on fixed days either at the new moon or the full moon, for they think these the most auspicious times to begin their undertakings. They do not reckon time by the number of days, as we do, but by the number of nights. So run their appointments, their contracts; the night introduces the day, so to speak. A disadvantage arises from their regard for liberty in that they do not come together at once as if commanded to attend, but two or three days are wasted by their delay in assembling. When the crowd is sufficient they take their places fully armed. Silence is proclaimed by the priests, who have on these occasions the right to keep order. Then the king or a chief addresses them, each being heard according to his age, noble blood, reputation in warfare and eloquence, though more because he has the power to persuade than the right to command. If an opinion is displeasing they reject if by shouting; if they agree to it they clash with their spears. The most complimentary form of assent is that which is expressed by means of their weapons.

It is also allowable in the assembly to bring up accusations, and to prosecute capital offenses. Penalties are distinguished according to crime. Traitors and deserters are hung to trees. Weaklings and cowards and those guilty of infamous crimes are cast into the mire of swamps. . . .

They undertake no business whatever either of a public or a private character save they be armed. But it is not customary for any one to assume arms until the tribe has recognized his competence to use them. Then in a full assembly some one of the chiefs or the father or relatives of the youth invest him with the shield and spear. This is the sign that the lad has reached the age of manhood; this is his first honor. . . .

In the intervals of peace they spend little time in hunting but much in idleness, given over to sleep and eating; all the bravest and most warlike doing nothing, while the hearth and home and the care of the fields is given over to the women, the old men and the various infirm members of the family. . . .

It is well known that none of the German tribes live in cities, nor even permit their dwellings to be closely joined to each other. They live separated and in various places, as a spring or a meadow or a grove strikes their fancy. They lay out their villages not as with us in connected or closely-joined houses, but each one surrounds his dwelling with an open space, either as a protection against conflagration or because of their ignorance of the art of building. They do not even make use of rough stones or tiles. They use for all purposes undressed timber, giving no beauty or comfort. Some parts they plaster carefully with earth of such purity and brilliancy as to form a substitute for painting and designs in color. They are accustomed also to dig out subterranean caves which they cover over with great heaps of manure as a refuge against the cold and a place for storing grain, for retreats of this sort render the extreme cold of their winters bearable and, whenever an enemy has come upon them, though he lays waste the open country he is either ignorant of what is hidden underground or else it escapes him for the very reason that is has to be searched for.

Generally their only clothing is a cloak fastened with a clasp, or if they haven't that, with a thorn; this being their only garment, they pass whole days about the hearth or near a fire. The richest of them are distinguished by wearing a tunic. . . . There are those, also, who wear the skins of wild beasts, those nearest the Roman border in a careless manner, but those further back more elegantly, as those do who have no better clothing obtained by commerce. They select certain animals, and stripping off their hides sew on them patches of spotted skins taken from those strange beasts that the distant ocean and the unknown sea bring forth. The women wear the same sort of dress as the men except that they wrap themselves in linen garments which they adorn with purple stripes and do not lengthen out the upper part of the tunic into sleeves, but leave the arms bare the whole length. The upper part of their breasts is also exposed. However, their marriage code is strict, and in no other part of their manners are they to be praised more than in this. For almost alone among barbarian peoples they are content with one wife each, expecting those few who because of their high position rather than out of lust enter into more than one marriage engagement.

The wife does not bring a dowry to the husband, but the husband to the wife. . . . Thus they live in well-protected virtue, uncorrupted by the allurements of shows or the enticement of banquets. Men and women alike know not the secrecy of correspondence. Though the race is so numerous, adultery is very rare, its punishment being immediate and inflicted by the injured husband. He cuts off the woman's hair in the presence of her kinsfolk, drives her naked from his house and flogs her through the whole village. Indeed, the loss of chastity meets with no indulgence. . . . To limit the number of children or to put any of the later children to death is considered a crime, and with them good customs are of more avail than good laws elsewhere.

In every household the children grow up naked and unkempt into that lusty frame and those sturdy limbs that we admire. Each mother nurses her own children; they are not handed over to servants and paid nurses. The lord and the slave are in no way to be distinguished by the delicacy of their bringing up. They live among the same flocks, they lie on the same ground, until age separates them and valor distinguishes the free born. The young men marry late and their vigor is thereby unimpaired. Nor is the marriage of girls hastened. They have the same youthful vigor, the same stature as the young men. Thus well-matched and strong when they marry, the children reproduce the robustness of their parents. . . .

A German is required to adopt not only the feuds of his father or of a relative, but also their friendships, though the enmities are not irreconcilable. For even homicide is expiated by the payment of a certain number of cattle, and the whole family accept the satisfaction, a useful practice as regards the state because feuds are more dangerous where there is no strong legal control.

No other race indulges more freely in entertainments and hospitality. It is considered a crime to turn any mortal man away from one's door. . . .

As soon as they awake from sleep, which they prolong till late in the day, they bathe, usually in warm water as their winter lasts a great part of the year. After the bath they take food, each sitting in a separate seat and having a table to himself. Then they proceed to their business or not less often to feasts, fully armed. It is no disgrace to spend the whole day and night in drinking. . . .

To trade with capital and to let it out at interest is unknown, and so it is ignorance rather than legal prohibition that protects them. Land is held by the villages as communities according to the number of the cultivators, and is then divided among the freemen according to their rank. The extent of their territories renders this partition easy. They cultivate fresh fields every year and there is still land to spare. They do not plant orchards nor lay off meadow-lands nor irrigate gardens so as to require of the soil more than it would naturally bring forth of its own richness and extent. Grain is the only tribute exacted from their land, whence they do not divide the year into as many seasons as we do. The terms winter, spring and summer have a meaning with them, but the name and blessings of autumn are unknown.

There is no pomp in the celebration of their funerals. The only custom they observe is that the bodies of illustrious men should be burned with certain kinds of wood. . . .

READING AND DISCUSSION QUESTIONS

1. According to Tacitus, why do the Germans fight with their families close by? What does this reveal about Germanic society?

2. What does the following passage tell you about *both* Germanic *and* Roman society: "To limit the number of children or to put any of the later children to death is considered a crime, and with them good customs are of more avail than good laws elsewhere"?

3. Describe three of the most important features of the Germanic economy.

COMPARATIVE QUESTIONS

1. Compare and contrast attitudes toward women as revealed in the *Corpus Juris Civilis* of Justinian to those evidenced in the story of the rape of Lucretia (Document 5-1) — documents with nearly 1,000 years of cultural history between them. What might account for such disparities or similarities?

2. Compare and contrast the visions of Christianity in Saint Benedict's rule and Saint Augustine's *City of God*.

3. Discuss the ways in which Saint Ambrose and Saint Augustine criticized the powerful classes or rulers of their time.

4. Tacitus' description of Germanic life predates the other documents in this chapter. Consider the order in which the sources were written. In what ways do the issues concerning Romans seem to shift over time? Does anything else stand out?

CHAPTER 8

Europe in the Early Middle Ages

600–1000

The period between 600 and 1000 witnessed the emergence of power-ful new empires. At the time of Muhammad's death in 632, Islam was largely confined to the Arabian peninsula, but the caliphs who fol-lowed him spread Islam throughout a vast empire. In Western Europe, conversion to Roman Catholicism helped spur the creation of new politi-cal entities. In the eighth and ninth centuries, Charlemagne created the Carolingian Empire, which included much of western and central Europe. Although a large part of this new empire was already Christian, Charle-magne forcibly converted pagans, most notably the Saxons, as he incorpo-rated new territories. In 800, the pope crowned Charlemagne Holy Roman Emperor. Following the reign of his son, Louis the Pious, the empire was split among Charlemagne's grandsons into three separate kingdoms. In Kievan Rus, the tenth-century conversion of the ruler Vladmir to the East-ern Orthodox Church laid the religious foundation for the eastern Slav states.

DOCUMENT 8-1

MUHAMMAD

From the Qur'an: *Call for Jihad*

ca. 650

Muslims believe that the Qur'an *is the direct word of God, which was trans-mitted to the Prophet Muhammad by the archangel Gabriel. Muslims be-*

Bernard Lewis, ed., *Islam: From the Prophet Muhammed to the Capture of Constan-tinople* (New York: Walker, 1987), 1:209–210.

lieve that the Hebrew Bible and the New Testament were revelations from God as well and that the Qur'an perfects rather than replaces those texts. Jihad of the sword, or struggle against non-Muslims, is principally meant for the defense and expansion of the Muslim community, rather than forcible conversion, and is only one kind of jihad. In one's personal life, the struggle for self-improvement is also a form of jihad.

Fight in the path of God against those who fight you, but do not transgress, for God does not love transgressors.

Kill them wherever you encounter them, and expel them from whence they have expelled you, for dissension [*fitna*] is worse than killing. But do not fight them by the Sacred Mosque unless they fight you first, and if they do fight you, then kill them. Such is the recompense of the unbelievers.

But if they desist, then God is forgiving and merciful.

Fight them until there is no more dissension, and religion is God's. If they desist, there is no enmity, save against the unjust.

When you meet those who are infidels, strike their necks until you have overwhelmed them, tighten their bonds, and then release them, either freely or for ransom, when war lays down its burdens. Thus it is, and if God wished, He would crush them Himself, but He tests you against one another. Those who are killed in the path of God, He does not let their good deeds go for nothing.

READING AND DISCUSSION QUESTIONS

1. The Qur'an instructs the faithful to "fight in the path of God against those who fight you," but at the same time it commands them not to "transgress." What limits does the Qur'an place on jihad?

2. According to this document, why doesn't God simply destroy His enemies Himself rather than commanding the faithful to do so?

WILLIBALD

Saint Boniface Destroys the Oak of Thor

ca. 750

Saint Boniface (680–754) is known as the apostle of the Germans. He was born in England, which was already a center of Christianity, and was commissioned by Pope Gregory II to spread the gospel and reorganize the church in what is now Germany. Boniface's descendant recounts that as the missionary prepared to chop down the sacred oak, he challenged the pagan god Thor to strike him down. Boniface's survival was proof enough to convert many of the locals. When Boniface destroyed the oak, he was consciously imitating the prophet Elijah from the Hebrew Bible, who had challenged the worship of the god Baal.

Many of the people of Hesse were converted [by Boniface] to the Catholic faith and confirmed by the grace of the spirit: and they received the laying on of hands. But some there were, not yet strong of soul, who refused to accept wholly the teachings of the true faith. Some men sacrificed secretly, some even openly, to trees and springs. Some secretly practiced divining, soothsaying, and incantations, and some openly. But others, who were of sounder mind, cast aside all heathen profanation and did none of these things; and it was with the advice and consent of these men that Boniface sought to fell a certain tree of great size, at Geismar, and called, in the ancient speech of the region, the oak of Jove [i.e., Thor].

The man of God was surrounded by the servants of God. When he would cut down the tree, behold a great throng of pagans who were there cursed him bitterly among themselves because he was the enemy of their gods. And when he had cut into the trunk a little way, a breeze sent by God stirred overhead, and suddenly the branching top of the tree was broken off, and the oak in all its huge bulk fell to the ground. And it was broken into four parts, as if by the divine will, so that the trunk was divided into four huge sections without any effort of the brethren who stood by. When the pagans who had cursed did see this, they left off cursing and, believing,

James Harvey Robinson, ed., *Readings in European History* (Boston: Ginn, 1904), 1:106–107.

blessed God. Then the most holy priest took counsel with the brethren: and he built from the wood of the tree an oratory, and dedicated it to the holy apostle Peter.

READING AND DISCUSSION QUESTIONS

1. How fully did the people of Hesse accept Christianity?
2. What first inspires Saint Boniface to cut down the oak?
3. How does this passage illustrate what people of the time considered to be a miracle?

DOCUMENT 8-3

EINHARD

From Life of Charlemagne

ca. 835

Although Einhard came from a humble family, he was educated at the monastery at Fulda, which was one of the centers of learning in Frankish lands. Brought to the Carolingian court as a man of learning, Einhard came to know Charlemagne well. After Charlemagne's death, Einhard became the private secretary of Charlemagne's son, Louis the Pious. It was Louis who asked Einhard to write the Life of Charlemagne, *which in a sense became an official biography. Einhard modeled his work on the* Life of Augustus *by the Roman historian Suetonius.*

Charles was large and robust, of commanding stature and excellent pro-portions, for it appears that he measured in height seven times the length of his own foot. The top of his head was round, his eyes large and ani-mated, his nose somewhat long. He had a fine head of gray hair, and his face was bright and pleasant; so that, whether standing or sitting, he showed great presence and dignity. Although his neck was thick and rather

Einhard, "Life of Charlemagne," in James Harvey Robinson, ed., *Readings in Euro-pean History* (Boston: Ginn, 1904), 1:126–128.

short, and his belly too prominent, still the good proportions of his limbs concealed these defects. His walk was firm, and the whole carriage of his body was manly. His voice was clear, but not so strong as his frame would have led one to expect. . . .

He took constant exercise in riding and hunting, which was natural for a Frank,[1] since scarcely any nation can be found to equal them in these pursuits. . . .

He wore the dress of his native country, that is, the Frankish; [and] he thoroughly disliked the dress of foreigners, however fine; and he never put it on except at Rome. . . .

In his eating and drinking he was temperate; more particularly so in his drinking, for he had the greatest abhorrence of drunkenness in anybody, but more especially in himself and his companions. He was unable to abstain from food for any length of time, and often complained that fasting was injurious to him. On the other hand, he very rarely feasted, only on great festive occasions, when there were very large gatherings. The daily service of his table consisted of only four dishes in addition to the roast meat, which the hunters used to bring in on spits, and of which he partook more freely than of any other food.

While he was dining he listened to music or reading. History and the deeds of men of old were most often read. He derived much pleasure from the works of St. Augustine, especially from his book called *The City of God*. . . .

While he was dressing and binding on his sandals, he would receive his friends; and also, if the count of the palace announced that there was any case which could only be settled by his decision, the suitors were immediately ordered into his presence, and he heard the case and gave judgment as if sitting in court. And this was not the only business that he used to arrange at that time, for he also gave orders for whatever had to be done on that day by any officer or servant.

He was ready and fluent in speaking, and able to express himself with great clearness. He did not confine himself to his native tongue, but took pains to learn foreign languages, acquiring such knowledge of Latin that he could make an address in that language as well as in his own. Greek he could better understand than speak. Indeed, he was so polished in speech that he might have passed for a learned man.

He was an ardent admirer of the liberal arts, and greatly revered their professors, whom he promoted to high honors. In order to learn grammar,

---

[1] **Frank**: A person of western Germanic origin or descent.

he attended the lectures of the aged Peter of Pisa, a deacon; and for other branches he chose as his preceptor Albinus, otherwise called Alcuin, also a deacon, — a Saxon by race, from Britain, the most learned man of the day, with whom the king spent much time in learning rhetoric and logic, and more especially astronomy. He learned the art of determining the dates upon which the movable festivals of the Church fall, and with deep thought and skill most carefully calculated the courses of the planets.

Charles also tried to learn to write, and used to keep his tablets and writing book under the pillow of his couch, that when he had leisure he might practice his hand in forming letters; but he made little progress in this task, too long deferred and begun too late in life.

READING AND DISCUSSION QUESTIONS

1. Why do you think Einhard describes Charlemagne's appearance at such great length? What does this description reveal about contemporary attitudes and about Einhard himself?

2. Charlemagne was a Frankish ruler. To what degree had the Franks assimilated the customs and practices of other people?

3. What is significant about the fact that Charlemagne, while dressing, would receive his friends and sometimes even hear cases?

4. What strikes you as most notable about Charlemagne's learning?

DOCUMENT 8-4

A Russian Chronicle of Religious Competition in Kievan Rus

ca. 1100

Vladimir the Great (r. 980–1015) became the ruler of Kievan Rus after a series of fratricidal wars. Originally, Vladimir had been a pious pagan, and some historians have argued that he had tried to reform Slavic religious

Serge A. Zenkovsky, ed., *Medieval Russia's Epics, Chronicles and Tales* (New York: Dutton, 1963), 66–72.

beliefs by worshipping Perun, the god of thunder, as the ruler of the gods. In 987, after consulting with his nobles, Vladimir sent emissaries to learn about other religions. Vladimir was also intent on establishing an alliance with the Byzantine Empire. His marriage to Anna, the sister of the Byzantine emperor Basil II, marked the first time that an imperial princess had married a barbarian.

987 [C.E.] . . . Vladimir summoned together his vassals and the city elders, and said to them: "Behold, the Bulgarians came before me urging me to accept their religion. Then came the Germans and praised their own faith; and after them came the Jews. Finally the Greeks appeared, criticizing all other faiths but commending their own, and they spoke at length, telling the history of the whole world from its beginning. Their words were artful, and it was wondrous to listen and pleasant to hear them. They preach the existence of another world. 'Whoever adopts our religion and then dies shall arise and live forever. But whosoever embraces another faith, shall be consumed with fire in the next world.' What is your opinion on this subject, and what do you answer?" The vassals and the elders replied: "You know, O Prince, that no man condemns his own possessions, but praises them instead. If you desire to make certain, you have servants at your disposal. Send them to inquire about the ritual of each and how he worships God."

Their counsel pleased the prince and all the people, so that they chose good and wise men to the number of ten, and directed them to go first among the Bulgarians [i.e., the Turkic Volga Bulgars] and inspect their faith. The emissaries went their way, and when they arrived at their destination they beheld the disgraceful actions of the Bulgarians and their worship in the mosque; then they returned to their own country. Vladimir then instructed them to go likewise among the Germans, and examine their faith, and finally to visit the Greeks. They thus went into Germany, and after viewing the German ceremonial, they proceeded to Constantinople where they appeared before the emperor. He inquired on what mission they had come, and they reported to him all that had occurred. When the emperor heard their words, he rejoiced, and did them great honor on that very day.

On the morrow, the emperor sent a message to the patriarch to inform him that a Russian delegation had arrived to examine the Greek faith, and directed him to prepare the church and the clergy, and to array himself in his sacerdotal robes, so that the Russians might behold the glory of the

God of the Greeks. When the patriarch received these commands, he bade the clergy assemble, and they performed the customary rites. They burned incense, and the choirs sang hymns. The emperor accompanied the Russians to the church, and placed them in a wide space, calling their attention to the beauty of the edifice, the chanting, and the offices of the archpriest and the ministry of the deacons, while he explained to them the worship of his God. The Russians were astonished, and in their wonder praised the Greek ceremonial. Then the Emperors Basil and Constantine invited the envoys to their presence, and said, "Go hence to your native country," and thus dismissed them with valuable presents and great honor.

Thus they returned to their own country, and the prince called together his vassals and the elders. Vladimir then announced the return of the envoys who had been sent out, and suggested that their report be heard. He thus commanded them to speak out before his vassals. The envoys reported: "When we journeyed among the Bulgarians, we beheld how they worship in their temple, called a mosque, while they stand ungirt.[2] The Bulgarian bows, sits down, looks hither and thither like one possessed, and there is no happiness among them, but instead only sorrow and a dreadful stench. Their religion is not good. Then we went among the Germans, and saw them performing many ceremonies in their temples; but we beheld no glory there. Then we went on to Greece, and the Greeks led us to the edifices where they worship their God, and we knew not whether we were in heaven or on earth. For on earth there is no such splendor or such beauty, and we are at a loss how to describe it. We know only that God dwells there among men, and their service is fairer than the ceremonies of other nations. For we cannot forget that beauty. Every man, after tasting something sweet, is afterward unwilling to accept that which is bitter, and therefore we cannot dwell longer here." Then the vassals spoke and said, "If the Greek faith were evil, it would not have been adopted by your grandmother Olga,[3] who was wiser than all other men." Vladimir then inquired where they should all accept baptism, and they replied that the decision rested with him. [However, Vladimir was not yet ready for baptism. He captured the Greek city of Kherson in the Crimea and demanded that the Byzantine emperor give him his daughter

---

[2] **ungirt**: With belt loosened, rather sloppily.
[3] **Olga**: Saint Olga of Kiev, grandmother of Vladimir the Great, who ruled Kievan Rus (ca. 945–963) as a regent following her husband's death. The first Russian ruler to convert to Christianity.

in marriage. The emperor refused unless Vladimir became a Christian. He gave his promise and the princess was dispatched to Russia, but still he refused to go through with the ceremony.]

By divine agency, Vladimir was suffering at that moment from a disease of the eyes, and could see nothing, being in great distress. The princess declared to him that if he desired to be relieved of this disease, he should be baptized with all speed, otherwise it could not be cured. When Vladimir heard her message, he said, "If this proves true, then of a surety is the God of the Christians great," and gave order that he should be baptized. The Bishop of Kherson, together with the princess's priests, after announcing the tidings, baptized Vladimir, and as the bishop laid his hand upon him, he straightway received his sight. Upon experiencing this miraculous cure, Vladimir glorified God, saying, "I have now perceived the one true God." When his followers beheld this miracle, many of them were also baptized.

READING AND DISCUSSION QUESTIONS

1. What does it reveal about Kievan Rus that its ruler would send out emissaries to learn about the faiths of other peoples?

2. What did the emissaries have to say about the various faiths they encountered?

3. What impressed the emissaries most about Greek Orthodoxy?

4. Why did Vladimir finally convert?

COMPARATIVE QUESTIONS

1. Compare the miracle of Saint Boniface with that of Vladimir of Kievan Rus. What similarities do these two events share? What are the differences?

2. Compare the Qur'an and Saint Boniface on the issue of religious disagreement. To what degree do these documents reveal a willingness to let people practice their own faiths?

3. Compare and contrast the courts of Charlemagne and of the Byzantine emperors that Vladimir's envoy studied.

CHAPTER 9

State and Church in the High Middle Ages

1000–1300

L ess than twenty years after the Norman conquest of England in 1066, William I ordered a thorough survey of the entire country. In the twelfth century, William's great-grandson Henry II reformed the legal system and laid the foundations of English common law. As royal power grew, however, the great barons of the realm sought to define and protect their rights, resulting in the Magna Carta of 1215. Within the Roman Catholic Church, the eleventh-century investiture controversy was a struggle for power pitting Pope Gregory VII against the Holy Roman emperor Henry IV. Gregory and his followers believed that they would never be able to reform the church if its bishops and abbots were appointed by secular rulers. Papal claims to authority over Christians reached its pinnacle with the call for the crusades as the Roman Church sought to regain Christian holy lands that had been controlled by Muslims for centuries.

DOCUMENT 9-1

William the Conqueror and the Domesday Book

1086

In 1066, William, duke of Normandy, conquered England, claiming to be the legitimate heir to the throne. Twenty years later, in December 1085, William ordered a complete survey of the entire kingdom. He wanted to

James Harvey Robinson, ed., *Readings in European History* (Boston: Ginn, 1904), 1:229–231.

define how much of England consisted of crown land and to describe the country in enough detail to be able to properly tax it. The survey, assembled into what became known as the Domesday Book, was remarkably thorough and stands as a testament to the Norman talent for administration.

At Midwinter the king was at Gloucester with his "witan" [advisors], and there held his court five days; and afterwards the archbishop and clergy had a synod [ecclesiastical assembly] three days. There was Maurice chosen bishop of London, and William, of Norfolk, and Robert, of Cheshire. They were all the king's clerks. After this the king had a great council, and very deep speech with his "witan" about this land, how it was peopled, or by what men; then he sent his men over all England, into every shire, and caused to be ascertained how many hundred hides were in the shire, or what land the king himself had, and cattle within the land, or what dues he ought to have, in twelve months, from the shire. Also he caused to be written how much land his archbishops had, and his suffragan bishops, and his abbots, and his earls: and — though I may narrate somewhat prolixly — what or how much each man had who was a landholder in England, in land, or in cattle, and how much money it might be worth. So very narrowly he caused it to be traced out, that there was not one single hide, nor one yard of land, nor even — it is shame to tell, though it seemed to him no shame to do — an ox, nor a cow, nor a swine, left that was not set down in his writ.

King William, about whom we speak, was a very wise man, and very powerful, more dignified and strong than any of his predecessors were. He was mild to the good men who loved God, and beyond all measure severe to the men who gainsaid his will. . . . He was also very dignified; thrice every year he wore his crown, as oft as he was in England. At Easter he wore it in Winchester; at Pentecost, in Westminster; at Midwinter, in Gloucester. And then were with him all the great men over all England, archbishops and suffragan bishops, abbots and earls, thanes and knights.

So also was he a very rigid and cruel man, so that no one durst do anything against his will. He had earls in bonds who had acted against his will; bishops he cast from their bishoprics, and abbots from their abbacies, and thanes into prison; and at last he spared not his own brother, named Odo: he was a very rich bishop in Normandy; at Bayeux was his episcopal see; and he was the foremost man besides the king; and he had an earldom in England, and when the king was in Normandy, then was he the most powerful in this land: and him the king put in prison.

Among other good things is not to be forgotten the good peace that he made in this land; so that a man who had any confidence in himself might go over his realm, with his bosom full of gold, unhurt. Nor durst any man slay another man had he done ever so great evil to the other. He reigned over England, and by his sagacity so thoroughly surveyed it that there was not a hide of land within England that he knew not who had it, or what it was worth, and afterwards set it in his writ.

Brytland [Wales] was in his power, and therein he built castles, and completely ruled over that race of men. In like manner he also subjected Scotland to him by his great strength. The land of Normandy was naturally his, and over the country which is called Le Maine he reigned; and if he might yet have lived two years he would, by his valor, have won Ireland, and without any weapons.

Certainly in his time men had great hardship and very many injuries. Castles he caused to be made, and poor men to be greatly oppressed. The king was very rigid, and took from his subjects many a mark of gold, and more hundred pounds of silver, all which he took, by right and with great unright, from his people, for little need. He had fallen into covetousness, and altogether loved greediness.

He planted a great preserve for deer, and he laid down laws therewith, that whosoever should slay hart or hind should be blinded. He forbade the harts and also the boars to be killed. As greatly did he love the tall deer as if he were their father. He also ordained concerning the hares that they should go free. His great men bewailed it, and the poor men murmured thereat; but he was so obdurate that he recked not of the hatred of them all; but they must wholly follow the king's will if they would live, or have land, or property, or even his peace. Alas that any man should be so proud, so raise himself up, and account himself above all men! May the Almighty God show mercy to his soul, and grant him forgiveness of his sins!

READING AND DISCUSSION QUESTIONS

1. The chronicler describes William as a "wise man" but also says that he was "very rigid and cruel." What does this reveal about what the chronicler seems to have expected from a king?

2. What were William's principal faults and virtues? How did they support or detract from one another?

3. How well had William established peace after conquering England? Give specific examples to support your position.

DOCUMENT 9-2

KING JOHN OF ENGLAND

From Magna Carta: *The Great Charter of Liberties*

1215

The English kings had extensive possessions in France and spent much of their resources trying to defend or expand these holdings. By 1215, King John — through a series of military defeats and poorly conducted alliances — had lost many of these French lands. To make up for his losses, John levied, to the point of abuse, the feudal payments that his vassals owed him. He also harshly enforced other traditional feudal rights, such as the laws governing the forests. In 1215, his nobles forced him to issue a charter that would clearly define both royal rights and the rights of subjects.

John, by the grace of God, king of England, lord of Ireland, duke of Normandy and Aquitaine, and count of Anjou, to the archbishops, bishops, abbots, earls, barons . . . and faithful subjects, greeting. . . .

We have . . . granted to all free men of our kingdom, for ourselves and our heirs, for ever, all the liberties written below, to be had and held by them and their heirs of us and our heirs. . . .

No widow shall be forced to marry so long as she wishes to live without a husband, provided that she gives security not to marry without our consent if she holds [a fief] of us, or without the consent of her lord of whom she holds, if she holds of another.

No scutage[1] or aid shall be imposed in our kingdom unless by common counsel of our kingdom, except for ransoming our person, for making our eldest son a knight, and for once marrying our eldest daughter; and for these only a reasonable aid shall be levied. . . .

Neither we nor our bailiffs will take, for castles or other works of ours, timber which is not ours, except with the agreement of him whose timber it is.

David C. Douglas, ed., *English Historical Documents*, vol. 3, ed. Harry Rothwell (London: Eyre and Spottiswoode, 1975), 316–321.

[1] **scutage:** Payment in lieu of performing military service.

We will not hold for more than a year and a day the lands of those convicted of felony, and then the lands shall be handed over to the lords of the fiefs.

No free man shall be arrested or imprisoned or disseised [dispossessed] or outlawed or exiled or in any way victimized, neither will we attack him or send anyone to attack him, except by the lawful judgment of his peers or by the law of the land.

To no one will we sell, to no one will we refuse or delay right or justice.

We will not make justices, constables, sheriffs or bailiffs save of such as know the law of the kingdom and mean to observe it well.

READING AND DISCUSSION QUESTIONS

1. In what ways does the Magna Carta limit how the king can raise money?
2. Discuss how the Magna Carta seeks to reform the administration of justice.
3. Judging from these selections, who in the kingdom seemed to have the strongest grievances against the king? Use examples to support your claim.

DOCUMENT 9-3

POPE GREGORY VII AND EMPEROR HENRY IV

Mutual Recriminations: The Investiture Controversy Begins

1076

The investiture controversy centered on who had the right to appoint the offi-cials of the Roman Catholic Church. In addition to being servants of the church, bishops and abbots were often great landowners. Because the clergy were the most extensive literate class, many royal or imperial officials were drawn from their ranks, and secular rulers sought to appoint men who were

James Harvey Robinson, ed., *Readings in European History* (Boston: Ginn, 1904), 1:276–281.

loyal to them. Those who were trying to reform the church from within, like Pope Gregory VII, argued that reform would be impossible if church officials owed their positions to secular rulers.

[POPE GREGORY VII TO EMPEROR HENRY IV]

Bishop Gregory, servant of the servants of God, to King Henry, greeting and apostolic benediction: — that is, if he be obedient to the apostolic chair as beseems a Christian king:

For we cannot but hesitate to send thee our benediction when we seriously consider the strictness of the Judge to whom we shall have to render account for the ministry intrusted to us by St. Peter, chief of the apostles. For thou art said knowingly to associate with men excommunicated by a judgment of the apostolic chair and by sentence of a synod. If this be true, thou thyself dost know that thou mayest not receive the favor of the divine, nor of the apostolic benediction, unless those who have been excommunicated be separated from thee and compelled to do penance, and thou, with condign repentance and satisfaction, obtain absolution and pardon for thy misdeeds. Therefore we counsel thy Highness that, if thou dost feel thyself guilty in this matter, thou shouldst seek the advice of some devout bishop, with prompt confession. He, with our permission, enjoining on thee a proper penance for this fault, shall absolve thee, and shall take care to inform us by letter, with thy consent, of the exact measure of thy penance.

In the next place, it seems strange to us that although thou dost so often send us such devoted letters; and although thy Highness dost show such humility in the messages of thy legates, — calling thyself the son of holy mother Church and of ourselves, subject in the faith, foremost in love and devotion; — although, in short, thou dost commend thyself with all the sweetness of devotion and reverence, yet in conduct and action thou dost show thyself most stubborn, and in opposition to the canonical and apostolic decrees in those matters which the religion of the Church deems of chief importance. . . . And now, indeed, inflicting wound upon wound, thou hast, contrary to the rules of the apostolic chair, given the churches of Fermo and Spoleto — if indeed a church can be given or granted by a mere man — to certain persons not even known to us, on whom, unless they are previously well known and proven, it is not lawful regularly to perform the laying on of hands.

It would have beseemed thy royal dignity, since thou dost confess thyself a son of the Church, to have treated more respectfully the master of the Church, — that is, St. Peter, the chief of the apostles. For to him, if thou art of the Lord's sheep, thou wast given over by the Lord's voice and authority to be fed; Christ himself saying, "Peter, feed my sheep." And again: "To thee are given over the keys of the kingdom of heaven; and whatsoever thou shalt bind on earth shall be bound in heaven; and whatsoever thou shalt loose on earth shall be loosed in heaven."

Inasmuch as in his seat and apostolic ministration we, however sinful and unworthy, do, by the providence of God, act as the representative of his power, surely he himself is receiving whatever, in writing or by word of mouth, thou hast sent to us. And at the very time when we are either perusing thy letters or listening to the voices of those who speak for thee, he himself is observing, with discerning eye, in what spirit the instructions were issued. Wherefore thy Highness should have seen to it that no lack of good will should appear toward the apostolic chair in thy words and messages. . . .

In this year a synod was assembled about the apostolic chair, over which the heavenly dispensation willed that we should preside, and at which some of thy faithful subjects were present. Seeing that the good order of the Christian religion has now for some time been disturbed, and that the chief and proper methods of winning souls have, at the instigation of the devil, long been neglected and suppressed, we, struck by the danger and impending ruin of the Lord's flock, reverted to the decrees and teachings of the holy fathers, — decreeing nothing new, nothing of our own invention. . . .

Lest these things should seem unduly burdensome or unjust to thee, we did admonish thee, through thy faithful servants, that the changing of an evil custom should not alarm thee; that thou shouldst send to us wise and religious men from thy land, to demonstrate or prove, if they could, by any reasoning, in what respects, saving the honor of the Eternal King and without danger to our soul, we might moderate the decree as passed by the holy fathers, and we would yield to their counsels. Even without our friendly admonitions it would have been but right that, before thou didst violate apostolic decrees, thou shouldst reasonably have appealed to us in cases where we oppressed thee or infringed thy prerogatives. But how little thou didst esteem our commands or the dictates of justice is shown by those things which thou afterwards didst.

But since the long-suffering patience of God still invites thee to amend thy ways, we have hopes that thy understanding may be awakened, and thy heart and mind be bent to obey the mandates of God: we exhort thee with paternal love to recognize the dominion of Christ over thee and to reflect how dangerous it is to prefer thine own honor to his.

[EMPEROR HENRY IV TO POPE GREGORY VII]

Henry, King not by usurpation but by holy ordination of God, to Hilde-brand, now no Pope but false monk:

Such greeting as this hast thou merited through thy disturbances, for there is no rank in the Church but thou hast brought upon it, not honor but disgrace, not a blessing but a curse. To mention a few notable cases out of the many, thou hast not only dared to assail the rulers of the holy Church, the anointed of the Lord, — archbishops, bishops, and priests, but thou hast trodden them under foot like slaves ignorant of what their master is doing. By so crushing them thou hast won the favor of the common herd; thou hast regarded them all as knowing nothing, — thyself alone as knowing all things. Yet this knowledge thou hast exerted, not for their advantage but for their destruction; so that with reason we believe St. Gregory, whose name thou hast usurped, prophesied of thee when he said, "The pride of the magistrate commonly waxes great if the number of those subject to him be great, and he thinks that he can do more than they all."

We, forsooth, have endured all this in our anxiety to save the honor of the apostolic see, but thou hast mistaken our humility for fear, and hast, accordingly, ventured to attack the royal power conferred upon us by God, and threatened to divest us of it. As if we had received our kingdom from thee! As if the kingdom and his empire were in thy hands, not in God's! For our Lord Jesus Christ did call us to the kingdom, although he has not called thee to the priesthood: that thou hast attained by the following steps.

By craft abhorrent to the profession of monk, thou hast acquired wealth; by wealth, influence; by influence, arms; by arms, a throne of peace. And from the throne of peace thou hast destroyed peace; thou hast turned subjects against their governors, for thou, who wert not called of God, hast taught that our bishops, truly so called, should be despised. Thou hast put laymen above their priests, allowing them to depose or condemn those whom they themselves had received as teachers from the hand of God through the laying on of bishops' hands.

Thou hast further assailed me also, who, although unworthy of anointing, have nevertheless been anointed to the kingdom, and who, according to the traditions of the holy fathers, am subject to the judgment of God alone, to be deposed upon no charge save that of deviation from the faith, — which God avert! For the holy fathers by their wisdom committed the judgment and deposition of even Julian the Apostate[2] not to them-

---

[2] **Julian the Apostate**: The last pagan Roman emperor (r. ca. 355–363), known for unsuccessfully trying to thwart the spread of Christianity within the empire.

selves but to God alone. Likewise the true pope, Peter, himself exclaims: "Fear God. Honor the king." But thou, who dost not fear God, art dishonoring me, his appointed one. Wherefore, St. Paul, since he spared not an angel of heaven if he should preach other than the gospel, has not excepted thee, who dost teach other doctrine upon earth. For he says, "If any one, whether I, or an angel from heaven, shall preach the gospel other than that which has been preached to you, he shall be damned."

Thou, therefore, damned by this curse and by the judgment of all our bishops and ourselves, come down and relinquish the apostolic chair which thou hast usurped. Let another assume the seat of St. Peter, who will not practice violence under the cloak of religion, but will teach St. Peter's wholesome doctrine. I, Henry, king by the grace of God, together with all our bishops, say unto thee: "Come down, come down, to be damned throughout all eternity!"

READING AND DISCUSSION QUESTIONS

1. Analyze the tone of the two letters. In what ways are they different? What are the similarities?

2. On what basis does Gregory claim the right to appoint church officials?

3. In what ways does the emperor claim that the pope was attacking both the church and imperial power?

DOCUMENT 9-4

ROBERT THE MONK OF RHEIMS
Urban II at the Council of Clermont: A Call for Crusade
ca. 1120

By the late eleventh century, Christians were pushing back Muslim forces in many parts of the Mediterranean world. The Normans conquered Sicily in

---

James Harvey Robinson, ed., *Readings in European History* (Boston: Ginn, 1904), 1:312–315.

1091, and the Christian kingdoms in Spain were expanding at the expense of their Muslim neighbors. The Byzantine emperor had appealed for mercenaries to fight against the Seljuk Turks, but Pope Urban II broadened this goal. He wanted to liberate Christians living under Muslim rule and to recapture the Holy Land — especially Jerusalem. The Crusaders captured the city in 1099 and established the Kingdom of Jerusalem and other Crusader states. In fewer than two hundred years, however, the Holy Land was once more under Muslim control.

"Oh, race of Franks, race from across the mountains, race beloved and chosen by God, — as is clear from many of your works, — set apart from all other nations by the situation of your country as well as by your Catholic faith and the honor which you render to the holy Church: to you our discourse is addressed, and for you our exhortations are intended. We wish you to know what a grievous cause has led us to your country, for it is the imminent peril threatening you and all the faithful which has brought us hither.

From the confines of Jerusalem and from the city of Constantinople a grievous report has gone forth and has repeatedly been brought to our ears; namely, that a race from the kingdom of the Persians, an accursed race, a race wholly alienated from God, 'a generation that set not their heart aright, and whose spirit was not steadfast with God,' has violently invaded the lands of those Christians and has depopulated them by pillage and fire. They have led away a part of the captives into their own country, and a part they have killed by cruel tortures. They have either destroyed the churches of God or appropriated them for the rites of their own religion. They destroy the altars, after having defiled them with their uncleanness. . . . The kingdom of the Greeks is now dismembered by them and has been deprived of territory so vast in extent that it could not be traversed in two months' time.

On whom, therefore, is the labor of avenging these wrongs and of recovering this territory incumbent, if not upon you, — you, upon whom, above all other nations, God has conferred remarkable glory in arms, great courage, bodily activity, and strength to humble the heads of those who resist you? Let the deeds of your ancestors encourage you and incite your minds to manly achievements: — the glory and greatness of King Charlemagne, and of his son Louis, and of your other monarchs, who have destroyed the kingdoms of the Turks and have extended the sway of the holy Church over lands previously pagan. Let the holy sepulcher of our

Lord and Savior, which is possessed by the unclean nations, especially arouse you, and the holy places which are now treated with ignominy and irreverently polluted with the filth of the unclean. Oh, most valiant soldiers and descendants of invincible ancestors, do not degenerate, but recall the valor of your progenitors.

But if you are hindered by love of children, parents, or wife, remember what the Lord says in the Gospel, 'He that loveth father or mother more than me is not worthy of me.' 'Every one that hath forsaken houses, or brethren, or sisters, or father, or mother, or wife, or children, or lands, for my name's sake, shall receive an hundredfold, and shall inherit everlasting life.' Let none of your possessions retain you, nor solicitude for your family affairs. For this land which you inhabit, shut in on all sides by the seas and surrounded by the mountain peaks, is too narrow for your large population; nor does it abound in wealth; and it furnishes scarcely food enough for its cultivators. Hence it is that you murder and devour one another, that you wage war, and that very many among you perish in intestine strife.

Let hatred therefore depart from among you, let your quarrels end, let wars cease, and let all dissensions and controversies slumber. Enter upon the road to the Holy Sepulcher; wrest that land from the wicked race, and subject it to yourselves. That land which, as the Scripture says, 'floweth with milk and honey' was given by God into the power of the children of Israel. Jerusalem is the center of the earth; the land is fruitful above all others, like another paradise of delights. This spot the Redeemer of mankind has made illustrious by his advent, has beautified by his sojourn, has consecrated by his passion, has redeemed by his death, has glorified by his burial.

This royal city, however, situated at the center of the earth, is now held captive by the enemies of Christ and is subjected, by those who do not know God, to the worship of the heathen. She seeks, therefore, and desires to be liberated and ceases not to implore you to come to her aid. From you especially she asks succor, because, as we have already said, God has conferred upon you above all other nations great glory in arms. Accordingly, undertake this journey eagerly for the remission of your sins, with the assurance of the reward of imperishable glory in the kingdom of heaven."

When Pope Urban had urbanely said these and very many similar things, he so centered in one purpose the desires of all who were present that all cried out, "It is the will of God! It is the will of God!" When the venerable Roman pontiff heard that, with eyes uplifted to heaven, he gave thanks to God and, commanding silence with his hand, said:

"Most beloved brethren, to-day is manifest in you what the Lord says in the Gospel, 'Where two or three are gathered together in my name, there am I in the midst of them'; for unless God had been present in your spirits, all of you would not have uttered the same cry; since, although the cry issued from numerous mouths, yet the origin of the cry was one. Therefore I say to you that God, who implanted this in your breasts, has drawn it forth from you. Let that then be your war cry in combats, because it is given to you by God. When an armed attack is made upon the enemy, let this one cry be raised by all the soldiers of God: 'It is the will of God! It is the will of God!' [*Deus vult! Deus vult!*]"

READING AND DISCUSSION QUESTIONS

1. Why would Urban II's claim that the land of the Franks was "too narrow for [its] large population" have been an important issue for the Crusaders?

2. In what ways were the Crusades examples of international cooperation?

3. What specific grievances does Urban II direct at the Muslims?

COMPARATIVE QUESTIONS

1. What do both the investiture controversy and the call for the First Crusade reveal about the new powers of the church?

2. What evidence is there from the Domesday Book and *Magna Carta* that England was evolving into a nation-state?

3. Based on the descriptions in the Domesday Book story and *Magna Carta*, discuss how English kings might be able to abuse royal power.

CHAPTER 10

The Changing Life of the People in the High Middle Ages

B y the year 1000, many social institutions of the later Middle Ages had taken root, although they had not yet borne fruit. Schools, often associated with the church, had emerged. Even though the majority of people were illiterate, almost everyone knew something about written documents and could turn for help to someone who was literate. Monasticism, which had long been an important part of European Christendom, experienced renewal and reform, especially with the founding of orders such as the Cistercians. For many peasants, however, social life became more constricted. Various forms of unfree servitude, including serfdom, tied them to the soil. In some parts of Europe, those who could escape to the cities might eventually gain freedom if they were not claimed by their masters within a specified period, often a year and a day.

DOCUMENT 10-1

On Laborers: A Dialogue Between Teacher and Student

ca. 1000

The following document was likely used to teach students Latin. It also provides a short explanation of social relations — information that would be useful for students who would later keep records or supervise workers. By

Thomas Wright, ed., *Anglo-Saxon and Old English Vocabularies* (London: Trubner, 1884), Vol. I, p. 88, reprinted in Roy C. Cave & Herbert H. Coulson, *A Source Book for Medieval Economic History* (New York: The Bruce Publishing Co., 1936; reprint ed., New York: Biblo & Tannen, 1965), 46–48.

The text has been modernized by Jerome S. Arkenberg, California State University–Fullerton.

1000, especially in the countryside, various forms of unfree status had been imposed, although outright slavery was one of the less common forms. Serfs, for instance, could not be bought and sold as individuals, but they also could not leave their land, and their duties to their masters were carefully prescribed. When the land they worked passed to another owner, they acquired a new master.

TEACHER: What do your companions know?

STUDENT: They are plowmen, shepherds, oxherds, huntsmen, fishermen, falconers, merchants, cobblers, salt-makers, and bakers.

TEACHER: What sayest thou plowman? How do you do your work?

PLOWMAN: O my lord, I work very hard: I go out at dawn, driving the cattle to the field, and I yoke them to the plow. Nor is the weather so bad in winter that I dare to stay at home, for fear of my lord: but when the oxen are yoked, and the plowshare and coulter attached to the plow, I must plow one whole field a day, or more.

TEACHER: Have you any assistant?

PLOWMAN: I have a boy to drive the oxen with a goad, and he too is hoarse with cold and shouting.

TEACHER: What more do you do in a day?

PLOWMAN: Certainly I do more. I must fill the manger of the oxen with hay, and water them and carry out the dung.

TEACHER: Indeed, that is a great labor.

PLOWMAN: Even so, it is a great labor for I am not free.

TEACHER: What have you to say shepherd? Have you heavy work too?

SHEPHERD: I have indeed. In the grey dawn I drive my sheep to the pasture and I stand watch over them, in heat and cold, with my dogs, lest the wolves devour them. And I bring them back to the fold and milk them twice a day. And I move their fold; and I make cheese and butter, and I am faithful to my lord.

TEACHER: Oxherd, what work do you do?

OXHERD: O my lord, I work hard. When the plowman unyokes the oxen I lead them to the pasture and I stand all night guarding them against thieves. Then in the morning I hand them over to the plowman well fed and watered.

TEACHER: What is your craft?

FISHERMAN: I am a fisherman.

TEACHER: What do you obtain from your work?

FISHERMAN: Food and clothing and money.

TEACHER: How do you take the fish?

FISHERMAN: I get into a boat, and place my nets in the water, and I throw out my hook and lines, and whatever they take I keep.

TEACHER: What if the fish should be unclean?

FISHERMAN: I throw out the unclean fish and use the clean as food.

TEACHER: Where do you sell your fish?

FISHERMAN: In the town.

TEACHER: Who buys them?

FISHERMAN: The citizens. I cannot catch as much as I can sell.

TEACHER: What fish do you take?

FISHERMAN: Herring, salmon, porpoises, sturgeon, oysters, crabs, mussels, periwinkles, cockles, plaice, sole, lobsters, and the like.

TEACHER: Do you wish to capture a whale?

FISHERMAN: No.

TEACHER: Why?

FISHERMAN: Because it is a dangerous thing to capture a whale. It is safer for me to go to the river with my boat than to go with many ships hunting whales.

TEACHER: Why so?

FISHERMAN: Because I prefer to take a fish that I can kill rather than one which with a single blow can sink or kill not only me but also my companions.

TEACHER: Yet many people do capture whales and escape the danger, and they obtain a great price for what they do.

FISHERMAN: You speak the truth, but I do not dare because of my cowardice.

READING AND DISCUSSION QUESTIONS

1. What can you deduce about the social status of the various speakers?

2. What are the duties of the plowman's helper?

3. In what ways does the social status of the fisherman differ from those of other speakers?

DOCUMENT 10-2

The Law of Brusthem

1175

Brusthem is located near Liège in present-day Belgium. This document is drawn from the cartulary (a collection of documents focused primarily on legal and property matters) of the Abbey de Saint-Trond. Although some medieval law, such as the English common law and the church's canonical law, extended over large areas, in many cases local law took precedent on particular local matters. This document reveals the complicated problems that could arise when people of different social statuses married. More generally, it reveals in detail how laws could treat people differently based on their social statuses.

In a mixed marriage between a freewoman and a serf living in Brusthem, her free condition was protected only if her husband was not claimed by his lord before his death. If the marriage was only discovered after the husband's death, then she had the rights of a freewoman. . . .

If the serf of another, living in this town, take in marriage a woman not his equal, and if his lord claim her while her husband is alive, she shall serve him as her lord, as justice demands. But if the serf die in peace, without being reclaimed by his lord, if the lord afterwards claim the goods of the dead man and exact a portion, the wife shall take as great a portion of them as she wishes and shall declare in the presence of the court that she has done so. And her unassisted oath will be taken that she has not more of her husband's goods (than she says she has). If, when she has taken the oath, she wishes for more, and has taken any of them, there will be a free division of the rest of her goods and all her possessions.

C. Piot, ed., *Cartulaire de l'Abbaye de Saint-Trond* (Brussels: Académie Royale de Belgique, 1870), 124; reprinted in Roy C. Cave & Herbert H. Coulson, eds., *A Source Book for Medieval Economic History* (Milwaukee: The Bruce Publishing Co., 1936; reprint ed., New York: Biblo & Tannen, 1965), 278.

The text has been modernized by Jerome S. Arkenberg, California State University–Fullerton.

READING AND DISCUSSION QUESTIONS

1. Why is it significant that marriage between a serf and a free person was permitted at all?

2. Why did it make a difference when the lord learned that his serf was married to a free woman?

3. Why is it significant that lords sometimes did not know about the marital status of their serfs?

4. In what way could a free woman lose her social status?

DOCUMENT 10-3

WILLIAM OF ST. THIERRY
On the Life of Saint Bernard
ca. 1140

Bernard of Clairvaux (1090–1153) was one of the principal figures of the Cistercian monastic order that was responsible for reforms that affected monastic life throughout Europe. Bernard was also an adviser to kings and popes and was one of the principal churchmen who preached in favor of the Second Crusade. In contrast to the rationalism of the Scholastics or to the ritualism of the earlier church, Bernard called for a more immediate, personal, relationship to God. He was especially devoted to the Virgin Mary, and his teaching emphasized her importance as an intercessor for humanity.

Saint Bernard was born at Fontaines in Burgundy, at the castle of his father. His parents were famed among the famous of that age, most of all because of their piety. His father, Tescelin, was a member of an ancient and knightly family, fearing God and scrupulously just. Even when engaged

Frederic Austin Ogg, ed., *A Source Book of Mediaeval History: Documents Illustrative of European Life and Institutions from the German Invasions to the Renaissance* (New York, 1907; reprinted by Cooper Square Publishers, New York, 1972), 251–258.

The text has been modernized by Jerome S. Arkenberg, California State University–Fullerton.

in holy war he plundered and destroyed no one; he contented himself with his worldly possessions, of which he had an abundance, and used them in all manner of good works. With both his counsel and his arms he served temporal lords, but so as never to neglect to render to the sovereign Lord that which was due him. Bernard's mother, Alith, of the castle Montbar, mindful of holy law, was submissive to her husband and, with him, governed the household in the fear of God, devoting herself to deeds of mercy and rearing her children in strict discipline. She bore seven children, six boys and one girl, not so much for the glory of her husband as for that of God; for all the sons became monks and the daughter a nun.

As soon as Bernard was of sufficient age his mother intrusted his education to the teachers in the church at Châtillon and did everything in her power to enable him to make rapid progress. The young boy, abounding in pleasing qualities and endowed with natural genius, fulfilled his mother's every expectation; for he advanced in his study of letters at a speed beyond his age and that of other children of the same age. But in secular matters he began already, and very naturally, to humble himself in the interest of his future perfection, for he exhibited the greatest simplicity, loved to be in solitude, fled from people, was extraordinarily thoughtful, submitted himself implicitly to his parents, had little desire to converse, was devoted to God, and applied himself to his studies as the means by which he should be able to learn of God through the Scriptures. . . .

Determined that it would be best for him to abandon the world, he began to inquire where his soul, under the yoke of Christ, would be able to find the most complete and sure repose. The recent establishment of the order of Cîteaux suggested itself to his thought. The harvest was abundant, but the laborers were few, for hardly any one had sought happiness by taking up residence there, because of the excessive austerity of life and the poverty which there prevailed, but which had no terrors for the soul truly seeking God. Without hesitation or misgivings, he turned his steps to that place, thinking that there he would be able to find seclusion and, in the secret of the presence of God, escape the importunities of men; wishing particularly there to gain a refuge from the vainglory of the noble's life, and to win purity of soul, and perhaps the name of saint.

When his brothers, who loved him according to the flesh, discovered that he intended to become a monk, they employed every means to turn him to the pursuit of letters and to attach him to the secular life by the love of worldly knowledge. Without doubt, as he has himself declared, he was not a little moved by their arguments. But the memory of his devout mother urged him importunately to take the step. It often seemed to him that she appeared before him, reproaching him and reminding him that she had not reared him for frivolous things of that sort, and that she had brought him up in quite another hope. Finally, one day when he was returning from the siege of a château called Grancey, and was coming to his brothers, who were with the duke of Burgundy, he began to be violently tormented by these thoughts. Finding by the roadside a church, he went in and there prayed, with flooded eyes, lifting his hands toward Heaven and pouring out his heart like water before the Lord. That day fixed his resolution irrevocably. From that hour, even as the fire consumes the forests and the flame ravages the mountains, seizing everything, devouring first that which is nearest but advancing to objects farther removed, so did the fire which God had kindled in the heart of his servant, desiring that it should consume it, lay hold first of his brothers (of whom only the youngest, incapable yet of becoming a monk, was left to console his old father), then his parents, his companions, and his friends, from whom no one had ever expected such a step. . . .

The number of those who decided to take upon themselves monastic vows increased and, as one reads of the earliest sons of the Church, "all the multitude of those who believed were of one mind and one heart." They lived together and no one else dared mingle with them. They had at Châtillon a house which they possessed in common and in which they held meetings, dwelt together, and held converse with one another. No one was so bold as to enter it, unless he were a member of the congregation. If anyone entered there, seeing and hearing what was done and said (as the Apostle declared of the Christians of Corinth), he was convinced by their prophecies and, adoring the Lord and perceiving that God was truly among them, he either joined himself to the brotherhood or, going away, wept at his own plight and their happy state. . . .

At that time, the young and feeble establishment at Cîteaux, under the venerable abbot Stephen, began to be seriously weakened by its paucity of numbers and to lose all hope of having successors to perpetuate the heritage of holy poverty, for everybody revered the life of these monks for its sanctity but held aloof from it because of its austerity. But the monastery was suddenly visited and made glad by the Lord in a happy and unhoped-for manner. In 1113, fifteen years after the foundation of the monastery, the servant of God, Bernard, then about twenty-three years of age, entered the establishment under the abbot Stephen, with his companions to the number of more than thirty, and submitted himself to the blessed yoke of Christ. From that day God prospered the house, and that vine of the Lord bore fruit, putting forth its branches from sea to sea.

Such were the holy beginnings of the monastic life of that man of God. It is impossible to any one who has not been imbued as he with the spirit of God to recount the illustrious deeds of his career, and his angelic conduct, during his life on earth. He entered the monastery poor in spirit, still obscure and of no fame, with the intention of there perishing in the heart and memory of men, and hoping to be forgotten and ignored like a lost vessel. But God ordered it otherwise, and prepared him as a chosen vessel, not only to strengthen and extend the monastic order, but also to bear His name before kings and peoples to the ends of the earth. . . .

At the time of harvest the brothers were occupied, with the fervor and joy of the Holy Spirit, in reaping the grain. Since he was not able to have part in the labor, they bade him sit by them and take his ease. Greatly troubled, he had recourse to prayer and, with much weeping, implored the Lord to grant him the strength to become a reaper. The simplicity of his faith did not deceive him, for that which he asked he obtained. Indeed from that day he prided himself in being more skillful than the others at that task; and he was the more given over to devotion during that labor because he realized that the ability to perform it was a direct gift from God. Refreshed by his employments of this kind, he prayed, read, or meditated continuously. If an opportunity for prayer in solitude offered itself, he seized it; but in any case, whether by himself or with companions, he preserved a solitude in his heart, and thus was everywhere alone. He read gladly, and always with faith and thoughtfulness, the Holy Scriptures, saying that they never seemed to him so clear as when read in the text alone, and he declared his ability to discern their truth and divine virtue much more readily in the source itself than in the commentaries which were derived from it. Nevertheless, he read humbly the saints and orthodox commentators and made no pretense of rivaling their knowledge; but, submitting his to theirs, and tracing it faithfully to its sources, he drank often at the fountain whence they had drawn. It is thus that, full of the spirit which has divinely inspired all Holy Scripture, he has served God to this day, as the Apostle says, with so great confidence, and such ability to instruct, convert, and sway. And when he preaches the word of God, he renders so clear and agreeable that which he takes from Scripture to insert in his discourse, and he has such power to move men, that everybody, both those clever in worldly matters and those who possess spiritual knowledge, marvel at the eloquent words which fall from his lips.

READING AND DISCUSSION QUESTIONS

1. Describe Bernard's social background.

2. What were the early signs of Bernard's future vocation?

3. What does William, the author of this biography, seem to praise as good features of monastic life? What makes a monastery particularly successful?

4. Why did Bernard choose the order of Cîteaux?

DOCUMENT 10-4

DUKE WILLIAM OF AQUITAINE
On the Foundation of Cluny
909

Cluny, founded by Duke William of Aquitaine in 910, became one of the leading abbeys in Europe and a model for monasteries in need of reform. According to the terms of its foundation, Cluny was subordinate only to the pope himself. This meant that the institution enjoyed a great deal of independence from local bishops and lords. In addition, Cluny became the "mother house" to other monasteries throughout Europe, and these subordinate houses came to enjoy the same privileges as Cluny itself. Cluny amassed such wealth that the monks eventually hired others to do the daily work of running the monastery and occupied themselves in almost constant prayer.

To all right thinkers it is clear that the providence of God has so provided for certain rich men that, by means of their transitory possessions, if they use them well, they may be able to merit everlasting rewards. As to which . . . I, William, count and duke by the grace of God, diligently pondering this, and desiring to provide for my own safety while I am still able, have considered it advisable — nay, most necessary, that from the temporal

E. F. Henderson, *Select Historical Documents of the Middle Ages* (London: 1892), 329–333.

goods which have been conferred upon me I should give some little portion for the gain of my soul. I do this, indeed, in order that I who have thus
increased in wealth, may not, perchance, at the last be accused of having
spent all in caring for my body, but rather may rejoice, when fate at last
shall snatch all things away, in having reserved something for myself.
Which end, indeed, seems attainable by no more suitable means than
that . . . I should support at my own expense a congregation of monks. And
this is my trust, this my hope, indeed, that although I myself am unable to
despise all things, nevertheless, by receiving despisers of the world, whom
I believe to be righteous, I may receive the reward of the righteous. Therefore be it known to all . . . that, for the love of God and of our Savior Jesus
Christ, I hand over from my own rule to the holy apostles, Peter, namely,
and Paul, the possessions over which I hold sway, the town of Cluny,
namely, with the court and demesne manor, and the church in honour of
St. Mary the mother of God and of St. Peter the prince of the apostles,
together with all the things pertaining to it, the vills, indeed, the chapels,
the serfs of both sexes, the vines, the fields, the meadows, the woods, the
waters and their outlets, the mills, the incomes and revenues, what is cultivated and what is not, all in their entirety. Which things are situated in or
about the country of Macon, each one surrounded by its own bounds. I
give, moreover, all these things to the aforesaid apostles — I, William, and
my wife Ingelberga — first for the love of God; then for soul of my lord
king Odo, of my father and my mother; for myself and my wife — for the
salvation, namely, of our souls and bodies; — and not least for that of Ava
who left me these things in her will; for the souls also of our brothers and
sisters and nephews, and of all our relatives of both sexes; for our faithful
ones who adhere to our service; for the advancement, also, and integrity
of the catholic religion. Finally, since all of us Christians are held together
by one bond of love and faith, let this donation be for all, — for the orthodox, namely, of past, present or future times. I give these things, moreover,
with this understanding, that in Cluny a regular monastery shall be constructed in honour of the holy apostles Peter and Paul, and that there the
monks shall congregate and live according to the rule of St. Benedict, and
that they shall possess, hold, have and order these same things unto all
time. . . . [The monks are to be under the protection of the pope, and no
one — not even the pope — is to dare to violate Cluny's rights.]

    If any one — which Heaven forbid, and which, through the mercy of
God and the protection of the apostles I do not think will happen, —
whether he be a neighbour or a stranger, no matter what his condition or
power, should, through any kind of wile, attempt to do any act of violence

contrary to this deed of gift which we have ordered to be drawn up for love of almighty God and for reverence of the chief apostles Peter and Paul: first, indeed, let him incur the wrath of almighty God, and let God remove him from the land of the living and wipe out his name from the book of life, and let his portion be with those who said to the Lord God: Depart from us; and, with Dathan and Abiron[1] whom the earth, opening its jaws, swallowed up, and hell absorbed while still alive, let him incur everlasting damnation. And being made a companion of Judas let him be kept thrust down there with eternal tortures, and, lest it seem to human eyes that he pass through the present world with impunity, let him experience in his own body, indeed, the torments of future damnation, sharing the double disaster with Heliodorus and Antiochus, of whom one being coerced with sharp blows scarcely escaped alive; and the other struck down by the divine will, his members putrefying and swarming with vermin, perished most miserably. . . .

I, William, commanded this act to be made and drawn up, and confirmed it with my own hand.

(Signed by Ingelberga and a number of bishops and nobles.)

READING AND DISCUSSION QUESTIONS

1. What is Duke William's stated motive for founding the abbey? What other motives could he have had?

2. Consider the following passage: "although I myself am unable to despise all things, nevertheless, by receiving despisers of the world, whom I believe to be righteous, I may receive the reward of the righteous." What does this reveal about William's religious beliefs?

3. Besides himself, who else does William expect will benefit from his gift? How does he expect they will benefit?

4. What specific punishments will befall anyone who defies the gift? Why is it significant that William includes these at the end of the document?

---

[1] **Dathan and Abiron**: Brothers who, as recounted in the Old Testament, tried to sabotage Moses during the exodus from Egypt. The earth swallowed them whole.

COMPARATIVE QUESTIONS

1. Compare and contrast the status of unfree persons as illustrated in the first two documents.

2. Compare and contrast the condition of serfs in the Middle Ages to the condition of slaves in the Roman Empire as evidenced in Document 5-2.

3. Compare the monastic reforms detailed in the last two documents to those of Saint Benedict (Document 7-3).

4. What were the personal qualities that made Saint Bernard a great spiritual leader, and which of these qualities would most appeal to William of Aquitaine? Why?

CHAPTER 11

The Creativity and Challenges of Medieval Cities

The Roman Empire had been organized around great cities, but as the empire crumbled in the West, cities declined. Beginning around 1100, however, cities in Western Europe were once again becoming important political, commercial, and intellectual centers. On the Italian peninsula, commercial cites such as Florence, Venice, and Milan rose to prominence as intellectual and artistic hubs. At various times during the Middle Ages, they became, in effect, independent city-states. France, too, witnessed an intellectual surge, often focused around the great cathedral schools such as Chartres and Laon. Most important was Paris, where the University of Paris became a center of theology and philosophy that drew students from all over Western Europe. At the same time, the courts of the kings and the great nobles offered patronage to writers and artists. Growing alongside medieval cities were religious institutions and rituals, including new religious orders ministering to city residents.

DOCUMENT 11-1

THE COMMUNE OF FLORENCE
A Sumptuary Law: Restrictions on Dress
1373

Sumptuary laws (laws regulating consumption) served a number of purposes — social, economic, and religious — and were most often associated with clothing. Sometimes religious or ethnic minorities, such as Jews at various times in European history, were required to wear distinctive clothing. In

---

Gene Brucker, *The Society of Renaissance Florence* (New York: Harper & Row, 1971), 46–47.

other cases, the hereditary aristocracy called for laws that forbade prosperous merchants or other some of the members of the bourgeoisie from adopting aristocratic fashions. A ruler who was concerned that too much wealth was leaving the country might pass ordinances that forbade his subjects from wearing silks or precious stones that had to be imported.

It is well known to all that the worthy men, Benozzo di Francesco di Andrea . . . [and fifteen others] . . . have been selected to discover ways and means by which money will accrue to the Commune. . . . Considering the Commune's need for revenue to pay current expenses . . . they have enacted . . . the following:

First, all women and girls, whether married or not, whether betrothed or not, of whatever age, rank, and condition . . . who wear — or who wear in future — any gold, silver, pearls, precious stones, bells, ribbons of gold or silver, or cloth of silk brocade on their bodies or heads . . . for the ornamentation of their bodies . . . will be required to pay each year . . . the sum of 50 florins . . . to the treasurer of the gabelle on contracts. . . . [The exceptions to this prohibition are] that every married woman may wear on her hand or hands as many as two rings. . . . And every married woman or girl who is betrothed may wear . . . a silver belt which does not exceed fourteen ounces in weight. . . .

So that the gabelle is not defrauded, and so that citizens — on account of clothing already made — are not forced to bear new expenditures, [the officials] have decreed that all dresses, gowns, coats, capes, and other items of clothing belonging to any women or girls above the age of ten years, which were made up to the present day and which are decorated in whatever manner, may be worn for ten years in the future without the payment of any gabelle. . . .

READING AND DISCUSSION QUESTIONS

1. What was the principal reason for passing this sumptuary law?

2. In what ways did the sumptuary laws create a kind of income tax?

3. In what ways did the sumptuary laws make social divisions more rigid? Less rigid?

4. Identify the grandfather clause (a provision that exempts certain people from the law) in this document. Why was it included?

ABBESS HELOISE OF THE PARACLETE
A Letter to Abelard
ca. 1135

Heloise (1101–1164) was a woman deeply learned in Greek, Latin, and Hebrew. At some point, perhaps in her middle or late twenties, she became the student of Peter Abelard (1079–1142), one of the best-known philosophers and theologians in Paris. They became lovers and eventually she gave birth to a son. At some later point, Abelard placed her in a convent and secretly married her. Accounts are not entirely clear, but many historians believe that her uncle Fulbert, believing that Abelard had abandoned her, hired men to attack Abelard in his sleep and castrate him. Their surviving correspondence began after these events.

To her master, nay father, to her husband, nay brother; his handmaid, nay daughter, his spouse, nay sister: to ABELARD, . . .

How many grave treatises in the teaching, or in the exhortation, or for the comfort of holy women the holy Fathers composed, and with what diligence they composed them, thine excellence knows better than our humility. Wherefore to no little amazement thine oblivion moves the tender beginnings of our conversion, that neither by reverence for God, nor by love of us, nor by the examples of the holy Fathers hast thou been admonished to attempt to comfort me, as I waver and am already crushed by prolonged grief, either by speech in thy presence or by a letter in thine absence. And yet thou knowest thyself to be bound to me by a debt so much greater in that thou art tied to me more closely by the pact of the nuptial sacrament; and that thou art the more beholden to me in that I ever, as is known to all, embraced thee with an unbounded love. Thou knowest, dearest, all men know what I have lost in thee, and in how wretched a case that supreme and notorious betrayal took me myself also from me with thee, and that my grief is immeasurably greater from the manner in which I lost thee than from the loss of thee. . . .

The Letters of Abelard and Heloise, trans. C. K. Scott Moncrieff (New York: Knopf, 1942), 53–61.

And if the name of wife appears more sacred and more valid, sweeter to me is ever the word friend, or, if thou be not ashamed, concubine or whore. To wit that the more I humbled myself before thee the fuller grace I might obtain from thee, and so also damage less the fame of thine excellence. And thou thyself wert not wholly unmindful of that kindness in the letter of which I have spoken, written to thy friend for his comfort. Wherein thou hast not disdained to set forth sundry reasons by which I tried to dissuade thee from our marriage, from an ill-starred bed; but wert silent as to many, in which I preferred love to wedlock, freedom to a bond. I call God to witness, if *Augustus*, ruling over the whole world, were to deem me worthy of the honor of marriage, and to confirm the whole world to me, to be ruled by me for ever, dearer to me and of greater dignity would it seem to be called thy strumpet than his empress.

For who among kings or philosophers could equal thee in fame? What kingdom or city or village did not burn to see thee? Who, I ask, did not hasten to gaze upon thee when thou appearedst in public, nor on the departure with straining neck and fixed eye follow thee? What wife, what maiden did not yearn for thee in thine absence, nor burn in thy presence? What queen or powerful lady did not envy me my joys and my bed? There were two things, I confess, in thee especially, wherewith thou couldst at once captivate the heart of any woman; namely the arts of making songs and of singing them. Which we know that other philosophers have seldom followed. Wherewith as with a game, refreshing the labour of philosophic exercise, thou hast left many songs composed in amatory measure or rhythm, which for the suavity both of words and of tune being oft repeated, have kept thy name without ceasing on the lips of all; since even illiterates the sweetness of thy melodies did not allow to forget thee. It was on this account chiefly that women sighed for love of thee. And as the greater part of thy songs descanted of our love, they spread my fame in a short time through many lands, and inflamed the jealousy of many women against me. For what excellence of mind or body did not adorn thy youth? What woman who envied me then does not my calamity now compel to pity one deprived of such delights? What man or women, albeit an enemy at first, is not now softened by the compassion due to me?

. . . While with thee I enjoyed carnal pleasures, many were uncertain whether I did so from love or from desire. But now the end shews in what spirit I began. I have forbidden myself all pleasures that I might obey thy will. I have reserved nothing for myself, save this, to be now entirely thine. Consider therefore how great is thine injustice, if to me who deserve more thou payest less, nay nothing at all, especially when it is a small thing that is demanded of thee, and right easy for thee to perform.

And so in His Name to whom thou hast offered thyself, before God I beseech thee that in whatsoever way thou canst thou restore to me thy presence, to wit by writing me some word of comfort. To this end alone that, thus refreshed, I may give myself with more alacrity to the service of God. When in time past thou soughtest me out for temporal pleasures, thou visitedst me with endless letters, and by frequent songs didst set thy *Heloise* on the lips of all men. With me every public place, each house resounded. How more rightly shouldst thou excite me now towards God, whom thou excitedst then to desire. Consider, I beseech thee, what thou owest me, pay heed to what I demand; and my long letter with a brief ending I conclude. Farewell, my all.

READING AND DISCUSSION QUESTIONS

1. In the opening why does Heloise address Abelard as "her master, nay father, . . . her husband, nay brother"? What does this indicate about their relationship?

2. Why does Heloise praise Abelard's talents so extravagantly?

3. Is Heloise ashamed of their sexual relationship? Explain.

4. What does she mean when she says, "With me every public place, each house resounded"?

DOCUMENT 11-3

SAINT THOMAS AQUINAS
From Summa Theologica: *On Dispensing the Eucharist*

1268

Thomas Aquinas (1225–1274) was one of the foremost theologians and philosophers of the Middle Ages. Although born in Sicily, he traveled widely, taught at great universities in France and Germany, and was an adviser to popes and kings. Thomas and the other Scholastic thinkers adapted the teachings of Aristotle to Christian purposes. In some of his works, Thomas deals with the most abstract issues of philosophy and theology. Here he addresses a more concrete issue — the exclusive role of the priest in the service of the Eucharist.

The dispensing of Christ's body[1] belongs to the priest for three reasons. First, because, as was said above, he consecrates as in the person of Christ. But as Christ consecrated His body at the supper, so also He gave it to others to be partaken of by them. Accordingly, as the consecration of Christ's body belongs to the priest, so likewise does the dispensing belong to him. Secondly, because the priest is the appointed intermediary between God and the people; hence as it belongs to him to offer the people's gifts to God, so it belongs to him to deliver consecrated gifts to the people. Thirdly, because out of reverence towards this sacrament, nothing touches it, but what is consecrated; hence the corporal and the chalice are consecrated, and likewise the priest's hands, for touching this sacrament. Hence it is not lawful for anyone else to touch it except from necessity, for instance, if it were to fall upon the ground, or else in some other case of urgency.

READING AND DISCUSSION QUESTIONS

1. Discuss the ways in which Aquinas compares the priest in the midst of the Eucharist to Christ at the Last Supper.

2. In what ways do the doctrines in this passage elevate the importance of priests?

3. On what occasion, if any, may ordinary lay people touch the sacrament? Explain the reasoning behind this doctrine.

Saint Thomas Aquinas, *Summa Theologica*, pt. 3, q. 82, art. 3., trans. Fathers of the English Dominican Province (London, 1912).

[1] **dispensing of Christ's body**: Serving the consecrated bread during Communion.

DOCUMENT 11-4

CHRÉTIEN DE TROYES

The Temptation of Sir Lancelot

ca. 1181

Many authors and traditions dealt with the legends of King Arthur and Sir Lancelot, his greatest knight. Although the Arthurian legends have their origin in Celtic lore, it is not known whether the Frenchman Chrétien de Troyes, whose work is represented here, drew on Celtic sources. In this episode, Lancelot is searching for his true love, Queen Guinevere, who has been kidnapped. Lancelot meets a beautiful young woman who offers him shelter in her home on the condition that he "lie with her" during the night. At first, he declines but then agrees to do what she asks.

When they had risen from the table, the damsel said to the knight: "Sire, if you do not object, go outside and amuse yourself; but, if you please, do not stay after you think I must be in bed. Feel no concern or embarrassment; for then you may come to me at once, if you will keep the promise you have made." And he replies: "I will keep my word, and will return when I think the time has come." Then he went out, and stayed in the courtyard until he thought it was time to return and keep the promise he had made.

Going back into the hall, he sees nothing of her who would be his mistress; for she was not there. Not finding or seeing her, he said: "Wherever she may be, I shall look for her until I find her." He makes no delay in his search, being bound by the promise he had made her.

Entering one of the rooms, he hears a damsel cry aloud, and it was the very one with whom he was about to lie. At the same time, he sees the door of another room standing open, and stepping toward it, he sees right before his eyes a knight who had thrown her down, and was holding her naked and prostrate upon the bed. She, thinking that he had come of course to help her, cried aloud: "Help, help, thou knight, who art my guest. If thou dost not take this man away from me, I shall find no one to do so; if thou dost not succour [help] me speedily, he will wrong me before thy eyes. Thou art the one to lie with me, in accordance with thy promise; and shall

---

Chrétien de Troyes, *Arthurian Romances*, trans. W. W. Comfort (London: Everyman's Library, 1914), 283–286.

this man by force accomplish his wish before thy eyes? Gentle knight, exert thyself, and make haste to bear me aid."

He sees that the other man held the damsel brutally uncovered to the waist, and he is ashamed and angered to see him assault her so; yet it is not jealousy he feels, nor will he be made a cuckold by him. At the door there stood as guards two knights completely armed and with swords drawn. Behind them there stood four men-at-arms, each armed with an axe — the sort with which you could split a cow down the back as easily as a root of juniper or broom. The knight hesitated at the door, and thought: "God, what can I do? I am engaged in no less an affair than the quest of Queen Guinevere. I ought not to have the heart of a hare, when for her sake I have engaged in such a quest. If cowardice puts its heart in me, and if I follow its dictates, I shall never attain what I seek. I am disgraced, if I stand here; indeed, I am ashamed even to have thought of holding back. My heart is very sad and oppressed: now I am so ashamed and distressed that I would gladly die for having hesitated here so long. I say it not in pride: but may God have mercy on me if I do not prefer to die honorably rather than live a life of shame! If my path were unobstructed, and if these men gave me leave to pass through without restraint, what honour would I gain? Truly, in that case the greatest coward alive would pass through; and all the while I hear this poor creature calling for help constantly, and reminding me of my promise, and reproaching me with bitter taunts."

Then he steps to the door, thrusting in his head and shoulders; glancing up, he sees two swords descending. He draws back, and the knights could not check their strokes: they had wielded them with such force that the swords struck the floor, and both were broken in pieces. When he sees that the swords are broken, he pays less attention to the axes, fearing and dreading them much less. Rushing in among them, he strikes first one guard in the side and then another. The two who are nearest him he jostles and thrusts aside, throwing them both down flat; the third missing his stroke at him, but the fourth, who attacked him, strikes him so that he cuts his mantle and shirt, and slices the white flesh on his shoulder so that the blood trickles down from the wound. But he, without delay, and without complaining of his wound, presses on more rapidly, until he strikes between the temples him who was assaulting his hostess. Before he departs, he will try to keep his pledge to her. He makes him stand up reluctantly. Meanwhile, he who has missed striking him comes at him as fast as he can, and, raising his arm again, expects to split his head to the teeth with the axe. But the other, alert to defend himself, thrusts the knight toward him in such a way that he receives the axe just where the shoulder joins the neck, so that they are cleaved apart. Then the knight seizes the axe, wresting it quickly from him who holds it; then he lets go the knight whom he still held, and looks to his own defence; for the knights from the door, and the three men with axes are all attacking him fiercely. So he leaped quickly between the bed and the wall, and called to them: "Come on now, all of you. If there were thirty-seven of you, you would have all the fight you wish, with me so favorably placed; I shall never be overcome by you." And the damsel watching him, exclaimed: "By my eyes, you need have no thought of that henceforth where I am." Then at once she dismisses the knights and the men-at-arms, who retire from there at once, without delay or objection. And the damsel continues: "Sire you have well defended me against the men of my household. Come now, and I'll lead you on." Hand in hand they enter the hall, but he was not at all pleased, and would have willingly dispensed with her.

In the midst of the hall a bed had been set up, the sheets of which were by no means soiled, but were white and wide and well spread out. The bed was not of shredded straw or of coarse spreads. But a covering of two silk cloths had been laid upon the couch. The damsel lay down first, but without removing her chemise. He had great trouble in removing his hose and in untying the knots. He sweated with the trouble of it all; yet, in the midst of all the trouble, his promise impels and drives him on. Is this then an actual force? Yes, virtually so; for he feels that he is in duty bound to take his place by the damsel's side. It is his promise that urges him and dictates his act. So he lies down at once, but like her, he does not remove his shirt. He takes good care not to touch her; and when he is in bed, he turns away from her as far as possible, and speaks not a word to her, like a monk to whom speech is forbidden. Not once does he look at her, nor show her any courtesy. Why not? Because his heart does not go out to her. She was certainly very fair and winsome, but not every one is pleased and touched by what is fair and winsome. The knight has only one heart, and this one is really no longer his, but has been entrusted to some one else, so that he cannot bestow it elsewhere.

Love, which holds all hearts beneath its sway, requires it to be lodged in a single place. All hearts? No, only those which it esteems. And he whom love deigns to control ought to prize himself the more. Love prized his heart so highly that it constrained it in a special manner, and made him so proud of this distinction that I am not inclined to find fault with him, if he lets alone what love forbids, and remains fixed where it desires.

The maiden clearly sees and knows that he dislikes her company and would gladly dispense with it, and that, having no desire to win her love, he would not attempt to woo her. So she said: "My lord, if you will not feel hurt, I will leave and return to bed in my own room, and you will be more comfortable. I do not believe that you are pleased with my company and society. Do not esteem me less if I tell you what I think. Now take your rest all night, for you have so well kept your promise that I have no right to make further request of you. So I commend you to God, and shall go away."

Thereupon she arises: the knight does not object, but rather gladly lets her go, like one who is the devoted lover of some one else; the damsel clearly perceived this, and went to her room, where she undressed completely and retired, saying to herself: "Of all the knights I have ever known, I never knew a single knight whom I would value the third part of an Angevin in comparison with this one. As I understand the case, he has on hand a more perilous and grave affair than any ever undertaken by a knight; and may God grant that he succeed in it." Then she fell asleep, and remained in bed until the next day's dawn appeared.

READING AND DISCUSSION QUESTIONS

1. According to this document, why does Lancelot hesitate so long before he takes action against the men who are assaulting the young woman?

2. What does the young woman think of Lancelot by the end of this passage? Why?

3. What does this document reveal about Arthurian and/or twelfth-century French attitudes toward sexual morality?

COMPARATIVE QUESTIONS

1. What similar attitudes toward sexuality are expressed in the letter of Heloise and the story of Lancelot? What are the differences?

2. How do you think Pope Gregory (Document 9-3) would have reacted to Aquinas's discussion of the Eucharist? Explain your reasoning.

3. Compare and contrast the story of Lancelot and the story of Odysseus (Document 3-1).

4. What do the four documents in this chapter, considered together, reveal about social tensions in the Middle Ages?

CHAPTER 12

The Crisis of the Later Middle Ages

1300–1450

B eginning around 1340, a series of disasters devastated much of Western Europe. The Black Death (or Black Plague), beginning in 1347, killed an estimated 30 to 60 percent of Western Europe's population. The Black Death proved so deadly for a number of reasons: some historians have argued that the plague struck a population that in many places was already malnourished and/or suffering the effects of war. Between 1337 and 1453, the Hundred Years' War — in actuality a series of wars and civil wars — wreaked havoc on France. These conflicts helped revolutionize warfare with new technologies, tactics, and strategies. Oddly enough, however, the ideals of chivalry, which were derived from older military practices, remained as popular as ever. New forms of popular piety emerged even as the papacy lost prestige, in part the result of its exile to Avignon, France, between 1309 and 1376, and also because of the conflicts over the papacy during the Great Schism (1378–1417).

DOCUMENT 12-1

GIOVANNI BOCCACCIO

From The Decameron: *The Plague Hits Florence*

ca. 1350

The first wave of the Black Death began in the late 1340s. The disease spread rapidly, and contemporaries understood very little about it, although they did

Giovanni Boccaccio, *The Decameron*, ed. Edward Hutton (London: Dent, 1955), 1:13–14.

associate it with rats. The only effective countermeasures were quarantine and isolation. The infection, which spread along trade routes from Central Asia, killed some 75 million people. Even after the first incidence receded, plague returned to Europe in many subsequent outbreaks until the 1700s, with varying mortality rates. In this document, excerpted from his famous collection of novellas, the Italian writer Giovanni Boccaccio detailed the chaos unleashed in Florence as a result of the plague.

"Dear ladies . . . here we tarry, as if, I think, for no other purpose than to bear witness to the number of the corpses that are brought here for intern-ment. . . . And if we quit the church, we see dead or sick folk carried about, or we see those, who for their crimes were of late condemned to exile . . . but who, now . . . well knowing that their magistrates are a prey to death or disease, have returned, and traverse the city in packs, making it hideous with their riotous antics; or else we see the refuse of the people, fostered on our blood, becchini, as they call themselves, who for our tor-ment go prancing about . . . making mock of our miseries in scurrilous songs. . . . Or go we home, what see we there? . . . where once were ser-vants in plenty, I find none left but my maid, and shudder with terror, and feel the very hairs of my head to stand on end; and turn or tarry where I may, I encounter the ghosts of the departed. . . . None . . . having means and place of retirement as we have, stays here . . . or if any such there be, they are of those . . . who make no distinction between things honorable and their opposites, so they but answer the cravings of appetite, and, alone or in company, do daily and nightly what things soever give promise of most gratification. Nor are these secular persons alone, but such as live recluse in monasteries break their rule, and give themselves up to carnal pleasures, persuading themselves that they are permissible to them, and only forbidden to others, and, thereby thinking to escape, are become un-chaste and dissolute."

READING AND DISCUSSION QUESTIONS

1. According to this account, how did civil order broke down during the plague?

2. What responses did people in religious orders have to plague as com-pared with other people?

3. What plan does the writer seem to have for the immediate future?

DOCUMENT 12-2

JEHAN FROISSART

The Sack of Limoges: On Warfare Without Chivalry

ca. 1400

The Hundred Years' War (1337–1453) broke out when Edward III of England claimed to be the legitimate heir to the French throne. Although there were extensive truces, France and England remained at war for most of this period. The war was also a civil war, in that large sections of France, especially Burgundy and Aquitaine, supported the English. Over the course of the conflict, medieval warfare changed radically, as new weapons and tactics were introduced, and both countries supported standing armies, which had not existed in Western Europe since the end of the Roman Empire. One ingeniously designed English attack on the French city of Limoges is described below.

[Having mined the town walls,] the miners set fire into their mine, and so the next morning, as the prince had ordained, there fell down a great piece of the wall and filled the moats, whereof the Englishmen were glad and were ready armed in the field to enter the town. The foot-men might well enter at their ease, and so they did, and ran to the gate and beat down the fortifying and barriers, for there was no defense against them: it was done so suddenly that they of the town were not aware thereof.

Then the prince,[1] the duke of Lancaster, the earl of Cambridge, the earl of Pembroke, Sir Guichard d'Angle, and all the others, with their companies, entered into the city, and all other foot-men ready apparelled to do evil, and to pill and rob the city, and to slay men, women, and children; for so it was commanded them to do. It was a great pity to see the men, women, and children that kneeled down on their knees before the prince for mercy. But he was so inflamed with ire that he took no heed of them,

---

John Froissart, *The Chronicles of England, France and Spain*, in James Harvey Robinson, ed., *Readings in European History* (Boston: Ginn, 1904), 1:472–473.

[1] **the prince**: Edward, Prince of Wales, Edward III's oldest son and the leader of the English armies, also known as the Black Prince.

so that none was heard, but all put to death as they were met withal, and such as were nothing culpable.

There was no pity taken of the poor people who wrought never no manner of treason, yet they bought it dearer than the great personages, such as had done the evil and trespass. There was not so hard a heart within the city of Limoges and if he had any remembrance of God, but that wept piteously for the great mischief that they saw before their eyen, for more than three thousand men, women, and children were slain that day. God have mercy on their souls, for I trow they were martyrs.

And thus entering into the city, a certain company of Englishmen entered into the bishop's palace, and there they found the bishop; and so they brought him to the prince's presence, who beheld him right fiercely and felly, and the best word that he could have of him was how he would have his head stricken off, and so he was had out of his sight. . . .

Thus the city of Limoges was pilled, robbed, and clean brent and brought to destruction.

READING AND DISCUSSION QUESTIONS

1. According to this document, how and why did the English troops destroy the town's fortifications?
2. Why is the scene with the bishop significant?
3. What does this passage reveal about the ideals of chivalry?

DOCUMENT 12-3

The Trial of Joan of Arc

1431

Joan of Arc (ca. 1412–1431), a peasant woman from eastern France, helped the French win important victories against the English in the Hundred Years' War. She claimed to have heard the voices of Saint Michael, Saint

Regine Pernoud, *Joan of Arc, By Herself and Her Witnesses* (New York: 1966), 30, 90–92.

Catherine, and Saint Margaret commanding her to drive out the English and to take the crown prince to Reims for coronation. Some historians argue that Joan was important symbolically for inspiring French morale while others argue that she was a skillful military strategist. After her capture by Burgundian trrops, the English put her on trial for heresy, and she was burned at the stake.

JOAN [*to her inquisitors*]: When I was thirteen years old, I had a voice from God to help me govern my conduct. And the first time I was very fearful. And came this voice, about the hour of noon, in the summertime, in my father's garden. . . . I heard the voice on the right-hand side . . . and rarely do I hear it without a brightness. . . . It has taught me to conduct myself well, to go habitually to church. . . . The voice told me that I should raise the siege laid to the city of Orleans . . . and me, I answered it that I was a poor girl who knew not how to ride nor lead in war.

JEAN PASQUEREL [*priest, Joan's confessor*]: "On the morrow, Saturday, I rose early and celebrated mass. And Joan went out against the fortress of the bridge where was the Englishman Classidas. And the assault lasted there from morning until sunset. In this assault . . . Joan . . . was struck by an arrow above the breast, and when she felt herself wounded she was afraid and wept. . . . And some soldiers, seeing her so wounded, wanted to apply a charm to her wound, but she would not have it, saying: "I would rather die than do a thing which I know to be a sin or against the will of God." . . . But if to her could be applied a remedy without sin, she was very willing to be cured. And they put on to her wound olive oil and lard. And after that had been applied, Joan made her confession to me, weeping and lamenting."

COUNT DUNOIS: "The assault lasted from the morning until eight . . . so that there was hardly hope of victory that day. So that I was going to break off and . . . withdraw. . . . Then the Maid [Joan] came to me and required me to wait yet a while. She . . . mounted her horse and retired alone into a vineyard. . . . And in this vineyard she remained at prayer. . . . Then she came back . . . at once seized her standard in hand and placed herself on the parapet of the trench, and the moment she was there the English trembled and were terrified. The king's soldiers regained courage and began to go up, charging against the boulevard without meeting the least resistance."

JEAN PASQUEREL: "Joan returned to the charge, crying and saying: 'Classidas, Classidas, yield thee, yield thee to the King of Heaven; thou hast called me 'whore'; I take great pity on thy soul and thy people's! Then Classidas, armed from head to foot, fell into the river of Loire and was drowned. And Joan, moved by pity, began to weep much for the soul of Classidas and the others who were drowned in great numbers." . . .

READING AND DISCUSSION QUESTIONS

1. Why is it important that at first the voice Joan heard seems principally to have been concerned with her good conduct?

2. Why would the claim that Joan was a "poor girl who knew not how to ride nor lead in war" have been an important issue at her trial?

3. What does the testimony of the two witnesses establish?

DOCUMENT 12-4

THOMAS À KEMPIS
From The Following of Christ:
On True Charity
1418

Thomas à Kempis (ca. 1379–1471) was the author of The Following of Christ, *one of the most influential spiritual tracts in Christian literature. He belonged to the Brothers and Sisters of the Common Life, a group that tried to imitate the simplicity of the earliest Christians. They were forbidden to beg; many of them earned a living by teaching or by copying manuscripts, as Thomas did. Thomas wrote as a time when many ordinary people throughout Western Europe were forming groups dedicated to Christian devotion and charitable activities.*

Thomas à Kempis, *The Following of Christ* (London: Burns and Oates, 1881), 30–32.

CHAPTER XV

Of works done out of charity.

Evil ought not to be done for anything in the world, nor for the love of any human being; but yet for the benefit of one that is in need, a good work is sometimes freely to be left undone, or rather to be changed for what is better.

For by this means a good work is not lost, but changed into a better. Without charity, the outward work provideth nothing; but whatever is done out of charity, be it ever so little and contemptible, it is all made fruitful, inasmuch as God regardeth more out of how much love a man doth a work, than how much he doth.

2. He doth much who loveth much.

He doth much who doth well what he hath to do.

He doth well, who regardeth rather the common good than his own will.

Oftentimes that seemeth to be charity which is rather carnality; for natural inclination, self-will, hope of reward, study of our own interests, will seldom be absent.

3. He that hath true and perfect charity, seeketh himself in nothing, but only desireth God to be glorified in all things.

And he envieth no man, for he loveth no joy for himself alone.

Neither doth he desire to rejoice in himself, but wisheth to find his blessedness above all good things in God.

He attributeth nothing of good to any man, but referreth it all to God, from whom, as from their fountain, all things proceed, and in whom, as in their end, all the Saints repose in fruition.

Oh, if one had but a spark of real charity, truly would he feel that all earthly things are full of vanity!

READING AND DISCUSSION QUESTIONS

1. Consider all the places where Thomas discusses charity. Explain what he means by this word.

2. According to this document, what is the relationship between "good works" and Christian devotion?

3. Explain why charity frees people from envy.

COMPARATIVE QUESTIONS

1. In what ways do the miracles of Joan of Arc resemble or differ from the miracles detailed in the stories of Saint Boniface (Document 8-2) and Vladimir the Great (Document 8-4)?

2. Compare the religious piety of Joan of Arc with the ideals espoused by Thomas à Kempis. Why do you think that *The Following of Christ* was such a popular spiritual guide?

3. Compare and contrast the ideas of honor and chivalry in the documents in this chapter. What common themes or actions can you identify?

4. Tragedy and warfare served as a breeding ground for Christian idealism and religious martyrdom, but also spurred less admiral behavior. Provide examples from both the description of the plague in Florence and the recounting of the sack of Limoges. Could one be both righteous and violent?

CHAPTER 13

European Society in the Age of the Renaissance

1350–1550

The Renaissance began as a revival and flourishing of learning and art in the Italian cities of the fourteenth century and spread throughout Europe. Many, though not all, of the Renaissance thinkers wrote in Latin, and successful authors such as the Dutchman Erasmus and the Englishman Thomas More acquired international reputations. Although the Italian peninsula was a center of learning and commerce, it was not a unified country. City-states such as Venice, Milan, and Florence often conflicted with one another. In 1494, Charles VIII of France invaded Italy, beginning a series of wars in which Italian states and outside powers were often at war. Although nationalism was still in its earliest stages, modern nation-states were beginning to take shape in France, England and Spain. Spanish rulers even attempted to impose uniformity of religion by expelling Jews and Muslims who resisted conversion to Christianity. In the context of these changes, many writers considered the role of the state and its leaders in creating a stable society.

DOCUMENT 13-1

NICCOLÒ MACHIAVELLI

From The Prince: *Power Politics During the Italian Renaissance*

1513

Niccolò Machiavelli (1469–1527) was a political philosopher and diplomat who had represented the Italian republic of Florence on numerous diplomatic missions. In 1512, when the powerful Medici family regained control of Florence, the anti-Medici Machiavelli was arrested and tortured. In 1513, he wrote The Prince, *a guide to gaining political power, and dedicated to Lorenzo di Medici, perhaps as a way to curry favor with the new rulers. Machiavelli claimed that he was simply drawing conclusions from his reading of history and from the example of successful contemporary rulers. The book circulated privately until after Machiavelli's death.*

Every one understands how praiseworthy it is in a prince to keep faith, and to live uprightly and not craftily. Nevertheless we see, from what has taken place in our own days, that princes who have set little store by their word, but have known how to overreach men by their cunning, have accomplished great things, and in the end got the better of those who trusted to honest dealing.

Be it known, then, that there are two ways of contending, — one in accordance with the laws, the other by force; the first of which is proper to men, the second to beasts. But since the first method is often ineffectual, it becomes necessary to resort to the second. A prince should, therefore, understand how to use well both the man and the beast. . . . But inasmuch as a prince should know how to use the beast's nature wisely, he ought of beasts to choose both the lion and the fox; for the lion cannot guard himself from the toils, nor the fox from wolves. He must therefore be a fox to discern toils, and a lion to drive off wolves.

To rely wholly on the lion is unwise; and for this reason a prudent prince neither can nor ought to keep his word when to keep it is hurtful to him and the causes which led him to pledge it are removed. If all men were good, this would not be good advice, but since they are dishonest and do not keep faith with you, you in return need not keep faith with them; and no prince was ever at a loss for plausible reasons to cloak a breach of faith. Of this numberless recent instances could be given, and it might be shown how many solemn treaties and engagements have been rendered inoperative and idle through want of faith among princes, and that he who has best known how to play the fox has had the best success.

It is necessary, indeed, to put a good color on this nature, and to be skilled in simulating and dissembling. But men are so simple, and governed so absolutely by their present needs, that he who wishes to deceive

Niccolò Machiavelli, *The Prince*, trans. N. H. Thomson, in James Harvey Robinson, ed., *Readings in European History* (Boston: Ginn, 1904), 2:10–13.

will never fail in finding willing dupes. One recent example I will not omit. Pope Alexander VI had no care or thought but how to deceive, and always found material to work on. No man ever had a more effective manner or asseverating, or made promises with more solemn protestations, or observed them less. And yet, because he understood this side of human nature, his frauds always succeeded. . . .

In his efforts to aggrandize his son the duke [Caesar Borgia], Alexander VI had to face many difficulties, both immediate and remote. In the first place, he saw no way to make him ruler of any state which did not belong to the Church. Yet, if he sought to take for him a state of the Church, he knew that the duke of Milan and the Venetians would withhold their consent, Faenza and Rimini [towns in the province of Romagna] being already under the protection of the latter. Further, he saw that the forces of Italy, and those more especially of which he might have availed himself, were in the hands of men who had reason to fear his aggrandizement, — that is, of the Orsini, the Colonnesi [Roman noble families] and their followers. These, therefore, he could not trust. . . .

And since this part of his [Caesar Borgia's] conduct merits both attention and imitation, I shall not pass it over in silence. After the duke had taken Romagna, finding that it had been ruled by feeble lords, who thought more of plundering than of governing their subjects, — which gave them more cause for division than for union, so that the country was overrun with robbery, tumult, and every kind of outrage, — he judged it necessary, with a view to rendering it peaceful, and obedient to his authority, to provide it with a good government. Accordingly he set over it Messer Remiro d'Orco, a stern and prompt ruler, who, being intrusted with the fullest powers, in a very short time, and with much credit to himself, restored it to tranquillity and order. But afterwards the duke, apprehending that such unlimited authority might become odious, decided that it was no longer needed, and established [at] the center of the province a civil tribunal, with an excellent president, in which every town was represented by its advocate. And knowing that past severities had generated ill feeling against himself, in order to purge the minds of the people and gain their good will, he sought to show them that any cruelty which had been done had not originated with him, but in the harsh disposition of this minister. Availing himself of the pretext which this afforded, he one morning caused Remiro to be beheaded, and exposed in the market place of Cesena with a block and bloody ax by his side. The barbarity of this spectacle at once astounded and satisfied the populace.

READING AND DISCUSSION QUESTIONS

1. Why must a prince be both a lion and a fox? What qualities do these animals represent?

2. Why does Machiavelli believe that sometimes a prince must break his word?

3. Explain why Machiavelli approves, or disapproves, of the execution of Remiro d'Orco.

4. Is there anything shocking about the examples Machiavelli uses to prove his point?

DOCUMENT 13-2

THOMAS MORE

From Utopia: On Diplomatic Advice

1516

Thomas More (1478–1535), a friend and collaborator of the prolific Erasmus (see Document 14-1), was one of the greatest English humanists. The son of a judge, More had a prominent career in the law and served the government in many capacities, eventually becoming the lord chancellor of England. In 1535, during the Protestant Reformation, he was executed when he refused to sign the Act of Supremacy that made Henry VIII head of the church in England. Utopia, *which was written in Latin, was intended for a European audience. A social satire, it is similar in some respects to Erasmus's* Praise of Folly *and other works of the time.*

"Do not you think that if I were about any king, proposing good laws to him, and endeavoring to root out all the cursed seeds of evil that I found in him, I should either be turned out of his court or at least be laughed at for my pains? For instance, what could it signify if I were about the King of France, and were called into his Cabinet Council, where several wise

Thomas More, "Dialogue of Counsel" in *Utopia* (New York: Colonial Press, 1901), 22–24.

men, in his hearing, were proposing many expedients, as by what arts and practices Milan may be kept, and Naples, that had so oft slipped out of their hands, recovered; how the Venetians, and after them the rest of Italy, may be subdued; and then how Flanders, Brabant, and all Burgundy, and some other kingdoms which he has swallowed already in his designs, may be added to his empire. One proposes a league with the Venetians, to be kept as long as he finds his account in it, and that he ought to communicate councils with them, and give them some share of the spoil, till his success makes him need or fear them less, and then it will be easily taken out of their hands. Another proposes the hiring [of] the Germans, and the securing [of] the Switzers by pensions. Another proposes the gaining [of] the Emperor by money, which is omnipotent with him. Another proposes a peace with the King of Aragon, and, in order to cement it, the yielding up [of] the King of Navarre's pretensions. Another thinks the Prince of Castile is to be wrought on, by the hope of an alliance; and that some of his courtiers are to be gained to the French faction by pensions. The hardest point of all is what to do with England: a treaty of peace is to be set on foot, and if their alliance is not to be depended on, yet it is to be made as firm as possible; and they are to be called friends, but suspected as enemies: therefore the Scots are to be kept in readiness, to be let loose upon England on every occasion: and some banished nobleman is to be supported underhand (for by the league it cannot be done avowedly) who had a pretension to the crown, by which means that suspected prince may be kept in awe.

"Now when things are in so great a fermentation, and so many gallant men are joining councils, how to carry on the war, if so mean a man as I should stand up, and wish them to change all their councils, to let Italy alone, and stay at home, since the Kingdom of France was indeed greater than could be well governed by one man; that therefore he ought not to think of adding others to it: and if after this, I should propose to them the resolutions of the Achorians, a people that lie on the southeast of Utopia, who long ago engaged in war, in order to add to the dominions of their prince another kingdom, to which he had some pretensions by an ancient alliance. This they conquered, but found that the trouble of keeping it was equal to that by which it was gained; that the conquered people were always either in rebellion or exposed to foreign invasions, while they were obliged to be incessantly at war, either for or against them, and consequently could never disband their army; that in the meantime they were oppressed with taxes, their money went out of the kingdom, their blood was spilt for the glory of their King, without procuring the least advantage to the people, who received not the smallest benefit from it even in time of peace; and that their manners being corrupted by a long war, robbery and murders everywhere abounded, and their laws fell into contempt; while their King, distracted with the care of two kingdoms, was the less able to apply his mind to the interests of either.

"When they saw this, and that there would be no end to these evils, they by joint councils made an humble address to their King, desiring him to choose which of the two kingdoms he had the greatest mind to keep, since he could not hold both; for they were too great a people to be governed by a divided king, since no man would willingly have a groom that should be in common between him and another. Upon which the good prince was forced to quit his new kingdom to one of his friends (who was not long after dethroned), and to be contented with his old one. To this I would add that after all those warlike attempts, the vast confusions, and the consumption both of treasure and of people that must follow them; perhaps upon some misfortune, they might be forced to throw up all at last; therefore it seemed much more eligible that the King should improve his ancient kingdom all he could, and make it flourish as much as possible; that he should love his people, and be beloved of them; that he should live among them, govern them gently, and let other kingdoms alone, since that which had fallen to his share was big enough, if not too big for him. Pray how do you think would such a speech as this be heard?"

"I confess," said I, "I think not very well."

READING AND DISCUSSION QUESTIONS

1.   In what ways do the fictional discussions in the French royal council reflect what you know about the European history of the time?

2.   What form of argument does More use, and where else have you seen it employed?

3.   To whom does More seem to be addressing his advice? How effective does he expect his advice to be?

DOCUMENT 13-3

CHRISTINE DE PIZAN

From The Book of the City of Ladies:
Advice for a Wise Princess

1404

Christine de Pizan (ca. 1363–1434) may have been the first European woman to earn her living as a writer. After de Pizan's birth in Venice, her father became a physician and astrologer at the French court, where Christine studied languages and the classics. In 1390, when her husband died in an epidemic and left her with three children, Christine began her literary career. She wrote a vast number of poems, often on romantic themes, and took part in an important literary debate over the merits of the great thirteenth-century allegorical poem, The Romance of the Rose, *which some claimed used vulgar language and slandered women.*

17. The Sixth Teaching: How the Wise Princess Will Keep the Women of Her Court in Good Order.

Just as the good shepherd takes care that his lambs are maintained in health, and if any of them becomes mangy, separates it from the flock for fear that it may infect the others, so the princess will take upon herself the responsibility for the care of her women servants and companions, who she will ensure are all good and chaste, for she will not want to have any other sort of person around her. Since it is the established custom that knights and squires and all men (especially certain men) who associate with women have a habit of pleading for love tokens from them and trying to seduce them, the wise princess will so enforce her regulations that there will be no visitor to her court so foolhardy as to dare to whisper privately with any of her women or give the appearance of seduction. If he does it or if he is noticed giving any sign of it, immediately she should take such an attitude towards him that he will not dare to importune them any more. The lady who is chaste will want all her women to be so too, on pain of being banished from her company.

Christine de Pizan, *The Book of the City of Ladies*, in Sarah Lawson, trans., *The Treasure of the City of Ladies* (New York: Penguin, 1985), 74–76.

She will want them to amuse themselves with decent games, such that men cannot mock, as they do the games of some women, though at the time the men laugh and join in. The women should restrain themselves with seemly conduct among knights and squires and all men. They should speak demurely and sweetly and, whether in dances or other amusements, divert and enjoy themselves decorously and without wantonness. They must not be frolicsome, forward, or boisterous in speech, expression, bearing or laughter. They must not go about with their heads raised like wild deer. This kind of behavior would be very unseemly and greatly derisory in a woman of the court, in whom there should be more modesty, good manners and courteous behavior than in any others, for where there is most honor there ought to be the most perfect manners and behavior. Women of the court in any country would be deceiving themselves very much if they imagined that it was more appropriate for them to be frolicsome and saucy than for other women. For this reason we hope that in time to come our doctrine in this book may be carried into many kingdoms, so that it may be valuable in all places where there might be any shortcoming.

We say generally to all women of all countries that it is the duty of every lady and maiden of the court, whether she be young or old, to be more prudent, more decorous, and better schooled in all things than other women. The ladies of the court ought to be models of all good things and all honor to other women, and if they do otherwise they will do no honor to their mistress nor to themselves. In addition, so that everything may be consistent in modesty, the wise princess will wish that the clothing and the ornaments of her women, though they be appropriately beautiful and rich, be of a modest fashion, well fitting and seemly, neat and properly cared for. There should be no deviation from this modesty nor any immodesty in the matter of plunging necklines or other excesses.

In all things the wise princess will keep her women in order just as the good and prudent abbess does her convent, so that bad reports about it may not circulate in the town, in distant regions or anywhere else. This princess will be so feared and respected because of the wise management that she will be seen to practice that no man or woman will be so foolhardy as to disobey her commands in any respect or to question her will, for there is no doubt that a lady is more feared and respected and held in greater reverence when she is seen to be wise and chaste and of firm behavior. But there is nothing wrong or inconsistent in her being kind and gentle, for the mere look of the wise lady and her subdued reception is enough of a sign to correct those men and women who err and to inspire them with fear.

READING AND DISCUSSION QUESTIONS

1. This passage is addressed "the wise princess." What other women, in addition to princesses, might find its advice useful?

2. Discuss the ways in which the princess must watch over the women of her court, especially in their relations with men. What does this reveal more generally about relations between men and women?

3. Why is reputation so important to the princess?

DOCUMENT 13-4

Account of an Italian Jew Expelled from Spain
1492

In 1492, the same year in which the last Islamic stronghold in Spain was overcome, Jews were given the choice of forcible conversion or expulsion. Even those who did convert endured persecution, because the authorities often believed that these conversos *continued to practice their old religion in secret. One of the principal tasks of the Inquisition in Spain was to root out secret Jews. The Jews who were expelled scattered over vast areas of the Muslim and Christian world. Muhammad had ordained that Muslims allow Jews to practice their religion, but there was no similar instruction for Christians.*

And in the year 1492, in the days of King Ferdinand [of Spain], the Lord visited the remnant of his people a second time and exiled them. After the King had captured the city of Granada from the Moors, . . . he ordered the expulsion of all the Jews in all parts of his kingdom — in the kingdoms of Castile, Catalonia, Aragon, Galicia, Majorca, Minorca, the Basque provinces, the islands of Sardinia and Sicily, and the kingdom of Valencia.

The King gave them three months' time in which to leave. . . .

About their number there is no agreement, but, after many inquiries, I found that the most generally accepted estimate is 50,000 families. . . .

Jacob Marcus, *The Jew in the Medieval World: A Sourcebook, 315–1791* (New York: JPS, 1938), 51–55.

They had houses, fields, vineyards, and cattle, and most of them were arti-sans. At that time there existed many academies in Spain, and at the head of the greatest of them were Rabbi Isaac Aboab in Guadalajara, Rabbi Isaac Veçudó in Leon, and Rabbi Jacob Habib in Salamanca. . . .

In the course of the three months' respite granted them they endeav-ored to effect an arrangement permitting them to stay on in the country, and they felt confident of success. Their representatives were the rabbi, Don Abraham Seneor, the leader of the Spanish congregations, who was attended by a retinue on thirty mules, and Rabbi Meïr Melamed, who was secretary to the King, and Don Isaac Abravanel, who had fled to Castile from the King of Portugal, and then occupied an equally prominent posi-tion at the Spanish royal court. He, too, was later expelled, went to Naples, and was highly esteemed by the King of Naples. . . .

The agreement permitting them to remain in the country on the pay-ment of a large sum of money was almost completed when it was frustrated by the interference of a prior who was called the Prior of Santa Cruz. Then the Queen gave an answer to the representatives of the Jews, similar to the saying of King Solomon: "The king's heart is in the hand of the Lord, as the rivers of water. God turneth it withersoever He will." She said further-more: "Do you believe that this comes upon you from us? The Lord hath put this thing into the heart of the king."

Then they saw that there was evil determined against them by the King, and they gave up the hope of remaining. But the time had become short, and they had to hasten their exodus from Spain. They sold their houses, their landed estates, and their cattle for very small prices, to save themselves. The King did not allow them to carry silver and gold out of his country, so that they were compelled to exchange their silver and gold for merchandise of cloths and skins and other things.

One hundred and twenty thousand of them went to Portugal, accord-ing to a compact which a prominent man, Don Vidal bar Benveniste del Cavalleria, had made with the King of Portugal, and they paid one ducat for every soul, and the fourth part of all the merchandise they had carried thither; and he allowed them to stay in his country six months. This King acted much worse toward them than the King of Spain, and after the six months had elapsed he made slaves of all those that remained in his coun-try, and banished seven hundred children to a remote island to settle it, and all of them died. . . .

Many of the exiled Spaniards went to Mohammedan countries, to Fez, Tlemçen, and the Berber provinces, under the King of Tunis. On account of their large numbers the Moors did not allow them into their cities, and many of them died in the fields from hunger, thirst, and lack of everything. The lions and bears, which are numerous in this country, killed some of them while they lay starving outside of the cities. . . .

When the edict of expulsion became known in the other countries, vessels came from Genoa to the Spanish harbors to carry away the Jews. The crews of these vessels, too, acted maliciously and meanly toward the Jews, robbed them, and delivered some of them to the famous pirate of that time who was called the Corsair of Genoa. To those who escaped and arrived at Genoa the people of the city showed themselves merciless, and oppressed and robbed them, and the cruelty of their wicked hearts went so far that they took the infants from the mothers' breasts.

Many ships with Jews, especially from Sicily, went to the city of Naples on the coast. The King of this country was friendly to the Jews, received them all, and was merciful towards them, and he helped them with money. The Jews that were at Naples supplied them with food as much as they could, and sent around to the other parts of Italy to collect money to sustain them. The Marranos[1] in this city lent them money on pledges without interest; even the Dominican Brotherhood acted mercifully toward them. On account of their very large number, all this was not enough. Some of them died by famine, others sold their children to Christians to sustain their life. Finally, a plague broke out among them, spread to Naples, and very many of them died, so that the living wearied of burying the dead. . . .

He who said unto His world, Enough, may He also say Enough unto our sufferings, and may He look down upon our impotence. May He turn again, and have compassion upon us, and hasten out salvation. Thus may it be Thy will!

READING AND DISCUSSION QUESTIONS

1. Why did the negotiations that might have allowed Jews to remain in Spain fail?

2. Which countries treated Jewish refugees best? Worst? Explain your answer.

---

[1] **Marranos:** Secret Jews, living under the guise of Christianity.

3. Jews suffered greatly even in countries where the rulers tried to act with some decency. What does this reveal about Europe's social and economic infrastructure?

4. How do you think contemporaries reacted to the outbreak of plague that accompanied the arrival of Jews and spread to Naples?

COMPARATIVE QUESTIONS

1. To what extent do Machiavelli and More agree or disagree about the ways that international politics are conducted?

2. Compare and contrast Christine de Pizan to Machiavelli and More. In what ways are they similar or different in their perceived audiences or in the advice they give?

3. "Rulers must be good examples to their subjects." To what extent would Machiavelli, More, and Pizan have agreed with this statement?

4. Ferdinand of Aragon, who ordered the expulsion of Jews described in Document 13-4, was one of the contemporary princes that Machiavelli most admired. What would Machiavelli have found to admire in a prince like Ferdinand?

5. The exodus of Jews from Spain was not the first Jewish exodus. Revisit Document 2-2. How had the plight of the Jewish people changed in the interim?

CHAPTER 14

Reformations and Religious Wars

1500–1600

E ven before Martin Luther posted his "Ninety-five Theses on the Power and Efficacy of Indulgences," numerous Catholic practices had come under widespread criticism. Erasmus, one of the most prestigious literary and scholarly figures of his time, had criticized many aspects of popular religion in *The Praise of Folly*. His scholarly work on the New Testament was important for those who believed that the Church had strayed from the teachings of the gospels. Reformers such as Luther and John Calvin believed that Christians should have a more immediate spiritual relationship with God. They argued that the Catholic sacrament of penance, as it was then practiced, could actually hinder spiritual growth. Some reformers, including Michael Servetus, adopted beliefs that were far more radical than the ideas of either Luther or Calvin, and were condemned by Protestants and Catholics alike.

DOCUMENT 14-1

DESIDERIUS ERASMUS

From The Praise of Folly: *On Popular Religious Practice*

1509

Desiderius Erasmus of Rotterdam (1466/1469–1536) was one of the leading scholars and writers of the Northern Renaissance, and produced important Greek and Latin translations of the New Testament. Erasmus wrote The Praise of Folly *in a single week while visiting Thomas More (Utopia,*

Erasmus, *The Praise of Folly*, in James Harvey Robinson, ed., *Readings in European History* (Boston: Ginn, 1904), 2:41–43.

Document 13-2) in England. The book quickly became popular throughout Europe, and, despite its criticism of religious beliefs, Pope Leo X was reported to have been amused by it. Although some expected that Erasmus would embrace the Protestant Reformation, he remained loyal to the Catholic Church.

To this same class of fools belong those who beguile themselves with the silly but pleasing notion that if they look upon a picture or image of St. Christopher, — that huge Polyphemus,[1] — they will not die that day; or that he who salutes an image of St. Barbara with the proper form of address will come back from battle safe; or that one who approaches St. Erasmus on certain days with wax candles and prayers will soon be rich. They have found a new Hercules in St. George, — a sort of second Hippolytus.[2] They seem to adore even his horse, which is scrupulously decked out with gorgeous trappings, and additional offerings are constantly being made in the hope of gaining new favors. His bronze helmet one would think half divine, the way people swear by it.

And what shall I say of those who comfortably delude themselves with imaginary pardons for their sins, and who measure the time in purgatory with an hourglass into years, months, days, and hours, with all the precision of a mathematical table? There are plenty, too, who, relying upon certain magical little certificates and prayers, — which some pious impostor devised either in fun or for the benefit of his pocket, — believe that they may procure riches, honor, future happiness, health, perpetual prosperity, long life, a lusty old age, — nay, in the end, a seat at the right hand of Christ in heaven; but as for this last, it matters not how long it be deferred: they will content themselves with the joys of heaven only when they must finally surrender the pleasures of this world, to which they lovingly cling.

The trader, the soldier, and the judge think that they can clean up the Augean stable[3] of a lifetime, once for all, by sacrificing a single coin from their ill-gotten gains. They flatter themselves that all sorts of perjury, debauchery, drunkenness, quarrels, bloodshed, imposture, perfidy, and treason can be compounded for by contract and so adjusted that, having paid off their arrears, they can begin a new score.

---

[1] **Polyphemus**: A Greek cyclops who appears in Homer's *Odyssey*.

[2] **Hippolytus**: A Greek horseman, praised for his chastity.

[3] **Augean stable**: An epically unclean cattle house. One of Hercules' twelve labors, performed as penance for murdering his family, was to clean the stables in a day.

How foolish, or rather how happy, are those who promise themselves more than supernal happiness if they repeat the verses of the seven holy psalms! Those magical lines are supposed to have been taught to St. Bernard by a demon, who seems to have been a wag; but he was not very clever, and, poor fellow, was frustrated in his attempt to deceive the saint. These silly things which even I, Folly, am almost ashamed of, are approved not only by the common herd but even by the teachers of religion.

How foolish, too, for religious bodies each to give preference to its particular guardian saint! Nay, each saint has his particular office allotted to him, and is addressed each in his special way: this one is called upon to alleviate toothache; that, to aid in childbirth; others, to restore a stolen article, bring rescue to the shipwrecked, or protect cattle, — and so on with the rest, who are much too numerous to mention. A few indeed among the saints are good in more than one emergency, especially the Holy Virgin, to whom the common man now attributes almost more than to her Son.

And for what, after all, do men petition the saints except for foolish things? Look at the votive offerings which cover the walls of certain churches and with which you see even the ceiling filled; do you find any one who expresses his gratitude that he has escaped Folly or because he has become a whit wiser? One perhaps was saved from drowning, another recovered when he had been run through by his enemy; another, while his fellows were fighting, ran away with expedition and success; another, on the point of being hanged, escaped, through the aid of some saintly friend of thieves, and lived to relieve a few more of those whom he believed to be overburdened with their wealth. . . .

These various forms of foolishness so pervade the whole life of Christians that even the priests themselves find no objection to admitting, not to say fostering, them, since they do not fail to perceive how many tidy little sums accrue to them from such sources. But what if some odious philosopher should chime in and say, as is quite true: "You will not die badly if you live well. You are redeeming your sins when you add to the sum that you contribute a hearty detestation of evil doers: then you may spare yourself tears, vigils, invocations, fasts, and all that kind of life. You may rely upon any saint to aid you when once you begin to imitate his life."

As for the theologians, perhaps the less said the better on this gloomy and dangerous theme, since they are a style of man who show themselves exceeding supercilious and irritable unless they can heap up six hundred conclusions about you and force you to recant; and if you refuse, they promptly brand you as a heretic, — for it is their custom to terrify by their thunderings those whom they dislike. It must be confessed that no other group of fools are so reluctant to acknowledge Folly's benefits toward them, although I have many titles to their gratitude, for I make them so in love with themselves that they seem to be happily exalted to the third heaven, whence they look down with something like pity upon all other mortals, wandering about on the earth like mere cattle. . . .

READING AND DISCUSSION QUESTIONS

1. In what ways does Erasmus criticize the veneration of saints?
2. According to this document, why and how do so many priests contribute to the follies of the world?
3. Describe Erasmus's attitude toward theologians.

DOCUMENT 14-2

MARTIN LUTHER

Ninety-five Theses on the Power and Efficacy of Indulgences

1517

Martin Luther (1483–1546), the acknowledged initiator of the Protestant Reformation, was a theologian, preacher, and pamphleteer. His German translation of the Bible was a shaping force in the development of the modern German language. Some historians argue that Luther had no intention of breaking with the Catholic Church when he developed the Ninety-five Theses — he had enclosed a copy in a letter to the archbishop of Mainz and Magdeburg, and the form in which he cast his ideas (the theses) was a common way for scholars to invite others to debate.

1. Our Lord and Master Jesus Christ in saying "Repent ye" etc., intended that the whole life of believers should be penitence.

Martin Luther, "Ninety-five Theses," in *Translations and Reprints from the Original Sources of European History* (Philadelphia: University of Pennsylvania Press, 1898), 2/6:12–18.

2. This word cannot be understood as sacramental penance, that is, of the confession and satisfaction which are performed under the ministry of priests.

3. It does not, however, refer solely to inward penitence; nay such inward penitence is naught, unless it outwardly produces various mortifications of the flesh.

4. The penalty thus continues as long as the hatred of self (that is, true inward penitence); namely, till our entrance into the kingdom of heaven.

5. The Pope has neither the will nor the power to remit any penalties except those which he has imposed by his own authority, or by that of the canons.

6. The Pope has no power to remit any guilt, except by declaring and warranting it to have been remitted by God; or at most by remitting cases reserved for himself; in which cases, if his power were despised, guilt would certainly remain.

7. Certainly God remits no man's guilt without at the same time subjecting him, humbled in all things, to the authority of his representative the priest. . . .

20. Therefore the Pope, when he speaks of the plenary remission of all penalties, does not mean really of all, but only of those imposed by himself.

21. Thus those preachers of indulgences are in error who say that by the indulgences of the Pope a man is freed and saved from all punishment.

22. For in fact he remits to souls in purgatory no penalty which they would have had to pay in this life according to the canons.

23. If any entire remission of all penalties can be granted to any one it is certain that it is granted to none but the most perfect, that is to very few.

24. Hence, the greater part of the people must needs be deceived by this indiscriminate and high-sounding promise of release from penalties. . . .

26. The Pope acts most rightly in granting remission to souls not by the power of the keys (which is of no avail in this case) but by the way of intercession.[4]

27. They preach man who say that the soul flies out of Purgatory as soon as the money thrown into the chest rattles.[5]

---

[4] **intercession**: A prayer to God on another's behalf.
[5] **They preach . . . rattles**: This was the claim being made by the indulgence seller Tetzel in Luther's Saxony.

28. It is certain that, when the money rattles in the chest, avarice and gain may be increased, but the effect of the intercession of the Church depends on the will of God alone.

29. Who knows whether all the souls in purgatory desire to be redeemed from it — witness the story told of Saints Severinus and Paschal?

30. No man is sure of the reality of his own contrition, much less of the attainment of plenary remission. . . .

35. They preach no Christian doctrine who teach that contrition is not necessary for those who buy souls [out of purgatory] or buy confessional licenses.

36. Every Christian who feels true compunction has of right plenary remission of punishment and guilt even without letters of pardon.

37. Every true Christian, whether living or dead, has a share in all the benefits of Christ and of the Church, given him by God, even without letters of pardon.

38. The remission, however, imparted by the Pope is by no means to be despised, since it is, as I have said, a declaration of the divine remission.

39. It is a most difficult thing, even for the most learned theologians, to exalt at the same time in the eyes of the people the ample effect of pardons and the necessity of true contrition.

40. True contrition seeks and loves punishment; while the ampleness of pardons relaxes it, and causes men to hate it, or at least gives occasion for them to do so. . . .

43. Christians should be taught that he who gives to a poor man, or lends to a needy man, does better than if he bought pardons.

44. Because by works of charity, charity increases, and the man becomes better; while by means of pardons, he does not become better, but only freer from punishment. . . .

49. Christians should be taught that the Pope's pardons are useful if they do not put their trust in them, but most hurtful if through them they lose the fear of God. . . .

54. Wrong is done to the Word of God when, in the same sermon, an equal or longer time is spent on pardons than on it.

55. The mind of the Pope necessarily is that, if pardons, which are a very small matter, are celebrated with single bells, single processions, and single ceremonies, the Gospel, which is a very great matter, should be preached with a hundred bells, a hundred processions, and a hundred ceremonies.

56. The treasures of the Church, whence the Pope grants indulgences, are neither sufficiently named nor known among the people of Christ.

57. It is clear that they are at least not temporal treasures, for these are not so readily lavished, but only accumulated, by many of the preachers. . . .

67. Those indulgences, which the preachers loudly proclaim to be the greatest graces, are seen to be truly such as regards the promotion of gain.

68. Yet they are in reality most insignificant when compared to the grace of God and the piety of the cross. . . .

75. To think that the Papal pardons have such power that they could absolve a man even if — by an impossibility — he had violated the Mother of God, is madness.

76. We affirm on the contrary that Papal pardons cannot take away even the least of venial sins, as regards its guilt. . . .

79. To say that the cross set up among the insignia of the Papal arms is of equal power with the cross of Christ, is blasphemy.

80. Those bishops, priests, and theologians who allow such discourses to have currency among the people will have to render an account. . . .

82. As for instance: Why does not the Pope empty purgatory for the sake of most holy charity and of the supreme necessity of souls — this being the most just of all reasons — if he redeems an infinite number of souls for the sake of that most fatal thing, money, to be spent on building a basilica — this being a very slight reason?

83. Again; why do funeral masses and anniversary masses for the deceased continue, and why does not the Pope return, or permit the withdrawal of, the funds bequeathed for this purpose, since it is a wrong to pray for those who are already redeemed?

84. Again; what is this new kindness of God and the Pope, in that, for money's sake, they permit an impious man and an enemy of God to re-deem a pious soul which loves God, and yet do not redeem that same pious and beloved soul out of free charity on account of its own need?

85. Again; why is it that the penitential canons, long since abrogated and dead in themselves, in very fact and not only by usage, are yet still redeemed with money, through the granting of indulgences, as if they were full of life?

86. Again; why does not the Pope, whose riches are at this day more ample than those of the wealthiest of the wealthy, build the single Basilica of St. Peter with his own money rather than with that of poor believers? . . .

89. Since it is the salvation of souls, rather than money, that the Pope seeks by his pardons, why does he suspend the letters and pardons granted long ago, since they are equally efficacious? . . .

91. If all these pardons were preached according to the spirit and mind of the Pope, all these questions would be resolved with ease; nay, would not exist. . . .

READING AND DISCUSSION QUESTIONS

1. In Thesis 36, Luther writes, "Every Christian who feels true compunction has of right plenary remission of punishment and guilt even without letters of pardon." Why would many interpret this as an attack on the papacy?

2. Luther claims that in some cases, people who buy indulgences are actually purchasing the anger of God (see Thesis 35). What does this suggest about his notions of charity?

3. According to the theses, in what ways have the leaders of the church failed to teach true Christian doctrine?

4. Based on your reading of Theses 82–91, how would you classify the sorts of reform that Luther would like to see within the church?

DOCUMENT 14-3

IMPERIAL DIET OF AUGSBURG
On the Religious Peace of Augsburg
1555

The Peace of Augsburg, a treaty between the Holy Roman emperor, Ferdinand I, and Protestant rulers who were nominally his subjects, was an attempt to end a series of religious wars. The treaty established the principle that each ruler could decide which religion — Catholicism or Lutheranism — would be practiced within his domain. It was a partial solution at best, particularly because it did not adequately deal with Protestant sects other than the Lutherans or divisions between Catholics and Protestants within individual political regions.

"The Religious Peace of Augsburg," in James Harvey Robinson, ed., *Readings in European History* (Boston: Ginn, 1904), 2:114–116.

In order that . . . peace, which is especially necessary in view of the divided religions, as is seen from the causes before mentioned, and is demanded by the sad necessity of the Holy Roman Empire of the German nation, may be the better established and made secure and enduring between his Roman Imperial Majesty and us, on the one hand, and the electors, princes, and estates of the Holy Empire of the German nation on the other, therefore his Imperial Majesty, and we, and the electors, princes, and estates of the Holy Empire will not make war upon any estate of the empire on account of the Augsburg Confession[6] and the doctrine, religion, and faith of the same, nor injure nor do violence to those estates that hold it, nor force them, against their conscience, knowledge, and will, to abandon the religion, faith, church usages, ordinances, and ceremonies of the Augsburg Confession, where these have been established, or may hereafter be established, in their principalities, lands, and dominions. Nor shall we, through mandate or in any other way, trouble or disparage them, but shall let them quietly and peacefully enjoy their religion, faith, church usages, ordinances, and ceremonies, as well as their possessions, real and personal property, lands, people, dominions, governments, honors, and rights. . . .

On the other hand, the estates that have accepted the Augsburg Confession shall suffer his Imperial Majesty, us, and the electors, princes, and other estates of the Holy Empire, adhering to the old religion, to abide in like manner by their religion, faith, church usages, ordinances, and ceremonies. They shall also leave undisturbed their possessions, real and personal property, lands, people, dominions, government, honors, and rights, rents, interest, and tithes. . . .

But all others who are not adherents of either of the above-mentioned religions are not included in this peace, but shall be altogether excluded. . . .

No estate shall urge another estate, or the subjects of the same, to embrace its religion.

But when our subjects and those of the electors, princes, and estates, adhering to the old religion or to the Augsburg Confession, wish, for the sake of their religion, to go with wife and children to another place in the lands, principalities, and cities of the electors, princes, and estates of the Holy Empire, and settle there, such going and coming, and the sale of property and goods, in return for reasonable compensation for serfdom and arrears of taxes, . . . shall be everywhere unhindered, permitted, and granted. . . .

---

[6] **Augsburg Confession:** The statement of faith in Lutheran churches.

READING AND DISCUSSION QUESTIONS

1. What does this decree pledge to do? Why?

2. To what extent does this decree support religious toleration? What are the limits of that toleration?

3. What provisions are made for people who remain true to the old religion?

4. What provisions are made for people who want to leave their homes because of their religion, and why were such measures necessary?

DOCUMENT 14-4

NICHOLAS DE LA FONTAINE
The Trial of Michael Servetus in Calvin's Geneva
1553

Michael Servetus (1511–1553) was a Spanish scientist, humanist, and theologian. Both Catholics and Protestants condemned his teachings, especially his rejection of both the doctrine of the Trinity and the practice of infant baptism. While fleeing from Catholic authorities in France, he passed through Geneva, which was then under the leadership of the Protestant reformer John Calvin. The author of this document, Nicholas de la Fontaine, took the most active role in the prosecution of Michael Servetus and drew up the list of charges. After being found guilty of heresy, Servetus was burned at the stake.

Nicholas de la Fontaine asserts that he has instituted proceedings against Michael Servetus, and on this account he has allowed himself to be held prisoner in criminal process.

1. In the first place that about twenty-four years ago the defendant commenced to annoy the churches of Germany with his errors and heresies, and was condemned and took to flight in order to escape the punishment prepared for him.

Nicholas de la Fontaine, in *Translations and Reprints from the Original Sources of European History* (Philadelphia: University of Pennsylvania Press, 1898), 3/2:12–15.

2. Item, that on or about this time he printed a wretched book, which has infected many people.
3. Item, that since that time he has not ceased by all means in his power to scatter his poison, as much by his construction of biblical text, as by certain annotations which he has made upon Ptolemy.[7]
4. Item, that since that time he has printed in secrecy another book containing endless blasphemies.
5. Item, that while detained in prison in the city of Vienne [in France], when he saw that they were willing to pardon him on condition of his recanting, he found means to escape from prison.

Said Nicholas demands that said Servetus be examined upon all these points.

And since he is able to evade the question by pretending that his blasphemies and heresies are nought else than good doctrine, said Nicholas proposes certain articles upon which he demands said heretic be examined.

6. To wit, whether he has not written and falsely taught and published that to believe that in a single essence of God there are three distinct persons, the Father, the Son, and the Holy Ghost, is to create four phantoms, which cannot and ought not to be imagined.
7. Item, that to put such distinction into the essence of God is to cause God to be divided into three parts, and that this is a threeheaded devil, like to Cerberus, whom the ancient poets have called the dog of hell, a monster, and things equally injurious. . . .
9. Item, whether he does not say that our Lord Jesus Christ is not the Son of God, except in so much as he was conceived of the Holy Ghost in the womb of the virgin Mary.
10. Item, that those who believe Jesus Christ to have been the word of God the Father, engendered through all eternity, have a scheme of redemption which is fanciful and of the nature of sorcery.
11. Item, that Jesus Christ is God, insomuch as God has caused him to be such. . . .
27. Item, that the soul of man is mortal, and that the only thing which is immortal is an elementary breath, which is the substance that Jesus Christ now possesses in heaven and which is also the elementary and divine and incorruptible substance of the Holy Ghost. . . .

---

[7] **certain annotations . . . Ptolemy:** Servetus wrote about the Roman-Egyptian's treatise *Geography*.

32. Item, that the baptism of little children is an invention of the Devil, an infernal falsehood tending to the destruction of all Christianity. . . .

37. Item, that in the person of M. Calvin, minister of the word of God in the Church of Geneva, he has defamed with printed book the doctrine which he preached, uttering all the injurious and blasphemous things which it is possible to invent. . . .

READING AND DISCUSSION QUESTIONS

1. When had Michael Servetus come into conflict with religious authorities on earlier occasions? Why are these earlier occasions mentioned in the present indictment?

2. Why is the charge that Michael Servetus argued that the human soul is mortal such an important part of the indictment? To what extent, if any, is this charge justified?

3. What are the major points on which Michael Servetus disagreed with orthodox Christian teachings?

COMPARATIVE QUESTIONS

1. Compare and contrast the views of Erasmus and Luther.

2. Which thinker, Luther or Servetus, posed the most serious threat to traditional Christianity? Why?

3. Compare and contrast the issues addressed in the Peace of Augsburg with those confronted during the investiture controversy (Document 9-3). Which posed a more serious threat to established authority and why?

4. In each of these documents, identify which doctrines or points seem to be most important to the author(s) of the document. How might their emphasis on these doctrines have influences other Christians?

CHAPTER 15

European Exploration and Conquest

1450–1650

I n the mid-1400s, Western Europe faced a rapidly expanding Muslim power in the east. The Ottoman Empire captured Constantinople in 1453 and over time came to rule, directly or indirectly, much of Eastern Europe. In the west, the Portuguese began exploring the west coast of Africa, eventually rounding the tip of Africa and reaching India. After the voyages of Columbus, the Spaniards and the Portuguese began to explore and conquer the Americas. The establishment of colonial empires in the Americas led to a new era of worldwide trade in African slaves. Europeans came into increasing contact with peoples of whom they had previously had little or no knowledge. In the context of threats from the Ottomans in the East and European competition in the West, a series of religious wars affecting all of Europe tore apart western Christendom.

DOCUMENT 15-1

DUCAS

From Historia Turcobyzantia: *The Fall of Constantinople to the Ottomans*

ca. 1465

On May 29, 1453, Constantinople, the city that had been "the second Rome" — the capital of the eastern half of the Roman Empire — and a center

Ducas, Historia Turcobyzantia, 1341–1462, in Deno John Geanokoplos, ed., *Byzantium: Church, Society, and Civilization Seen Through Contemporary Eyes* (Chicago: University of Chicago Press, 1984), 389.

of Christian learning throughout the Middle Ages, fell to the Ottoman Turks. In the years that followed Constantinople's fall, the Ottomans continued to advance into Central Europe, seizing control of the Balkan Peninsula and even besieging Vienna, once in the sixteenth century and again in the seventeenth century. The account excerpted here is from a member of a prominent Byzantine family.

And the entire City [its inhabitants and wealth] was to be seen in the tents of the [Turkish] camp, the city deserted, lying lifeless, naked, soundless, without either form or beauty. O City, City, head of all cities! O City, City, center of the four corners of the world! O City, City, pride of the Romans, civilizer of the barbarians! O City, second paradise planted toward the west, possessing all kinds of vegetation, laden with spiritual fruits! Where is your beauty, O paradise, where the beneficent strength of the charms of your spirit, soul, and body? Where are the bodies of the Apostles of my Lord, which were implanted long ago in the always-green paradise, having in their midst the purple cloak, the lance, the sponge, the reed, which, when we kissed them, made us believe that we were seeing him who was raised on the Cross? Where are the relics of the saints, those of the martyrs? Where the remains of Constantine the Great and the other emperors? Roads, courtyards, crossroads, fields, and vineyard enclosures, all teem with the relics of saints, with the bodies of nobles, of the chaste, and of male and female ascetics. Oh what a loss! "The dead bodies of thy servants, O Lord, have they given to be meat unto the fowls of the heaven, the flesh of thy saints unto the beasts of the earth round about New Sion and there was none to bury them." [Psalm 78:2–3]

O temple [Hagia Sophia]! O earthly heaven! O heavenly altar! O sacred and divine places! O magnificence of the churches! O holy books and words of God! O ancient and modern laws! O tablets inscribed by the finger of God! O Scriptures spoken by his mouth! O divine discourses of angels who bore flesh! O doctrines of men filled with the Holy Spirit! O teachings of semi-divine heroes! O commonwealth! O citizens! O army, formerly beyond number, now removed from sight like a ship sunk into the sea! O houses and palaces of every type! O sacred walls! Today I invoke you all, and as if incarnate beings I mourn with you, having Jeremiah[1] as [choral] leader of this lamentable tragedy!

---

[1] **Jeremiah**: The famously "broken-hearted prophet."

READING AND DISCUSSION QUESTIONS

1. This account was written more than ten years after the fall of Constantinople. How does this affect its value as an eyewitness account?

2. What does the reference to Psalm 78 at the end of the first paragraph tell you about both the siege and the author of this account?

3. How does Ducas describe the destruction of Constantinople, both physical and spiritual?

4. What does Ducas's account reveal about the place of Constantinople in the Christian world?

DOCUMENT 15-2

HERNANDO CORTÉS

Two Letters to Charles V: On the Conquest of the Aztecs

1521

In a number of letters to his sovereign, the Holy Roman emperor Charles V, who was also king of Spain, Hernando Cortés described his conquest of the Aztec Empire of Mexico. While Cortés was surprised, even impressed by the advanced culture he encountered, his conquests were not without considerable violence. In one incident, one of his men ordered the massacre of thousands of unarmed members of the Aztec nobility who had assembled peaceably. Under examination, Cortés claimed that this act was done to instill fear and prevent future treachery. Some contemporaries speculated that Cortés embellished his accounts in order to retain the favor of the king.

This great city of Tenochtitlan is built on the salt lake. . . . It has four approaches by means of artificial causeways. . . . The city is as large as Seville or Cordoba. Its streets . . . are very broad and straight, some of these, and all the others, are one half land, and the other half water on which they go about in canoes. . . .There are bridges, very large, strong, and well constructed,

Letters of Cortés, trans. Francis A. MacNutt (New York: 1908), 1:256–257, 2:244.

so that, over many, ten horsemen can ride abreast. . . . The city has many squares where markets are held. . . . There is one square, twice as large as that of Salamanca, all surrounded by arcades, where there are daily more than sixty thousand souls, buying and selling . . . in the service and manners of its people, their fashion of living was almost the same as in Spain, with just as much harmony and order; and considering that these people were barbarous, so cut off from the knowledge of God and other civilized peoples, it is admirable to see to what they attained in every respect. [Second letter]

It happened . . . that a Spaniard saw an Indian . . . eating a piece of flesh taken from the body of an Indian who had been killed. . . . I had the culprit burned, explaining that the cause was his having killed that Indian and eaten him which was prohibited by Your Majesty, and by me in Your Royal name. I further made the chief understand that all the people . . . must abstain from this custom. . . . I came . . . to protect their lives as well as their property, and to teach them that they were to adore but one God . . . that they must turn from their idols, and the rites they had practiced until then, for these were lies and deceptions which the devil . . . had invented. . . . I, likewise, had come to teach them that Your Majesty, by the will of Divine Providence, rules the universe, and that they also must submit themselves to the imperial yoke, and do all that we who are Your Majesty's ministers here might order them. . . . [Fifth letter]

READING AND DISCUSSION QUESTIONS

1. Although Cortés describes the people of Tenochtitlan as "barbarous" and laments that they are "cut off from the knowledge of God and other civilized peoples," what positive qualities does he attribute to the city and its people?

2. Why do you think Cortés chooses to describe an act of cannibalism? What does his commentary on this incident reveal about his conception of his mission?

3. What different images of Mexico was Cortés trying to impress upon Charles?

ALVISE DA CA' DA MOSTO

Description of Capo Bianco and the Islands Nearest to It: Fifteenth-Century Slave Trade in West Africa

1455–1456

Alvise da Ca' da Mosto (ca. 1428–1483) was an Italian trader and explorer. After Alvise's father was banished from Venice, Alvise took up service with Prince Henry of Portugal, who was promoting exploration of the West African coast. In 1455, he traveled to the Canary and Madeira Islands and sailed past Cape Verde to the Gambia River. During another voyage in 1456, Alvise discovered islands off Cape Verde and sailed sixty miles up the Gambia River. In the excerpt that follows, Alvise describes trade with African Muslim middlemen that included the traffic in humans for the Atlantic slave trade.

You should also know that behind this Cauo Bianco on the land, is a place called Hoden,[2] which is about six days inland by camel. This place is not walled, but is frequented by Arabs, and is a market where the caravans arrive from Tanbutu [Timbuktu], and from other places in the land of the Blacks, on their way to our nearer Barbary. The food of the peoples of this place is dates, and barley, of which there is sufficient, for they grow in some of these places, but not abundantly. They drink the milk of camels and other animals, for they have no wine. They also have cows and goats, but not many, for the land is dry. Their oxen and cows, compared with ours, are small.

Alvise da Ca' da Mosto, "Description of Capo Bianco and the Islands Nearest to It," in J. H. Parry, *European Reconnaissance: Selected Documents* (New York: Walker, 1968), 59–61.

[2] **Hoden**: Wadan, an important desert market about 350 miles east of Arguim. Later, in 1487, when the Portuguese were endeavoring to penetrate the interior they attempted to establish a trading factory at Wadan which acted as a feeder to Arguim, tapping the northbound caravan traffic and diverting some of it to the west coast.

They are Muhammadans, and very hostile to Christians. They never remain settled, but are always wandering over these deserts. These are the men who go to the land of the Blacks, and also to our nearer Barbary. They are very numerous, and have many camels on which they carry brass and silver from Barbary and other things to Tanbuto and to the land of the Blacks. Thence they carry away gold and pepper, which they bring hither. They are brown complexioned, and wear white cloaks edged with a red stripe: their women also dress thus, without shifts. On their heads the men wear turbans in the Moorish fashion, and they always go barefooted. In these sandy districts there are many lions, leopards, and ostriches, the eggs of which I have often eaten and found good.

You should know that the said Lord Infante of Portugal [the crown prince, Henry the Navigator] has leased this island of Argin to Christians [for ten years], so that no one can enter the bay to trade with the Arabs save those who hold the license. These have dwellings on the island and factories where they buy and sell with the said Arabs who come to the coast to trade for merchandise of various kinds, such as woollen cloths, cotton, silver, and "alchezeli," that is, cloaks, carpets, and similar articles and above all, corn, for they are always short of food. They give in exchange slaves whom the Arabs bring from the land of the Blacks, and gold tiber. The Lord Infante therefore caused a castle to be built on the island to protect this trade for ever. For this reason, Portuguese caravels are coming and going all the year to this island.

These Arabs also have many Berber horses, which they trade, and take to the Land of the Blacks, exchanging them with the rulers for slaves. Ten or fifteen slaves are given for one of these horses, according to their quality. The Arabs likewise take articles of Moorish silk, made in Granata and in Tunis of Barbary, silver, and other goods, obtaining in exchange any number of these slaves, and some gold. These slaves are brought to the market and town of Hoden; there they are divided: some go to the mountains of Barcha, and thence to Sicily, [others to the said town of Tunis and to all the coasts of Barbary], and others again are taken to this place, Argin, and sold to the Portuguese leaseholders. As a result every year the Portuguese carry away from Argin a thousand slaves. Note that before this traffic was organized, the Portuguese caravels, sometimes four, sometimes more, were wont to come armed to the Golfo d'Argin, and descending on the land by night, would assail the fisher villages, and so ravage the land. Thus they took of these Arabs both men and women, and carried them to Portugal for sale: behaving in a like manner along all the rest of the coast, which stretches from Cauo Bianco to the Rio di Senega and even beyond. . . .

READING AND DISCUSSION QUESTIONS

1. What evidence can you discern from this document as to why Alvise wrote it?

2. Describe the principal patterns of commerce in northern Africa.

3. Describe the groups that were involved in the various facets of the slave trade.

4. In what ways did the Portuguese change slavery and the slave trade?

DOCUMENT 15-4

MICHEL DE MONTAIGNE

From Essays: *On the Fallibility of Human Understanding*

1580

The essayist Michel de Montaigne lived in the midst of the religious civil wars that tore France apart. Although a Catholic, Montaigne supported the Protestant prince Henry of Navarre, who later became King Henry IV of France. As a statesman, Montaigne was respected by Protestants and Catholics alike. Montaigne's writings focus on skepticism, secularism (nonreligious thinking), and toleration, thus foreshadowing the Enlightenment of the eighteenth century. In the excerpt that follows, Montaigne takes on a variety of ideas and writers, from the Greek philosophers to Martin Luther.

I do not know what to say about it, but it is evident from experience that so many interpretations disperse the truth and shatter it. Aristotle wrote to be understood; if he did not succeed, still less will another man, less able, and not treating his own ideas. By diluting the substance we allow it to escape and spill it all over the place; of one subject we make a thousand, and, multiplying and subdividing, fall back into Epicurus' infinity of atoms. Never did two men judge alike about the same thing, and it is impossible to find

Michel de Montaigne, *Essays*, trans. Donald Frame (Stanford, Cal.: Stanford University Press, 1957), 817, 818–819.

two opinions exactly alike, not only in different men, but in the same man at different times. Ordinarily I find subject for doubt in what the commentary has not deigned to touch on. I am more apt to trip on flat ground, like certain horses I know which stumble more often on a smooth road.

Who would not say that glosses [interpretations, translations, annotations] increase doubts and ignorance, since there is no book to be found, whether human or divine, with which the world busies itself, whose difficulties are cleared up by interpretation? The hundredth commentator hands it on to his successor thornier and rougher than the first one had found it. When do we agree and say, "There has been enough about this book; henceforth there is nothing more to say about it"?

This is best seen in law practice. We give legal authority to numberless doctors, numberless decisions, and as many interpretations. Do we therefore find any end to the need of interpreting? Do we see any progress and advance toward tranquillity? Do we need fewer lawyers and judges than when this mass of law was still in its infancy? On the contrary, we obscure and bury the meaning; we no longer find it except hidden by so many enclosures and barriers.

Men do not know the natural infirmity of their mind: it does nothing but ferret and quest, and keeps incessantly whirling around, building up and becoming entangled in its own work, like our silkworms, and is suffocated in it. A *mouse in a pitch barrel* [Erasmus's allegory]. It thinks it notices from a distance some sort of glimmer of imaginary light and truth; but while running toward it, it is crossed by so many difficulties and obstacles, and diverted by so many new quests, that it strays from the road, bewildered. . . .

It is more of a job to interpret the interpretations than to interpret the things, and there are more books about books than about any other subject: we do nothing but write glosses about each other. The world is swarming with commentaries; of authors there is a great scarcity.

Is it not the chief and most reputed learning of our times to learn to understand the learned? Is that not the common and ultimate end of all studies?

Our opinions are grafted upon one another. The first serves as a stock for the second, the second for the third. Thus we scale the ladder, step by step. And thence it happens that he who has mounted highest has often more honor than merit; for he has only mounted one speck higher on the shoulders of the next last.

How often and perhaps how stupidly have I extended my book to make it speak for itself! Stupidly, if only for this reason, that I should have remembered what I say of others who do the same: that these frequent sheep's eyes at their own work testify that their heart thrills with love for it, and that even the rough, disdainful blows with which they beat it are only the love taps and affectations of maternal fondness; in keeping with Aristotle, to whom self-appreciation and self-depreciation often spring from the same sort of arrogance. For as for my excuse, that I ought to have more liberty in this than others, precisely because I write of myself and my writings as of my other actions, because my theme turns in upon itself — I do not know whether everyone will accept it.

I have observed in Germany that Luther has left as many divisions and altercations over the uncertainty of his opinions, and more, as he raised about the Holy Scriptures.

Our disputes are purely verbal. I ask what is "nature," "pleasure," "circle," "substitution." The question is one of words, and is answered in the same way. "A stone is a body." But if you pressed on: "And what is a body?" — "Substance." — "And what is substance?" and so on, you would finally drive the respondent to the end of his lexicon. We exchange one word for another word, often more unknown. I know better what is man than I know what is animal, or mortal, or rational. To satisfy one doubt, they give me three; it is the Hydra's head.[3]

Socrates asked Meno what virtue was. "There is," said Meno, "the virtue of a man and a woman, of a magistrate and of a private individual, of a child and of an old man." "That's fine," exclaimed Socrates; "we were in search of one virtue, and here is a whole swarm of them."

READING AND DISCUSSION QUESTIONS

1. What does Montaigne see as being inherently flawed in commentaries on difficult texts or laws?

2. How does Montaigne assess Martin Luther's writings on the Scriptures?

3. Why do you think Montaigne wrote this essay? What larger point is he trying to make?

---

[3] **Hydra's head**: In Greek mythology, a hydra was a many-headed water monster. Heracles (Hercules) killed the Lerneaen Hydra as the second of his twelve labors.

COMPARATIVE QUESTIONS

1. Compare and contrast the fall of Constantinople as portrayed by Ducas and Cortés's capture of Tenochtitlan, taking into consideration the different perspective of each account.

2. Compare and contrast the descriptions of non-European peoples by the conqueror Cortés and the explorer Alvise.

3. Based on your reading of these documents, which distinctions among peoples seem most important for Europeans of the fifteenth and sixteenth centuries?

4. Compare and contrast the account of an Italian Jew expelled from Spain (Document 13-4) to the letters by Cortés. What differences between European Christians and "others" do these two documents highlight?

CHAPTER 16

Absolutism and Constitutionalism in Western Europe

ca. 1589–1715

The fundamental political struggle in early modern Europe in the 1500–1600s was the battle for power between absolutist rulers and the institutions put in place as representative forms of government. Many factors influenced the course of these struggles, and the outcomes varied from country to country. In France, Kings Henry IV, Louis XIII, and Louis XIV gradually managed to suppress much of the opposition to their royal power. Although these absolutist monarchs lacked the power and authority to exert their will over all of their subjects — the great nobles in particular — they achieved far greater success in consolidating and extending royal authority than did their counterparts in the Netherlands or England.

DOCUMENT 16-1

HENRY IV

From Edict of Nantes: *Limited Toleration for the Huguenots*

1598

Prince Henry of Navarre (1553–1610) was a Huguenot, or Protestant, in an overwhelmingly Roman Catholic country. He ascended to the French throne as Henry IV in 1589 in the midst of the French wars of religion. A pragma-

---

King Henry of Navarre, "Edict of Nantes," excerpted in James Harvey Robinson, ed., *Readings in European History* (Boston: Ginn, 1904), 2:183–185.

tist, Henry realized that the country's Catholic majority would never accept a Protestant as their legitimate ruler, so he converted to Catholicism. However, in order to protect the Huguenots against religiously motivated attacks, as well as to establish peace among the people he was determined to rule, he issued the Edict of Nantes. In so doing, Henry legally sanctioned a degree of religious tolerance in a Europe previously characterized by the formula "one king, one people, one faith."

Among the infinite benefits which it has pleased God to heap upon us, the most signal and precious is his granting us the strength and ability to withstand the fearful disorders and troubles which prevailed on our advent in this kingdom. The realm was so torn by innumerable factions and sects that the most legitimate of all the parties was fewest in numbers. God has given us strength to stand out against this storm; we have finally surmounted the waves and made our port of safety, — peace for our state. For which his be the glory all in all, and ours a free recognition of his grace in making use of our instrumentality in the good work. . . . We implore and await from the Divine Goodness the same protection and favor which he has ever granted to this kingdom from the beginning. . . .

We have, by this perpetual and irrevocable edict, established and proclaimed and do establish and proclaim:

I. First, that the recollection of everything done by one party[1] or the other between March, 1585, and our accession to the crown, and during all the preceding period of troubles, remain obliterated and forgotten, as if no such things had ever happened. . . .

III. We ordain that the Catholic Apostolic and Roman religion shall be restored and reestablished in all places and localities of this our kingdom and countries subject to our sway, where the exercise of the same has been interrupted, in order that it may be peaceably and freely exercised, without any trouble or hindrance; forbidding very expressly all persons, of whatsoever estate, quality, or condition, from troubling, molesting, or disturbing ecclesiastics in the celebration of divine service, in the enjoyment or

---

[1] **one party**: Henry's reference to "party" refers to the three factions, two of them Catholic, one of them Protestant, struggling for control of the French throne in the French Wars of Religion (1561–1598).

collection of tithes, fruits, or revenues of their benefices, and all other rights and dues belonging to them; and that all those who during the troubles have taken possession of churches, houses, goods or revenues, belonging to the said ecclesiastics, shall surrender to them entire possession and peaceable enjoyment of such rights, liberties, and sureties as they had before they were deprived of them. . . .

VI. And in order to leave no occasion for troubles or differences between our subjects, we have permitted, and herewith permit, those of the said religion called Reformed [Protestant] to live and abide in all the cities and places of this our kingdom and countries of our sway, without being annoyed, molested, or compelled to do anything in the matter of religion contrary to their consciences, . . . upon conditions that they comport themselves in other respects according to that which is contained in this our present edict.

VII. It is permitted to all lords, gentlemen, and other persons making profession of the said religion called Reformed, holding the right of high justice [or a certain feudal tenure], to exercise the said religion in their houses. . . .

IX. We also permit those of the said religion to make and continue the exercise of the same in all villages and places of our dominion where it was established by them and publicly enjoyed several and divers times in the year 1597, up to the end of the month of August, notwithstanding all decrees and judgments to the contrary. . . .

XIII. We very expressly forbid to all those of the said religion its exercise, either in respect to ministry, regulation, discipline, or the public instruction of children, or otherwise, in this our kingdom and lands of our dominion, otherwise than in the places permitted and granted by the present edict.

XIV. It is forbidden as well to perform any function of the said religion on our court or retinue, or in our lands and territories beyond the mountains, or in our city of Paris, or within five leagues of the said city. . . .

XVIII. We also forbid all our subjects, of whatever quality and condition, from carrying off by force or persuasion, against the will of their parents, the children of the said religion, in order to cause them to be baptized or confirmed in the Catholic Apostolic and Roman Church; and the same is forbidden to those of the said religion called Reformed, upon penalty of being punished with special severity. . . .

XXI. Books concerning the said religion called Reformed may not be printed and publicly sold, except in cities and places where the public exercise of the said religion is permitted.

XXII. We ordain that there shall be no difference or distinction made in respect to the said religion, in receiving pupils to be instructed in universities, colleges, and schools; or in receiving the sick and poor into hospitals, retreats and public charities.

XXIII. Those of the said religion called Reformed shall be obliged to respect the laws of the Catholic Apostolic and Roman Church, recognized in this our kingdom, for the consummation of marriages contracted, or to be contracted, as regards to the degrees of consanguinity and kinship.

READING AND DISCUSSION QUESTIONS

1. Why was Henry so intent on "obliterating" memory of "everything done by one party or the other" in the years immediately prior to his coronation as king of France?
2. Was the Edict of Nantes consistent with Henry's aim of increasing the monarchy's and the state's power? Why or why not?
3. Why might Henry's son, Louis XIII, have regarded the Huguenots as "a state within a state"?
4. Based on the details of the edict regarding ceremonies, property, literature, and education, what sorts of practices defined a religion before and during Henry's reign? What, if any practices did he consider irreligious, or purely civil?

DOCUMENT 16-2

JEAN-BAPTISTE COLBERT

The Advantages of Colonial Trade

1664

Jean-Baptiste Colbert (1619–1683) came from a family of wealthy French merchants. He first achieved political prominence during the early years of Louis XIV's reign, in the service of Cardinal Jules Mazarin, Louis's political mentor and advisor. Following Mazarin's death in 1661 until his own in 1683, Colbert served Louis XIV as both minister of finance and minister of marine and colonies. He was a staunch proponent of mercantilism, in which the government regulates economic activities in order to increase the wealth of the state. To this end, he commissioned a pamphlet from which the following excerpt is drawn, in which he tried to encourage French merchants to invest in the state's East India Company.

Now of all commerces whatsoever throughout the whole world, that of the East Indies[2] is one of the most rich and considerable. From thence it is (the sun being kinder to them, than to us) that we have our merchandise of greatest value and that which contributes the most not only to the pleasure of life but also to glory, and magnificence. From thence it is that we fetch our gold and precious stones and a thousand other commodities (both of a general esteem and a certain return) to which we are so accustomed that it is impossible for us to be without them, as silk, cinnamon, pepper, ginger, nutmegs, cotton cloth, ouate [cotton wadding], porcelain, woods for dyeing, ivory, frankincense, bezoar [poison antidote], etc. So that having an absolute necessity upon us, to make use of all these things, why we should not rather furnish ourselves, than take them from others, and apply that profit hereafter to our own countrymen, which we have hitherto allowed to strangers, I cannot understand.

Jean-Baptiste Colbert, "A Discourse . . . ," trans. R. L'Estrange (London: 1664), in Geoffrey Symcox, ed., *War, Diplomacy, and Imperialism, 1618–1763* (New York: Walker, 1974), 257–260.

[2] **East Indies**: That is to say, modern-day Malaysia and Indonesia. In Colbert's time, and for more than two centuries afterward, they were known as the Dutch East Indies and included the islands of Java, Sumatra, Borneo, and the Celebes.

Why should the Portuguese, the Hollanders [Dutch], the English, the Danes, trade daily to the East Indies possessing there, their magazines, and their forts, and the French neither the one nor the other? . . . To what end is it *in fine* that we pride ourselves to be subjects of the prime monarch of the universe, if being so, we dare not so much as show our heads in those places where our neighbors have established themselves with power? . . .

What has it been, but this very navigation and traffic that has enabled the Hollanders to bear up against the power of Spain,[3] with forces so unequal, nay, and to become terrible to them and to bring them down at last to an advantageous peace? Since that time it is that this people, who had not only the Spaniards abroad, but the very sea and earth at home to struggle with, have in spite of all opposition made themselves so considerable, that they begin now to dispute power and plenty with the greatest part of their neighbors. This observation is no more than truth, their East India Company being known to be the principal support of their state and the most sensible cause of their greatness.

READING AND DISCUSSION QUESTIONS

1. Why do you think Colbert found it so objectionable that the French depended on middlemen ("the Portuguese, the Hollanders, the English, the Danes") to provide France with the riches of India, rather than obtaining them themselves?

2. Why do you think Colbert stressed "the pleasure of life *but also to glory, and magnificence*" that Indian goods provided to France? What does his emphasis tell us about the culture of French absolutism?

3. Based on the language of his treatise, whom does Colbert seem to blame for the absence of direct French trade with the West Indies?

---

[3] **Hollanders to bear up against . . . Spain**: Owing to their financial and naval strength, part of which derived from their lucrative East India trade, the Dutch prevailed in their long struggle (1568–1648) to gain independence from Spain.

DOCUMENT 16-3

MOLIÈRE

From Le Bourgeois Gentilhomme

1671

Molière (1622–1673) was an outstanding playwright at the court of Louis XIV, and among the very greatest in French history. Unlike his contemporary Jean Racine, who wrote tragedies, Molière excelled at satirical comedies such as Tartuffe, *which played on the prejudices of his employer and mocked the foibles of humankind. In this excerpt from* Le Bourgeois Gentilhomme (The Middleclass Gentleman), *Molière ridicules the aspirations Monsieur Jourdain entertains for his daughter, at the same time depicting Madame Jourdain as a mouthpiece for a social order in which everyone "knows their place."*

M. JOURDAIN: Shut up, saucebox. You're always sticking your oar in the conversation. I have enough property for my daughter; all I need is honor; and I want to make her a marquise.[4]

MME. JOURDAIN: Marquise?

M. JOURDAIN: Yes, marquise.

MME. JOURDAIN: Alas, God forbid!

M. JOURDAIN: It's something I've made up my mind to.

MME. JOURDAIN: As for me, it's something I'll never consent to. Alliances with people above our own rank are always likely to have very unpleasant results. I don't want to have my son-in-law able to reproach my daughter for her parents, and I don't want her children to be ashamed to call me their grandma. If she should happen to come and visit me in her grand lady's carriage, and if by mistake she should fail to salute some one of the neighbors, you can imagine how they'd talk. "Take a look at that fine Madame la Marquise showing off," they'd say. "She's the daughter of Monsieur Jourdain, and when she was little, she was only too glad to play at being a fine lady. She wasn't always so high and mighty as she is now, and both her grandfathers sold dry goods besides

Molière, *Le Bourgeois Gentilhomme*, in Morris Bishop, trans., *Eight Plays by Molière* (New York: Modern Library, 1957), 372.

[4] **make her a marquise**: In other words, to marry her to a nobleman.

the Porte Saint Innocent. They both piled up money for their children, and now perhaps they're paying dear for it in the next world; you don't get so rich by being honest." Well, I don't want that kind of talk to go on; and in short, I want a man who will feel under obligation to my daughter, and I want to be able to say to him: "Sit down there, my boy, and eat dinner with us."

M. JOURDAIN: Those views reveal a mean and petty mind, that wants to remain forever in its base condition. Don't answer back to me again. My daughter will be a marquise in spite of everyone; and if you get me angry, I'll make her a duchess.

READING AND DISCUSSION QUESTIONS

1. Monsieur Jourdain states that he has property enough for his daughter's dowry. Why is he so eager to secure "honor" for her as well?

2. Why does Madame Jourdain object to her daughter marrying "above her own rank"?

3. What does Molière's satire suggest about the relative importance of wealth and social origins in determining one's status in Louis XIV's France? Does Molière seem to prefer Monsieur or Madame Jourdain's opinion?

DOCUMENT 16-4

JOHN LOCKE

From Second Treatise of Civil Government: Vindication for the Glorious Revolution

1690

John Locke (1632–1704) was, along with Thomas Hobbes, one of the two greatest English political theorists of the seventeenth century. Unlike Hobbes, however, whose Leviathan *(1651) provided a justification for monarchical absolutism, Locke's* Second Treatise of Government, *published anonymously*

John Locke, *Two Treatises of Government* (London: Awnsham Churchill, 1690).

in 1690, argued that government is an agreement between the governed, who submitted to governmental authority in return for protection of their life, liberty, and property, and the governors, whose fundamental task is provide those essential protections. According to Locke, a government that failed to do so or became tyrannical lost its claim to legitimacy, and could therefore be cast off by the governed.

87. Man being born, as has been proved, with a Title to perfect Freedom, and an uncontroled enjoyment of all the Rights and Privileges of the Law of Nature, equally with any other Man, or Number of Men in the World, hath by Nature a Power, not only to preserve his Property, that is, his Life, Liberty and Estate, against the Injuries and Attempts of other Men; but to judge of, and punish the breaches of that Law in others, as he is perswaded the Offense deserves, even with Death it self, in Crimes where the heinousness of the Fact, in his Opinion, requires it. But because no *Political Society* can be, nor subsist without having in it self the Power to preserve the Property, and in order thereunto punish the Offenses of all those of that Society; there, and there only is *Political Society*, where every one of the Members hath quitted this natural Power, resign'd it up into the hands of the Community in all cases that exclude him not from appealing for Protection to the Law established by it. And thus all private judgment of every particular Member being excluded, the Community comes to be Umpire, by settled standing Rules, indifferent, and the same to all Parties; and by Men having Authority from the Community, for the execution of those Rules, decides all the differences that may happen between any Members of that Society, concerning any matter of right; and punishes those Offences, which any Member hath committed against the Society, with such Penalties as the Law has established: Whereby it is easie to discern who are, and who are not, in *Political Society* together. Those who are united into one Body, and have a common establish'd Law and Judicature to appeal to, with Authority to decide Controversies between them, and punish Offenders, *are in Civil Society* one with another: but those who have no such common Appeal, I mean on Earth, are still in the state of Nature, each being, where there is no other, Judge for himself, and Executioner; which is, as I have before shew'd it, the perfect *state of Nature.*

88. And thus the Commonwealth comes by a Power to set down, what punishment shall belong to the several transgressions which they think worthy of it, committed amongst the Members of that Society, (which is the *power of making Laws*) as well as it has the power to punish any Injury done unto any of its Members, by any one that is not of it, (which is the

power of War and Peace;) and all this for the preservation of the property of all the Members of that Society, as far as is possible. But though every Man who has enter'd into civil Society, and is become a member of any Commonwealth, has thereby quitted his power to punish Offenses against the Law of Nature, in prosecution of his own private Judgment; yet with the Judgment of Offenses which he has given up to the Legislative in all Cases, where he can Appeal to the Magistrate, he has given a right to the Commonwealth to imploy his force, for the Execution of the Judgments of the Commonwealth, whenever he shall be called to it; which indeed are his own Judgments, they being made by himself, or his Representative. And herein we have the original of the *Legislative* and *Executive Power* of Civil Society, which is to judge by standing Laws how far Offenses are to be punished, when committed within the Commonwealth; and also to determin, by occasional Judgments founded on the present Circumstances of the Fact, how far Injuries from without are to be vindicated, and in both these to imploy all the force of all the Members when there shall be need.

89. Where-ever therefore any number of Men are so united into one Society, as to quit every one his Executive Power of the Law of Nature, and to resign it to the publick, there and there only is a *Political, or Civil Society*. And this is done where-ever any number of Men, in the state of Nature, enter into Society to make one People, one Body Politick under one Supreme Government, or else when any one joyns himself to, and incorporates with any Government already made. For hereby he authorizes the Society, or which is all one, the Legislative thereof to make Laws for him as the publick good of the Society shall require; to the Execution whereof, his own assistance (as to his own Decrees) is due. And this *puts Men* out of a State of Nature *into* that of a *Commonwealth*, by setting up a Judge on Earth, with Authority to determine all the Controversies, and redress the Injuries, that may happen to any Member of the Commonwealth; which Judge is the Legislative, or Magistrates appointed by it. And where-ever there are any number of Men, however associated, that have no such decisive power to appeal to, there they are still *in the state of Nature*.

90. Hence it is evident, that *Absolute Monarchy*, which by some Men is counted the only Government in the World, is indeed *inconsistent with Civil Society*, and so can be no Form of Civil Government at all. For the *end of Civil Society*, being to avoid, and remedy those inconveniencies of the State of Nature, which necessarily follow from every Man's being Judge in his own Case, by setting up a known Authority, to which every one of that Society may Appeal upon any injury received, or Controversie that may arise, and which every one of the Society ought to obey; where-ever

any persons are, who have not such an Authority to Appeal to, for the decision of any difference between them, there those persons are still *in the state of Nature*. And so is every *Absolute Prince* in respect of those who are under his *Dominion*.

91. For he being suppos'd to have all, both Legislative and Executive Power in himself alone, there is no Judge to be found, no Appeal lies open to any one, who may fairly, and indifferently, and with Authority decide, and from whose decision relief and redress may be expected of any Injury or Inconveniency, that may be suffered from the Prince or by his Order: So that such a Man, however intitled, *Czar*, or *Grand Signior*, or how you please, is as much *in the state of Nature* with all under his Dominion, as he is with the rest of Mankind. For where-ever any two Men are, who have no standing Rule, and common Judge to Appeal to on Earth for the determination of Controversies of Right betwixt them, there they are still *in the state of Nature*, and under all the inconveniencies of it, with only this woeful difference to the Subject, or rather Slave of an Absolute Prince: That whereas, in the ordinary State of Nature, he has a liberty to judge of his Right, and according to the best of his Power, to maintain it; now whenever his Property is invaded by the Will and Order of his Monarch, he has not only no Appeal, as those in Society ought to have, but as if he were degraded from the common state of Rational Creatures, is denied a liberty to judge of, or to defend his Right, and so is exposed to all the Misery and Inconveniencies that a Man can fear from one, who being in the unrestrained state of Nature, is yet corrupted with Flattery, and armed with Power.

92. For he that thinks *absolute Power purifies Mens Bloods*, and corrects the baseness of Humane Nature, need read but the History of this, or any other Age to be convinced of the contrary. He that would have been insolent and injurious in the Woods of *America*, would not probably be much better in a Throne; where perhaps Learning and Religion shall be found out to justifie all, that he shall do to his Subjects, and the Sword presently silence all those that dare question it. For what the *Protection of Absolute Monarchy* is, what kind of Fathers of their Countries it makes Princes to be, and to what a degree of Happiness and Security it carries Civil Society where this sort of Government is grown to perfection, he that will look into the late Relation of *Ceylon*,[5] may easily see.

---

[5] **Relation of *Ceylon***: Locke was referring to Robert Knox's *An Historical Relation of the Island Ceylon in the East Indies Together with an Account of the Detaining in Captivity the Author and Divers other Englishmen Now Living There, and of the Author's Miraculous Escape* (1681).

READING AND DISCUSSION QUESTIONS

1. What, according to Locke, distinguishes *"Political, or Civil Society"* from "a state of nature"?

2. What, in Locke's opinion, led to the creation of *"Political, or Civil Society"*?

3. Why does he argue that *"Absolute Monarchy,* which by some Men is counted the only Government in the World, is indeed *inconsistent with Civil Society,* and so can be no Form of Civil Government at all"?

4. Why do you think Locke published this work anonymously, rather than publicly claiming credit for what is now generally regarded as one of the classics of Western political theory?

COMPARATIVE QUESTIONS

1. What do you think Madame Jourdain would say to Locke's argument in the *Second Treatise of Civil Government* that all men are born "with a Title to perfect Freedom, and an uncontrouled enjoyment of all the Rights and Privileges of the Law of Nature, equally with any other Man"?

2. What do the *Le Bourgeois Gentilhomme* and Colbert's argument for direct French trade with India tell us about the structure of early modern European society and the economy?

3. Given the four documents in this chapter, list a few of the techniques that writers, politicians, and citizens used to call for change in a monarchy.

CHAPTER 17

Absolutism in Central and Eastern Europe

to 1740

Although historians use the term *absolutist* to describe the governments of Prussia, Austria, Russia, and the Ottoman Empire, there were important social and political differences between the absolutism of these states and that of France. Whereas serfdom — a status closer to slavery than to freedom — had largely vanished from northwest Europe by 1600, it expanded and grew more oppressive in central and eastern Europe. Similarly, while towns grew in size and economic importance in western Europe, they declined east of the Elbe River in central Germany, due in part to the devastating wars that wracked the region. While Louis XIV could turn to the educated urban middle class to staff his bureaucracy, his Prussian, Austrian, and Russian counterparts could not; in return for uncontested power at the national level, monarchs left local power entirely in the hands of the aristocrats, who also staffed the state's bureaucracy — a "service nobility." The losers in this bargain were the voiceless serfs, who made up more than 95 percent of the population.

DOCUMENT 17-1

LUDWIG FABRITIUS
The Revolt of Stenka Razin
1670

With the rise of the Romanov family to the Russian monarchy in 1613, Russian autocracy expanded rapidly. In 1649, Tsar Alexei (r. 1645–1676)

From Anthony Glenn Cross, ed., *Russia under Western Eyes, 1517–1825* (London: Elek Books, 1971), 120–123.

enacted the Code of 1649, making millions of formerly free peasants and urban workers into serfs bound to the land and their aristocratic owners. In 1667, Stenka Razin (ca. 1630–1671), from southern Russia, led a revolt of urban laborers, peasants, and soldiers who resisted becoming serfs. Ludwig Fabritius (1648–1729), a Dutch soldier employed in the Russian army at the time, wrote an account of the revolt.

Then Stenka with his company started off upstream, rowing as far as Tsaritsyn, whence it took him only one day's journey to Panshin, a small town situated on the Don [River]. Here he began straightaway quietly collecting the common people around him, giving them money, and promises of riches if they would be loyal to him and help to exterminate the treacherous boyars.

This lasted the whole winter, until by about spring he had assembled 4,000 to 5,000 men. With these he came to Tsaritsyn and demanded the immediate surrender of the fortress; the rabble soon achieved their purpose, and although the governor tried to take refuge in a tower, he soon had to give himself up as he was deserted by one and all. Stenka immediately had the wretched governor hanged; and all the goods they found belonging to the Tsar and his officers as well as to the merchants were confiscated and distributed among the rabble.

Stenka now began once more to make preparations. Since the plains are not cultivated, the people have to bring their corn [grain] from Nizhniy-Novgorod and Kazan down the Volga in big boats known as *nasady*, and everything destined for Astrakhan has first to pass Tsaritsyn. Stenka Razin duly noted this, and occupied the whole of the Volga, so that nothing could get through to Astrahkan. Here he captured a few hundred merchants with their valuable goods, taking possession of all kinds of fine linen, silks, striped silk material, sables, soft leather, ducats, talers, and many thousands of rubles in Russian money and merchandise of every description. . . .

In the meantime four regiments of *streltsy* [sharpshooters] were dispatched from Moscow to subdue these brigands. They arrived with their big boats and as they were not used to the water, were easily beaten. Here Stenka Razin gained possession of a large amount of ammunition and artillery-pieces and everything else he required. While the above-mentioned [sharpshooters] were sent from Moscow, about 5,000 men were ordered up from Astrakhan by water and land to capture Stenka Razin. As soon as he finished with the former, he took up a good position, and being in possession of reliable information regarding our forces, he left Tsaritsyn and came to meet us half way at Chernyy Yar, confronting us before we had suspected his presence or received any information about him. We stopped at Chernyy Yar for a few days and sent out scouts by water and by land, but were unable to obtain any definite information. On 10 July [sic: June] a council of war was held at which it was decided to advance and seek out Stenka. The next morning, at 8 o'clock, our look-outs on the water came hurriedly and raised the alarm as the Cossacks were following at their heels. We got out of our boats and took up battle positions, General Knyaz Semen Ivanovich Lvov went through our ranks and reminded all the men to do their duty and to remember the oath they had taken to His Majesty the Tsar, to fight like honest soldiers against these irresponsible rebels, whereupon they all unanimously shouted: "Yes, we will give our lives for His Majesty the Tsar, and will fight to the last drop of our blood."

In the meantime Stenka prepared for battle and deployed on a wide front; to all those who had no rifle he gave a long pole, burnt a little at one end, and with a rag or small hook attached. They presented a strange sight on the plain from afar, and the common soldiers imagined that, since there were so many flags and standards, there must be a host of people. They [the common soldiers] held a consultation and at once decided that this was the chance for which they had been waiting so long, and with all their flags and drums they ran over to the enemy. They began kissing and embracing one another and swore with life and limb to stand together and to exterminate the treacherous boyars, to throw off the yoke of slavery, and to become free men.

The general looked at the officers and the officers at the general, and no one knew what to do; one said this, and another that, until it was finally decided that they and the general should get into the boats and withdraw to Astrakhan. But the rascally [sharpshooters] of Chernyy Yar stood on the walls and towers, turning their weapons on us and opened fire; some of them ran out of the fortress and cut us off from the boats, so that we had no means of escape. In the meantime those curs of ours who had gone over to the Cossacks came up from behind. We numbered about eighty men, officers, noblemen, and clerks. Murder at once began. Then, however, Stenka Razin ordered that no more officers were to be killed, saying that there must be a few good men among them who should be pardoned, whilst those others who had not lived in amity with their men should be condemned to well-deserved punishment by the Ataman[1] and his *Krug*. A

---

[1] **Ataman**: A Cossack political and military leader, in this case Stenka Razin himself. Atamans were usually elected by the Cossack groups they led.

Krug is a meeting convened by the order of the Ataman, at which the Cossacks stand in a circle with the standard in the center; the Ataman then takes his place beside his best officers, to whom he divulges his wishes, ordering them to make these known to the common brothers and to hear their opinion on the matter. . . .

A *Krug* was accordingly called and Stenka asked his chiefs how the general and his officers had treated the soldiers under their command. Thereupon the unscrupulous curs [sharpshooters], as well as soldiers, unanimously called out that there was not one of them who deserved to remain alive, and they all asked that their father Stepan [i.e., Stenka] Timofeyevich Razin should order them to be cut down. This was granted with the exception of General Knyaz Semem Ivanovich Lvov, whose life was specially spared by Stenka himself. The officers were now brought in order of rank out of the tower, into which they hand been thrown bound hand and foot the previous day, their ropes were cut and they were led outside the gate. When all the bloodthirsty curs had lined up, each was eager to deal his former superior the first blow, one with the sword, another with the lance, another with the scimitar, and others again with martels, so that as soon as an officer was pushed into the ring, the curs immediately killed him with their many wounds; indeed, some were cut to pieces and straightaway thrown into the Volga. My stepfather, Paul Rudolf Beem, and Lt. Col. Wundrum and many other officers, senior and junior, were cut down before my eyes.

My own time had not yet come: this I could tell by the wonderful way in which God rescued me, for as I — half-dead — now awaited the final blow, my [former] orderly, a young soldier, came and took me by my bound arms and tried to take me down the hill. As I was already half-dead, I did not move and did not know what to do, but he came back and took me by the arms and led me, bound as I was, through the throng of curs, down the hill into the boat and immediately cut my arms free, saying that I should rest in peace here and that he would be responsible for me and do his best to save my life. . . . Then my guardian angel told me not to leave the boat, and left me. He returned in the evening and brought me a piece of bread which I enjoyed since I had had nothing to eat for two days.

The following day all our possessions were looted and gathered together under the main flag, so that both our bloodthirsty curs and the Cossacks got their share.

READING AND DISCUSSION QUESTIONS

1. What is Fabritius's attitude toward Stenka and his followers? Why?

2. What do his descriptions of the soldiers suggest about why they deserted?

3. Why, on the basis of Fabritius's account, do you think Peter the Great reformed his army?

4. What does Fabritius's account suggest to you about the political structure of Razin's army?

DOCUMENT 17-2

FREDERICK II (THE GREAT) AND FREDERICK WILLIAM I

Letters Between a Son and Father

1728

Frederick William I (r. 1713–1740) and his grandfather, Frederick William the Great Elector (r. 1640–1688), were most responsible for elevating Prussia to the status of a major European power. Both men realized that Prussia's security rested almost solely on the strength of its army, and both, especially Frederick William I, devoted immense sums and energy to make the army the best, if not the largest, in Europe. Frederick William's eldest son, the future Frederick the Great (r. 1740–1788), would eventually demonstrate his military genius, but as a young man he seemed far more interested in the cultural, rather than the military, arts, greatly displeasing his notoriously difficult father.

Frederick, Prince of Prussia to his Father, Frederick William I, September 11, 1728

I have not ventured for a long time to present myself before my dear papa, partly because I was advised against it, but chiefly because I anticipated an

James Harvey Robinson, *Readings in European History* (Lexington, Mass.: Ginn & Co., 1934).

even worse reception than usual and feared to vex my dear papa still further by the favor I have now to ask; so I have preferred to put it in writing.

I beg my dear papa that he will be kindly disposed toward me. I do assure him that after long examination of my conscience I do not find the slightest thing with which to reproach myself; but if, against my wish and will, I have vexed my dear papa, I hereby beg most humbly for forgiveness, and hope that my dear papa will give over the fearful hate which has appeared so plainly in his whole behavior and to which I cannot accustom myself. I have always thought hitherto that I had a kind father, but now I see the contrary. However, I will take courage and hope that my dear papa will think this all over and take me again into his favor. Meantime I assure him that I will never, my life long, willingly fail him, and in spite of his disfavor I am still, with most dutiful and childlike respect, my dear papa's Most obedient and faithful servant and son.
Frederick

FREDERICK WILLIAM I TO FREDERICK, PRINCE OF PRUSSIA

A bad, obstinate boy, who does not love his father, for when one does one's best, and especially when one loves one's father, one does what he wishes not only when he is standing by but when he is not there to see. Moreover you know I cannot stand an effeminate fellow who has no manly tastes, who cannot ride or shoot (to his shame be it said!), is untidy about his person, and wears his hair curled like a fool instead of cutting it; and that I have condemned all these things a thousand times, and yet there is no sign of improvement. For the rest, haughty, offish as a country lout, conversing with none but a favored few instead of being affable and popular, grimacing like a fool, and never following my wishes out of love for me but only when forced into it, caring for nothing but to have his own way, and thinking nothing else is of any importance.

This is my answer.
Frederick William

READING AND DISCUSSION QUESTIONS

1. What, according to Frederick William I, are properly masculine virtues and pursuits? What do these suggest about his personality and priorities?

2. What, if any, statements are there in Prince Frederick's letter that might indicate why his father was so mad at him? Are there any clues in Frederick William I's reply? If so, what are they?

DOCUMENT 17-3

A Song to Lost Lands: Russia's Conquest by the Mongols

ca. 1240–1300

During the period 880–1200, a Russian principality developed in what is the Ukraine, its capital at Kiev. This poem recounts the glories of that state and the might of its princes, to whom even the Eastern Roman Empire paid homage, as well as the beauty of the lands it ruled. The "great misfortune" to which the unknown author refers in the final line of this excerpt was the Mongol conquest of the Kievan state in 1240. The Mongols were a nomadic people from north-central Asia who, between 1160 and 1250 conquered a vast swath of Asia and eastern Europe, stretching from China to Poland.

O Russian land, brightest of the bright,
most beautifully adorned,
thou art marvelous to us, with thy many beauties.
Marvelous are thy numerous lakes,
thy rivers and venerated springs,
steep mountains, high hills,
oak forests, beautiful fields,
many beasts and countless birds,
great cities, wonderful villages, and monastery gardens,
honorable boyars[2] and countless lords,
Christian churches and stern princes.
Thou, Russian land, art rich in wealth

"Orison on the Downfall of Russia," in Serge A. Zenkovsky, ed., *Medieval Russia's Epics, Chronicles and Tales* (New York: 1963), 173–174.

[2] **boyars**: The greatest nobles.

Thou spreadest from Hungary to Poland and Bohemia,
from Bohemia to the land of the Yatvags,[3]
from the land of the Yatvags to the Lithuanians and Germans,
from the land of the Germans to Karelia,[4]
from Karelia to Ustiug[5]
where live the pagan Toymians,
and beyond the breathing sea,
and from the sea to the Bulgars,[6]
from the Bulgars to the Burtasians,
from the Burtasians to the Cheremiss, and
from the Cheremiss to the Mordvians.[7]
All these vast areas and the people that live on them
were subjugated by God to the Christian people (of Russia)
and to Great Prince Vsevolod[8]
and to his father, Yury,[9] Prince of Kiev,
and to his grandfather, Vladimir Monomakh,[10]
with whose name the Kumans[11] frightened their children in their cradles,
and in whose reign the Lithuanians
did not dare show themselves from their swamps,
and in whose reign the Hungarians fortified
the stone walls of their cities with their iron gates
so that great Vladimir might not pass through.
And at that time the Germans did rejoice
in being so far (from the Russians) beyond the sea.
And the Burtasians, Cheremiss, Votiaks,[12] and Mordvians

---

[3] **Yatvags**: A non-Slavic people who inhabited the Baltic region.
[4] **Karelia**: The isthmus between the Gulf of Finland and Lake Ladoga; the Karelians were Finns.
[5] **Ustiug**: A settlement in northeastern corner of the modern-day Russian province of Vologda.
[6] **Bulgars**: A nomadic people originating in central Asia, perhaps of Turkic descent. They settled in the Caucasus, and along the north shore of the Black Sea.
[7] **Burtasians . . . Cheremiss . . . Mordvians**: Finnish peoples living in eastern Russia.
[8] **Vsevolod**: Vsevolod III, r. 1176–1212.
[9] **Yury**: Yuri Dolgoruki, r. 1154–1157.
[10] **Vladimir Monomakh**: Vladimir II Monomakh, r. 1113–1125; a ruthless ruler under whom the Kievan reached its highest power.
[11] **Kumans**: A Turkic people, settled in the lower Don, Donets, and Volga river basins.
[12] **Votiaks**: Another Finnish people, who inhabited the region between the Baltic and upper Volga river basin.

worked hard to pay tribute to Vladimir the Great.
And even the Emperor of Byzantium, Manuel,
fearing lest Vladimir the Great take Constantinople,
was sending rich presents to him.
And so it used to be.
But now a great misfortune has befallen the Russian land. . . .

READING AND DISCUSSION QUESTIONS

1. If the princes of Kiev were as powerful as the poet claims, what are some reasons the state may have succumbed to the Mongols?

2. Who, aside from the Mongols, were the chief beneficiaries of Kiev's collapse, and why?

DOCUMENT 17-4

PETER THE GREAT

Edicts and Decrees: Imposing Western Styles on the Russians

1699–1723

Peter the Great's reign (1682–1725) marked Russia's emergence as a major European power. Russia defeated Sweden in the grueling Great Northern War (1700–1721) and acquired a "window on Europe" at the head of the Gulf of Finland, where Peter built a new capital, St. Petersburg. In order to defeat the Swedes, who had routed his ill-trained army at Narva in 1700, Peter had reformed and modernized his military along western European lines. His enthusiasm for western technology and tactics extended also to other realms, including education, dress, and economic programs, as can be seen from the following excerpts.

L. Jay Oliva, *Peter the Great* (Englewood Cliffs, NJ: Prentice-Hall, 1970).

Decree on the New Calendar, 1699

It is known to His Majesty that not only many European Christian lands, but also Slavic nations which are in total accord with our Eastern Orthodox Church . . . agree to count their years from the eighth day after the birth of Christ, that is from the first day of January, and not from the creation of the world,[13] because of the many difficulties and discrepancies of this reckoning. It is now the year 1699 from the birth of Christ, and from the first of January will begin both the new year 1700 and a new century; and so His Majesty has ordered, as a good and useful measure, that from now on time will be reckoned in government offices and dates be noted on documents and property deeds, starting from the first of January 1700. And to celebrate this good undertaking and the new century . . . in the sovereign city of Moscow . . . let the reputable citizens arrange decorations of pine, fir, and juniper trees and boughs along the busiest main streets and by the houses of eminent church and lay persons of rank. . . . Poorer persons should place at least one shrub or bough on their gates or on their house. . . . Also . . . as a sign of rejoicing, wishes for the new year and century will be exchanged, and the following will be organized: when fireworks are lit and guns fired on the great Red Square, let the boyars [nobles], the Lords of the Palace, of the Chamber, and the Council, and the eminent personages of Court, Army, and Merchant ranks, each in his own grounds, fire three times from small guns, if they have any, or from muskets and other small arms, and shoot some rockets into the air.

Decree on the Invitation of Foreigners, 1702

Since our accession to the throne all our efforts and intentions have tended to govern this realm in such a way that all of our subjects should, through our care for the general good, become more and more prosperous. For this end we have always tried to maintain internal order, to defend the state against invasion, and in every possible way to improve and to extend trade. With this purpose we have been compelled to make some necessary and salutary changes in the administration, in order that our subjects might more easily gain a knowledge of matters of which they were before ignorant, and become more skillful in their commercial relations. We have therefore given orders, made dispositions, and founded institutions

---

[13] **agree to count their years . . . world:** Before January 1, 1700, the Russian calendar started from the date of the creation of the world, which was reckoned at 5508 B.C.E. The year began on September 1.

indispensable for increasing our trade with foreigners, and shall do the same in the future. Nevertheless we fear that matters are not in such a good condition as we desire, and that our subjects cannot in perfect quietness enjoy the fruits of our labors, and we have therefore considered still other means to protect our frontier from the invasion of the enemy, and to preserve the rights and privileges of our State, and the general peace of all Christians. . . .

To attain these worthy aims, we have endeavored to improve our military forces, which are the protection of our State, so that our troops may consist of well-drilled men, maintained in perfect order and discipline. In order to obtain greater improvement in this respect, and to encourage foreigners, who are able to assist us in this way, as well as artisans profitable to the State, to come in numbers to our country, we have issued this manifesto, and have ordered printed copies of it to be sent throughout Europe. . . . And as in our residence of Moscow, the free exercise of religion of all other sects, although not agreeing with our church, is already allowed, so shall this be hereby confirmed anew in such manner that we, by the power granted to us by the Almighty, shall exercise no compulsion over the consciences of men, and shall gladly allow every Christian to care for his own salvation at his own risk.

An Instruction to Russian Students Abroad Studying Navigation, 1714

1. Learn how to draw plans and charts and how to use the compass and other naval indicators.
2. Learn how to navigate a vessel in battle as well as in a simple maneuver, and learn how to use all appropriate tools and instruments; namely, sails, ropes, and oars, and the like matters, on row boats and other vessels.
3. Discover . . . how to put ships to sea during a naval battle. . . . Obtain from foreign naval officers written statements, bearing their signatures and seals, of how adequately you are prepared for naval duties.
4. If, upon his return, anyone wishes to receive from the Tsar greater favors, he should learn, in addition to the above enumerated instructions, how to construct those vessels [aboard] which he would like to demonstrate his skills.
5. Upon his return to Moscow, every foreign-trained Russian should bring with him at his own expense, for which he will later be reimbursed, at least two experienced masters of naval science. They [the

returnees] will be assigned soldiers, one soldier per returnee, to teach them what they have learned abroad. . . .

Decree on Western Dress, 1701

Western dress shall be worn by all the boyars, members of our councils and of our court . . . gentry of Moscow, secretaries . . . provincial gentry, gosti,[14] government officials, streltsy,[15] members of the guilds purveying for our household, citizens of Moscow of all ranks, and residents of provincial cities . . . excepting the clergy and peasant tillers of the soil. The upper dress shall be of French or Saxon cut, and the lower dress . . . — waistcoat, trousers, boots, shoes, and hats — shall be of the German type. They shall also ride German saddles. Likewise the womenfolk of all ranks, including the priests', deacons', and church attendants' wives, the wives of the dragoons, the soldiers, and the streltsy, and their children, shall wear Western dresses, hats, jackets, and underwear — undervests and petticoats — and shoes. From now on no one of the abovementioned is to wear Russian dress or Circassian[16] coats, sheepskin coats, or Russian peasant coats, trousers, boots, and shoes. It is also forbidden to ride Russian saddles, and the craftsmen shall not manufacture them or sell them at the marketplaces.

Decree on Shaving, 1705

Henceforth, in accordance with this, His Majesty's decree, all court attendants . . . provincial service men, government officials of all ranks, military men, all the gosti, members of the wholesale merchants' guild, and members of the guilds purveying for our household must shave their beards and moustaches. But, if it happens that some of them do not wish to shave their beards and moustaches, let a yearly tax be collected from such persons; from court attendants. . . . Special badges shall be issued to them from the Administrator of Land Affairs of Public Order . . . which they must wear. . . . As for the peasants, let a toll of two half-copecks[17] per beard be collected at the town gates each time they enter or leave a town; and do not let the peasants pass the town gates, into or out of town, without paying this toll.

---

[14] gosti: Merchants who often served the tsar in some capacity.
[15] streltsy: Members of the imperial guard stationed in Moscow.
[16] Circassian: Circassia was a Russian territory between the Caspian and Black Seas.
[17] half-copecks: One-twentieth a ruble, the basic unit of Russian money.

Decree on Promotion to Officer's Rank, 1714

Since there are many who promote to officer rank their relatives and friends — young men who do not know the fundamentals of soldiering, not having served in the lower ranks — and since even those who serve [in the ranks] do so for a few weeks or months only, as a formality; therefore . . . let a decree be promulgated that henceforth there shall be no promotion [to officer rank] of men of noble extraction or of any others who have not first served as privates in the Guards. This decree does not apply to soldiers of lowly origin who, after long service in the ranks, have received their commissions through honest service or to those who are promoted on the basis of merit, now or in the future. . . .

Statute for the College of Manufactures,[18] 1723

His Imperial Majesty is diligently striving to establish and develop in the Russian Empire such manufacturing plants and factories as are found in other states, for the general welfare and prosperity of his subjects. He [therefore] most graciously charges the College of Manufactures to exert itself in devising the means to introduce, with the least expense, and to spread in the Russian Empire these and other ingenious arts, and especially those for which materials can be found within the empire. . . .

His Imperial Majesty gives permission to everyone, without distinction of rank or condition, to open factories wherever he may find suitable. . . .

Factory owners must be closely supervised, in order that they have at their plants good and experienced [foreign] master craftsmen, who are able to train Russians in such a way that these, in turn, may themselves become masters, so that their produce may bring glory to the Russian manufactures. . . .

By the former decrees of His Majesty commercial people were forbidden to buy villages [i.e., to own serfs], the reason being that they were not engaged in any other activity beneficial for the state save commerce; but since it is now clear to all that many of them have started to found manufacturing establishments and build plants, . . . which tend to increase the welfare of the state . . . therefore permission is granted both to the gentry and to men of commerce to acquire villages for these factories without hindrance. . . .

[18]**College of Manufactures**: One of several administrative boards created by Peter in 1717. Modeled on Swedish practice.

In order to stimulate voluntary immigration of various craftsmen from other countries into the Russian Empire, and to encourage them to establish factories and manufacturing plants freely and at their own expense, the College of Manufactures must send appropriate announcements to the Russian envoys accredited at foreign courts. The envoys should then, in an appropriate way, bring these announcements to the attention of men of various professions, urge them to come to settle in Russia, and help them to move.

READING AND DISCUSSION QUESTIONS

1. Why do you think Peter decreed that the nobles, merchants, and towns-people wear German, rather than French, clothes, seeing that the French kings and their palaces were objects of emulation throughout Europe?

2. What does Peter's decree encouraging foreign soldiers and artisans to emigrate to Russia and his Statute for the College of Manufactures suggest about the state of its military forces and economy as of the early 1700s?

3. Why didn't Russia have a navy prior to 1700?

4. What, according to Peter, was wrong with the system of promotion in the Russian army, and how did he intend to redress it? What does his decree on promotion suggest about the power and benefits granted to the Russian nobility?

COMPARATIVE QUESTIONS

1. In what ways were the absolutist states of eastern Europe — Russia, Austria, and Prussia — and their societies similar to France? In what ways did they differ, and how do you account for those differences?

2. What do Peter the Great's decrees about clothes and beards and Frederick William I's letter to his son suggest about their personalities and their methods of ruling?

3. In 1240, Kiev quickly succumbed to Mongol invaders; by the early eighteenth century Peter the Great was able to defeat the Swedes,

expand his empire, and bring Russia into the ranks of the great european powers. What had the Romanov rulers, especially Peter, learned from past events, and how had they reformed their state, society, and military forces?

4. According to the principles set forth in John Locke's *Second Treatise of Civil Government* (Document 16-4), was Stenka Razin's bloody revolt justified?

Acknowledgments *(continued from p. iv)*

CHAPTER 1

1-4. The Egyptian Book of the Dead's Declaration of Innocence, Anonymous. Excerpt from *Ancient Egyptian Literature: A Book of Readings*, Volume 2; The New Kingdom, translated and edited by Miriam Lichteim. Copyright © 1973 University of California Press. Reproduced with permission of the University of California Press, in the format Textbook via Copyright Clearance Center.

CHAPTER 2

2-4. Inscription Honoring Cyrus, King of Persia, Anonymous. Excerpt from *Ancient Near East Texts Relating to the Old Testament*, 3rd edition, edited by James B. Pritchard (pp. 315–316). Copyright © 1950 Princeton University Press, 1978 Renewed, 2nd Edition 1955, 1983 renewed PUP. Reprinted by permission of Princeton University Press.

CHAPTER 5

5-3. Seneca, The Sounds of a Roman Bath. From *Roman Civilization: Selected Readings*, edited by Naphtali Lewis and Meyer Reinhold. Copyright © 1951 Columbia University Press. Reprinted with permission of the publisher.

5-5. Cicero, *Philippius:* Cicero Offers Faint Praise for Antony. From *Cicero: Volume XV*, Loeb Classical Library® Volume 189, translated by Walter A. C. Ker (pp. 21–25). Cambridge, Mass.: Harvard University Press. Copyright © 1926 by the President and Fellows of Harvard College. Reprinted with the permission of the publishers and the Trustees of the Loeb Classical Library. The Loeb Classical Library is a registered trademark of the President and Fellows of Harvard College.

CHAPTER 11

11-2. Abbess Heloise of the Paraclete, Letter to Abelard: "I beseech thee. . . ." From *The Letters of Abelard and Heloise* by Peter Abelard & Heloise, translated by C. K. Moncrieff, translation copyright © 1926, copyright renewed 1954 by Alfred A. Knopf, a division of Random House, Inc. Used by permission of Alfred A. Knopf, a division of Random House, Inc.

CHAPTER 13

13-3. The Book of the City of Ladies: Advice for a "Wise Princess," Christine de Pizan. Excerpt from *Treasure of the City of Ladies*, by Christine de Pisan, translated with an introduction by Sarah Lawson (Penguin Classics, 1985). This translation copyright © Sarah Lawson, 1985. Reprinted with permission of Penguin Books Ltd.

13-4. Account of an Italian Jew Expelled from Spain, Anonymous. Excerpt from *The Jew in the Medieval World: A Sourcebook, 315–1791* by Jacob Marcus (New York: JPS, 1938), 51–55. Revised edition copyright © 1999 by the Hebrew Union College Press. Reprinted 1990 by the Hebrew Union College Perss, Hebrew Union College Jewish Institute of Religion, by agreement with Jacob Rader Marcus. First published in 1938 by Jacob Marcus. Reprinted by permission of the Hebrew Union College Press.

CHAPTER 15

15-4. Michel de Montaigne, *On the Fallibility of Human Understanding*, from *The Complete Works of Montaigne, Essays, Travel Journal*, Letters by Michel de Montaigne, translated by Donald M. Frame (pp. 817, 818–819). Copyright © 1943 by Donald M. Frame, renewed 1971; © 1948, 1957, 1958 by the Board of Trustees of the Leland Stanford Junior University. Used with the permission of Stanford University Press. www.sup.org. All rights reserved.

CHAPTER 17
17-1. Ludwig Fabritius, The Revolt of Stenka Razin. Excerpt from *Russia Under Western Eyes, 1517–1825*, edited with an introduction by Anthony Glenn Cross (pp. 121–123). Copyright © 1971, Elek Books. Reprinted with permission of Anthony Glenn Cross.